Julian Mather was an ABC cameraman based in Brisbane for twenty-seven years. He has worked on more than 100 ABC programs, as well as on ABC co-productions with the BBC, National Geographic, Discovery Channel, Canadian Broadcasting Corporation and TVNZ. He regularly shot for *Australian Story* and *Catalyst*, and wrote a chapter of the book *Australian Story: Off the Record* (ABC Books 2007), in which he revealed himself as a storyteller of some flair and talent. He lives in Brisbane.

# THE SECOND BEST JOB IN THE WORLD

# THE SECOND BEST JOB IN THE WORLD

## Adventures of an ABC Cameraman

### JULIAN MATHER

ABC Books

The ABC 'Wave' device is a trademark of the Australian Broadcasting Corporation and is used under licence by HarperCollins*Publishers* Australia.

First published in 2010
by HarperCollins*Publishers* Australia Pty Limited
ABN 36 009 913 517
harpercollins.com.au

Copyright © Julian Mather 2010

The right of Julian Mather to be identified as the author of this work has been asserted by him in accordance with the *Copyright Amendment (Moral Rights) Act 2000*.

This work is copyright. Apart from any use as permitted under the *Copyright Act 1968*, no part may be reproduced, copied, scanned, stored in a retrieval system, recorded, or transmitted, in any form or by any means, without the prior written permission of the publisher.

**HarperCollins*Publishers***
25 Ryde Road, Pymble, Sydney, NSW 2073, Australia
31 View Road, Glenfield, Auckland 0627, New Zealand
A 53, Sector 57, Noida, UP, India
77–85 Fulham Palace Road, London, W6 8JB, United Kingdom
2 Bloor Street East, 20th floor, Toronto, Ontario M4W 1A8, Canada
10 East 53rd Street, New York NY 10022, USA

National Library of Australia Cataloguing-in-Publication data

Mather, Julian Myles Wilson, 1961.
   The second best job in the world : the extraordinary
aventures of an ABC cameraman / Julian Mather.
   ISBN: 978 0 7333 2526 7 (pbk.)
   Mather, Julian Myles Wilson, 1961.
   Australian Broadcasting Corporation – Employees – Biography.
   Television camera operators – Australia – Biography.
778.59092

Cover design by Matt Stanton
Cover images courtesy of
Author pic courtesy R. Smith
Typeset in 11 on 16 pt Sabon by Kirby Jones

To Vicky, Georgia and Sophie —
the best thing that ever happened to me.

# Preface

The cremator door opened with a whoosh. An invisible wall of heat kept me from inching closer. It was hot. What was I expecting? My eyes took a moment to adjust to the maelstrom of white and yellow flame. No doubt about it, that's a burning body. Head, ribcage, legs all in the last moments of their earthly form. Fifteen minutes earlier I'd found out something I never knew. They burn the coffin as well. What a waste. No time to dwell, get the shot, another hearse waits.

'Is this one suitable?' We chose carefully. We wanted one that looks good on camera. 'Look at that grain, look at that finish; this is q-u-a-l-i-t-y.' Brimming with professional achievement, the funeral directors polished away some fingermarks and proudly slid the coffin into the open hearse. 'Better get moving, we have mourners arriving soon,' urged another dark-suited funeral worker. He helped me into my position alongside the casket, handed me my camera, laid the flowers in place and closed the tailgate of the hearse. I tried to reposition myself in my narrow slot but my trouser pocket had caught on one of the polished chrome handles. Snagged on a coffin – sheesh! No time to dwell, get the shot then hurry to the hospital delivery rooms.

The PR woman desperately wanted to roll her eyes. Behind the feigned smile I knew she was muttering, 'Why me?' I reiterated our request: 'Yep, you understand perfectly. We need one of these women to give us permission to film their baby's first breaths …

No, not actually coming out, just when you slap it and it cries.' It was to be a long night of pacing the corridor with expectant fathers.

Without my camera I guess I looked like any other would-be dad. An exhausted-looking candidate for imminent fatherhood asked me, 'What are you hoping for?' My honest answer would have been, 'To film your wife having a baby and get home because I have a naked woman waiting for me,' but that would have been inappropriate. I said it anyway. He laughed. In between groans his wife agreed and I captured the miracle of life all before morning peak hour. Thank goodness. I'm to meet Françoise soon. She's the naked woman I mentioned. Though a complete stranger, she had agreed to disrobe her eight months of pregnancy and stand naked, uncomfortably, on a box in my living room as I fiddled with lights to get the shot just right. No time to dwell. 'Gee, thanks … Françoise, isn't it? Yes of course, bye …'

## The next morning

'Could you try and find me a brush? Jesus is really dusty.' The Catholic church official assigned to babysit us smiled up at me in acknowledgement. Atop my precarious five-metre tower in the cathedral, I had a meeting with Jesus up close and personal in a way few do. The image in the viewfinder was certainly dramatic. This was, after all, the opening shot of a film called *The Darkest Hour*, a documentary about birth, death and the tenuous moments many face as they teeter between the two. Our church helper understood the importance of my request. 'You don't get a second chance at a first impression,' he chortled in appreciation of my respect for the House of God. It didn't seem the time to tell him that within the hour we would be trading the sanctity of the church for the Red Garter, a strip club. No time to dwell, the Amazing Miss Sandy finished her shift in under two hours.

Miss Sandy was a stripper and, yes, she was amazing. She was also very accommodating in performing her overly gymnastic act for the camera. We were in a nightclub, a temporary misnomer, as it was one in the afternoon. It was a favourite haunt of another of the documentary's subjects, a burnt-out taxi driver who never recovered from the horrors of the Vietnam War, and the sight of Miss Sandy somehow soothed his pain. Not a bad argument if you can get away with it. Get the shot, no time to ... OK, we can dwell a bit.

That was two days in 1993 and that, folks, is my job: a never-ending eclectic mix of people and places and I love it. Mind you, it has its dull moments, like sitting on cold concrete, endlessly waiting, day after day, for a jury to return on a high-profile case. Viewed monthly, at least one thing of anecdotal worth happens. Yearly you end up with a bucketful of stories. A few decades later and you could write a book about it, especially if you wrote it all down at the time, which is what I did. In part this book is possible because of my unshakeable urge to make lists, something I have done on almost every trip, something that drives me crazy and points to an obsessive flaw in my make-up.

I love being a cameraman. It's something I've wanted to do for most of my life. It is odd then that my photographic career should have started on the other side of the camera, in front of it. My father was a home-movie buff, something he applied himself to with vigour as attested to by the small mountain of metal canisters that document my life from birth to teens. Each can holds two hundred feet of jumpy, grainy vignettes of my short time of relative innocence. The smell of memories and acetate rise every time the cans are prised open. Those tiny frames, eight millimetres across and eighteen of them for every second of my recorded life, spool off the reel as I hold them to the light. Striking are the saturated colours after nearly half a century of sarcophagial containment. Striking too is their clarity. That's what I looked like. I stand there gawky, shy, unsure and obviously resigned to the fact that this is part of my family duty. Gathering in genealogical clusters and posing unnaturally in the centre of a freshly mown lawn, while wearing clothes I was patently not accustomed to wearing was very much one of my family duties for many years.

I cannot report that the memories in my head are as clear. There are lots of them. Lots and lots and lots. That's the legacy of twenty-five years with the ABC as a cameraman. It really is a jumble of experiences way beyond anything I might have imagined possible. It is strange, too, that for someone who angled so much for this lifestyle, who lived and breathed photography and travel, relatively few of the experiences came from a conscious decision to be part of them. I was told to be part of them. Being an ABC cameraman has many things going for it but self-determination isn't one of them. This lack of self-determination caused me much inner conflict.

For many years it was easy to resolve this as I unflinchingly enjoyed the benefits of my job: knowledge, excitement, world travel, moderate prestige, access-all-area passes, rubbing shoulders with the rich and famous. As it is, time changed my needs and attitudes. I stood atop the sum of my experiences and realised the view I have of life is a privileged and often-sought-after one. It was here I found myself, straddling a knife edge. On one side a job made for me, on the other a huge pit of dissatisfaction that was growing by the day. It took this job and a quarter of a century for me to find out what my purpose is.

You're welcome on the ride but before you buy a ticket I warn that you may not like me by the end. The one thing above all that this job has shown me is that behind every façade there is a fallible human stumbling their way through life. I am no different. I could paint myself in a rosy light but that would serve no purpose. For starters, I don't invest in people and I'm poorer for it. On more than one occasion I have shown cold indifference to those who have extended their hand in friendship – never through malice, it's just that sometimes focus and enthusiasm get the better of me. At times I am a truly miserable person. Then there is my objectionable

Queensland jingoism and blunt descriptions of bodily functions that will have you slamming the book closed on occasion. Despite all this I hope to lure you back with measured amounts of wit and charm, you wait and see.

I should mention my propensity for proverbs and sayings, and they litter this book. My grandmother loved using them and the habit took root with me. Colleagues and my children call me 'proverb man' or names to that effect. Before she died, my grandmother gave me a handwritten book full of quotes she thought relevant to me, and most in this book originate from it. It's in the genes.

There is one thing you can do for me. No doubt the temptation will arise to place this book next to treasured family photos on the mantelpiece, as it will have gained a special place in your affections, but I must caution you against that. Books are tools and there is much utility in this one. Please find someone who needs the flame inside them lit, someone who could benefit from my ability to apply enthusiasm to an idea and turn it into action, and pass this book on to them.

# 1

## A picture is a poem without words.

**HORACE**

The one thing that distinguishes ABC cameramen from their commercial counterparts is their love of and deep interest in photography and filmmaking. That's not to say the ABC is any better than the commercial networks, which have fantastic shooters, ones I aspire to be as good as. But in general their reasons for getting into the industry are different. If I were to have an anecdotal whiparound, their top three reasons would most likely be: it looked more fun than what I was doing; my uncle/dad/neighbour works in the industry and got me the job; I can get into the footy for free. Make no mistake, though, they are a talented, fun and gregarious group.

By and large the ABC recruited from tertiary film schools, which should then have excluded me. How did I get in? In a word: passion. A passion for photography. I've got oodles of it. I can thank my father for that. Nothing could dampen my fascination for the process of photography; not even being forced to endure the staged family clusters for Dad's home movie-making; not even his constant pleas of 'Don't just stand there, do something for the camera' that spurred my brother and I on to our monkey impersonations; not even being forced to wear our matching white shirts and bow ties so generations hence could have a chuckle.

Cameras from the 1950s and '60s came from a golden age of fine engineering. Made essentially from metal and glass, they had weight commensurate with their bulk. German design and Japanese manufacturing excellence meant that even as a domestic consumer you were treated to the best there was. And you respected your purchase as you knew it would likely be your one camera for the better part of your life and it could easily go the distance.

I was intrigued by this design brilliance. I clearly recall my silent forays into the forbidden camera cupboard where I would carefully open every box (my dad kept every box – and I mean *every* box – anything ever came in) and delight in the guilty pleasure of winding things that I shouldn't have been winding, popping open viewfinders that would 'click' just so. There were large ground-glass screens that could magically turn everything upside down. Dollops of unfocused light snapped into recognisable images and as quickly dissolved again as I played with the big knurled focus knob. I had secretly committed this knob's position to memory during our many family photo sessions. Its actual purpose was uncertain to me but that it was important was abundantly clear. I never had any problem looking at the camera for our family photos – quite the opposite: I couldn't take my eyes off it.

My father must have recognised this interest because on my eleventh birthday he presented me with an old rangefinder camera. With that gesture, my photographic career nearly fell stillborn from the womb. He had polished up the metallic body to look like new except for one thing: it wasn't new. The camera was missing its rear viewfinder lens, a small but vital piece of glass that differentiates a camera from a paperweight. In his perfectly reasoned belief that such a small thing shouldn't dampen the moment he had found a suitable prism of glass that was oh, say, six times too large and glued it over the vacant hole. In his defence clear glues weren't as widely available then so he had used yellow contact which, as anyone who has ever tried it knows, creates an unsightly mess. This cancerous looking lump of glass and glue defeated me. Even though I could see through it I could never see past it. The embarrassment it caused me was insurmountable. I was sure it was a magnet for stares and whispers. The problem was not theirs, but mine.

I had self-confidence issues growing up. Where these came from I'm not sure. I just felt different to others. I do remember my best friends and their families lived lives full of weekly traditions that I felt excluded from, like church on weekends, Sunday dinners as they called them, and membership of the cricket club. I never knew what any of them meant except my friends all knew some secret code that I didn't. We didn't belong to anything. I think we were quite insular. Only once can I remember my parents having friends around for a barbecue. No one would ever have called the Mathers a gregarious lot. My parents taught us many things but social skills weren't on the list.

My mother did all the things any child would want. We felt loved and she made the best-fancy dress costumes out of nothing. We struggled a lot for money. I never wanted for too much, except to be like other families which I thought were 'normal'. Normal to me meant not having to go to elocution lessons to overcome stuttering. Normal meant not having to wear hideous home-made board shorts because most things were simply out of our price range. Yes, they were eye-catching, but for all the wrong reasons. Normal was not having a name like Julian, which might be popular now, but in the sixties and seventies was like a neon light attracting every bug of a bully for kilometres. Vintage was the easiest way to describe our cars when everyone else drove sleek. My life was one huge comparison with others and, no matter how I looked at it, it didn't measure up. That said, I was very happy.

Mine was a typical subtropical Brisbane childhood: T-shirt and shorts, bare feet (thongs on formal occasions), a staple diet of sandwiches and ice blocks, multiple sodden towels fermenting in the bottom of my school swimming bag, endless adventures with mates on bicycles and copping hidings for getting back after dark, way after dark. This was the Brisbane that earned the moniker 'It's just a big country town'. My big brother Shane was older by a year and a half, and little sister Vanessa was dragging her feet as my junior of five years. We seemed a well balanced unit; Shane would beat me up at home but stand up for me when it mattered. We teased Vanessa mercilessly because that's what little sisters were for.

Entering our modest house you parted the curtains of Brisbane normality and set foot in a slightly exotic world of aromas, by 1960s standards at least. The rich smell of artist's oils and curry would always evoke a 'What's t-h-a-t smell?' from my urchin-like friends. My father was an amateur artist and would unwind at the easel by mixing colours on the palette with a spatula and applying them directly to the canvas with the blade. These rough, chopped wads of oil seemed to take my entire growing up to dry. I was forever sneaking a touch to discover 'not yet'. I did discover that oil paint has chemical binding properties like nothing else. My evidence-ridden finger lived permanently under the armpit of my T-shirt. As a prelude to my getting a hiding the said paint-riddled shirt would be held aloft the laundry basket like Exhibit A in the courtroom. I enjoyed his paintings but what intrigued me more were the intense colours and textures of the palette itself. My aesthetic leanings were kicking in.

The curry smells that so assaulted my friends' xenophobic sensibilities resulted directly from my father's diet. He was an Englishman by law and skin colour, but as the handwritten slip of paper from the Gundlupet Pharmacy that is attached to his birth certificate indicates, he was born in India. Julian Shaun Fawcett Mather – Shaun to everyone – and his siblings were all born in southern India. My grandparents had moved there. My grandmother was to take up a post as governess to the Maharani (the female of a Maharaja) of Mysore. The 1930s were still a time of the Raj. For me to open a family photo album was to journey in my mind to a truly romantic place, page upon page teasing me with the majesty of elephants bedecked in ceremonial garb below towering domes of excessive Indian architecture. It was exotic and entrancing, a sideshow of colour and spectacle, but it was not the India my father loved: his was the simple farm life and elderly Indian folk of gentle nature who helped raise him and whom he never stopped talking about.

Every second photo of Dad as a toddler has a dead tiger in it. Dad's eldest brother, whom I had always called Uncle Mickey, was much older than Dad and made his living as a game hunter. Our family photo albums were a who's who of Indian wildlife. Unfortunately for the most part they were dead. For years I was torn between pride and slight embarrassment about this heritage. I've ended up with a cobra skin and tiger's claws as my hand-me-downs of family history. I've never been quite sure what to do with them. I would studiously trawl the pages of these albums marvelling at the stories the pictures told. There seemed to be a lot of guns in the photos. 'There's Uncle Mickey again, quietly going about his business of depopulating India's natural wealth … and there's Uncle Andy in the Spanish Foreign Legion with bandoliers and bullets, the West African desert behind him, looking quite the mercenary fighter … and there's Dad in his paratrooper uniform with a gun.' These images were at odds with the sedate, unremarkable life we lived.

Even at an early age I sensed a paradox within my father; now I can articulate it, then it was a nagging mystery. Dad seemed to be a really clever bloke and, in the eyes of a nine year old, able to turn his hand to anything. My grandparents once bought a few acres of weeds close to our house. Dad took on the job of whipping them into shape so they could agist a few horses and soften the bank repayments. My brother Shane and I were press-ganged into helping, as this qualified as quality family time and a cheap outing to boot.

I marvelled at how Dad knew how to cut the posts with a big double-ended saw, the way the sweat would bead and accelerate into rivulets as he twisted the hand auger bit to create holes in the posts to accept the wire. He just seemed so knowledgeable and capable; so too my brother Shane – he had a physical strength and a 'nuts and bolts' know-how that had eluded me. I envied my brother's luxury of being firstborn, as I was the sensitive one and crying never got a fence finished. The land was infested with a prickly weed called Noogoora burr. With scythe, sickle and mattock Dad would single-handedly keep it under control, weekend after steamy, hot Queensland weekend. How he knew where to start amazed me, but he did, and would only stop for a drink of steaming hot tea from his thermos flask. 'It cools you down,' he'd say – another mystery to me. No one ever called my dad lazy.

Later, to relax, he would mix his oil colours and before my eyes a tube of purple paint and a tube of white paint would become jacaranda flowers. Why he chose to paint trees and not tigers was a mystery too but that it was real on the canvas was undeniable. Convention taught me to draw a picture then colour it in but Dad just painted in splotches. Viewed closely they looked like splotches. Take one step back though and the colours suddenly fused and the shapes breathed. My father understood the subtleties of light, and I understood that he understood them. It was a language that had no words.

What I couldn't understand was that if my dad was so talented, why didn't we have much money? He had qualifications as a probate valuer but didn't use them. He worked mainly unpleasant jobs that required him to wear overalls, leave early and arrive back grubby. He had so much going for him but he was missing a key ingredient: self-esteem. Only I didn't know that at the time.

Neither did I know that at the tender age of six he was sent on a ship to boarding school in England, his dreams left behind in India. It was a poor trade: the nurturing cradle of his family for an entrenched system of bastardisation that destabilised the lives of many young boys.

By age eleven I had a camera, albeit one I would only dare use within the confines of our house. My father was my mentor during my photographic awakening, always at hand and on call. Though frustrated by my family's financial shortcomings I was becoming aware that I had something others didn't: a heritage of adventure. The ingredients of my future were coming together. Something was brewing. But little did I know there was another pot bubbling away.

That same year my parents separated. I had an inkling of their differences, with my mother's wandering quest for religious fulfilment and my father's agnostic indifference with eastern overtones. Of course there was more to it than that. There was somebody else. Well actually 'two' someone elses. I handled it all matter-of-factly, as generous doses of pragmatism and resilience were given to me upon entering this life. I did, however, find it odd and trying when, for about six months, my mother, her new partner, my father, his new partner, her three kids and we three kids all lived in the same little weatherboard-clad house. Something had to give.

Like the Clampetts movin' to Beverly, Dad and his new partner loaded up the car and drove off to Melbourne to begin anew. Unexpectedly they included my brother Shane in the packing list. It wasn't the best day of the year for my little sister Vanessa and me. With stiff upper lips we made light of his departure. As a superficial coping mechanism it worked but I felt let down. Blame didn't come into it. I became acutely aware that even those with your best interests at heart could be unreliable. From that moment on I started to put up a wall of independence around myself that would protect me from disappointment. It has stayed standing to this day.

The upside to all this was that it did give me somewhere to travel to and so started my yearly pilgrimage to Melbourne. By age fourteen I was doing the two-day train trip by myself. I would overnight to Sydney, loving every minute of my time in a sleeper compartment. First thing at Central Station in Sydney was to find the storage lockers. I say lockers because I have never found it easy to travel light. Clothes aren't the problem, it's possessions. A clutter of instruments and tools. Things for doing things. Then it was a guitar, camera and tripod, lots of books, magazines, mask and snorkel. I like to be prepared. This is something that I've never been able to shake and it's been both a blessing and a curse as a professional cameraman. My booty safely stowed I'd spend the day roaming Sydney's back alleys trying to take in some of the gritty underbelly of city life that seemed to be the staple of the photography magazines I was becoming addicted to. My dad kept his photographic mentorship alive from afar by paying for my magazine subscriptions. I read, reread and wrung every last drop of information I could from those pages.

The travel bug bit early. By sixteen I was a veteran of the long road trip to Melbourne and elsewhere interstate. Though I was too young to have a licence my friends weren't – having older friends has been a constant in my life – and I would encourage those with newly acquired licences to drive me. And if they couldn't, train travel was cheap, fun and liberating. I was already aware there was a big world out there and I wanted desperately to be a part of it.

My mind was everywhere else except where I was. As far as school was concerned I did pretty well, if you don't count learning. An oversight by someone, somewhere, enabled me to attend Brisbane State High School, long known for its top-level academic and sporting achievements. Capitalising on my lack of self-esteem, my refusal to be a team player and an immaturity that came from being the youngest in my year, I earned a place as one of the school's finest underachievers. In my final year I knew that staring at the ceiling and playing the class fool to hide my inadequacies was wasting everyone's time. I decided to take matters into my own hands.

With six months to go I embarked upon a systematic campaign of wagging school that enabled me to develop my own curriculum. Every minute of my truancy was spent at the William Street State Library poring over every book on photography and every book on travel I could find. The die was cast. Every page I turned strengthened my resolve. Grainy black and white photo essays of the Vietnam War entranced me. Time lost meaning as a single photo engrossed me for hours. Where maths left me unmoved, the numbers for the technical details of each photo spoke to me. Patterns of time and place, aperture and shutter speed revealed themselves and were committed to memory. The jigsaw was taking shape. It was time to leave my self-made classroom and hit the gritty streets. But this was Brisbane in the seventies and nothing happened in Brisbane, or so I thought.

# 2

## Opportunity is missed by most people because it is dressed in overalls and looks like hard work.

THOMAS EDISON

A barking dog is annoying. A barking policeman is worse. 'GET BACK ON THE FOOTPATH,' he hollered. All but a handspan away from my face, I could see the fillings in his back teeth. There was no mistaking that he was talking to me. Half crouching, as if this would somehow protect me from the law's burning gaze, I weaselled my way back into the crowd.

A human fence had self-erected upon the roadside's edge, providing me with enough cover to sneak along. Sorry, sorry, sorry. I squeezed and weaved and apologised my way through the tightening crowd of shoppers all rubber-necking for a glimpse of the gladiatorial spectacle playing out on the road alongside. I made a mental note to myself: I need to learn to be more pushy.

A safe distance down I re-entered from whence I came, into a river of protesters surging along inner Brisbane's Adelaide Street. Like a bobbing log fated to drop over the falls I was sucked into the river of grown men fighting, spitting and swearing, each one of them fired with anger and hatred and all inevitably headed to the thin blue line where police and protesters clashed. The sheer animality of it intrigued me. I raised Dad's hand-me-down SLR camera, vainly trying to find focus and work out when I should push the shutter button. I had no idea.

Whatever my failings I've never had a problem acting upon ideas. There was to be a street march in Brisbane city that afternoon in 1977. I knew it was to protest Queensland's new anti-protest laws brought in by the Bjelke-Petersen government, but I didn't know what any of that meant either. I just knew that photojournalists took those sort of photos and if I wanted to be a photojournalist that's where I needed to be.

I did know one thing about photojournalists, though – how they dressed. I took my cue from the likes of *Playboy*, which shaped many of my adolescent opinions. Wagging yet another day off school I dressed in my best chambray denim top and faded denim flares, unbuttoned my shirt one button too many, slung my blue and tan cordura camera bag (complete with brass corner protectors) onto my shoulder, hotfooted it to the city, took a deep breath and stepped into the fray. There, displaying equally bad 1970s Brisbane fashion sense, safari-suited middle-aged men with helmet-like displays of mutton chops and moustaches fought alongside beer-gutted, stubby-shorted, rubber-thong-wearing comrades from the workers' unions. The other side sported ill-fitting short-sleeved business shirts and ties, the standard detective outfit of the day. This was battle: it wasn't schoolwork and I was slap bang in the middle.

It was all new to me. Having a camera and using it with a dose of attitude let me be where I patently didn't belong. I'd found a portal to an eye-popping new world. I didn't know a man's three-day stubble made a loud scratching as it bristled against an equally hairy forearm that forcibly cradled it in a choker hold. CLICK. I had never before seen an adult lose their dignity and this shocked me. CLICK. It happens when an angry person is physically restrained in a way they can't escape. They snort and produce unpleasant guttural sounds as they are carried prone by four burly policemen, their pants stretched so far down that half their bum crack points skyward for all to see. CLICK. Bubbles of snot uncontrollably bluster and pop from their flaring nostrils as they are wrestled into the back of a waiting paddy van presenting an image they want few to see, let alone photograph. CLICK. CLICK.

I was immediately struck by the self-imposed, self-serving discipline that separated the onlookers from the protesters. The area defined itself into an arena. You were either in or out. I was on the inside. It felt good being on the inside and bearing witness from close quarters. Deep down I knew I was destined for more than just spectating. I wasn't part of the fight but part of the action. I liked it. Unfortunately this wasn't a sentiment shared by the same police sergeant, who again thrust his face closer to mine than I thought possible. 'IF I HAVE TO TELL YOU AGAIN I'LL ARREST YOU. GET BACK ON THE FOOTPATH.'

With my tail between my legs and my face beetroot red with embarrassment I disappeared into the anonymity of the crowd. I drove away in my VW Beetle complete with a 'Save the Whale' sticker. My head buzzed from continually recalling the event and my body was still anaesthetised from the adrenaline rush. I had a new taste in my mouth. It was slightly unpleasant but nonetheless I licked my lips the whole way home.

Next to me on the front seat rode my camera where I had proudly angled it to show off its best side. I marvelled at its bulk, its dials and numbers, its magenta and green reflections typical of many a lens. I relived the sounds of the camera's shutter and mirror mechanism clunking loudly and how people reacted to that, moving aside to let me do my job. At the time I simply felt 'bloody good'. Looking back I can see I was going through a rite of passage all professional shooters experience: the moment your camera ceases to be a toy and becomes a tool.

My expectations weren't high. I would've been happy enough if the photos were simply in focus and correctly exposed. Of course I had grand visions of a magazine placement but I knew these images were for private viewing only. For me they were damning evidence that I had wagged school and so were destined for the bottom drawer. But now at least I was blooded. My destiny was clear.

I finished school and moved seamlessly onto the dole. Unbeatable as it was for getting a good tan going, unemployment didn't sit well with me. I'm one of the least idle people I know, and very thin-skinned, which is why my stint as a restaurant photographer was short. Trying to beat the flower seller to the table to interrupt someone's perfectly good dinner with, 'Evening, folks, care for a photo?' was not what I had in mind when I visualised my career. I never knew there were so many creative ways to say fuck off.

The federal government did start insisting I attend some job interviews. As hard as I tried to be everything an employer didn't desire, I still got the job at the ACI Glass factory. Having someone watch thousands and thousands of beer bottles rattle past a light box at three am to check them for faults is not a good idea, especially when that person is me. The general public have an expectation that bottles fresh from the factory don't contain shards of glass. I had never done nightshift and consequently I slept at inappropriate times. Had I been awake I would have lived up to my 'quality control' name tag. Ten minutes here and ten minutes there added up to a lot of faulty bottles that slipped through. Someone out there may have got a little more glass than they bargained for when they swigged on their stubbie. Still, if I was to listen to the Turkish and Vietnamese workers who formed the majority of the factory floor, I had hit the jackpot. All I had to do was volunteer to do double shifts for just thirty years and I could retire pretty.

With photography still in the forefront of my mind I hatched a plan to escape my indenture to the glassworks. I simply didn't turn up for seven days. I did return and was summarily despatched through the 'you've broken your side of the contract' door. There I was befriended by a shop steward type fellow who was obviously bored and itching for a tussle with management. He convinced me there must have been a really 'good' reason why I didn't turn up for seven days. Not to disappoint him I got my creative juices going. 'My mum's had a brain tumour and I had to stay at home and look after my sister' is what came out of my mouth. With that he stormed into my supervisor's office and demanded this and threatened that. An hour later I was clicking my heels down the street with an envelope full of cash and no doubt one very happy union official was gloating to a sycophantic audience about how he 'stuck it up management' yet again. I was also happy my photographic career had a chance of getting back on track.

At this stage of my life I used to prance around wearing cheesecloth, drive that 'Save the Whale' sticker-clad VW Beetle, carry a calico shoulder bag with a fife in it and listen to Donovan records. In short I was a wanker. So the next step in my photographic quest came as somewhat of a surprise to those who endured my ideological pretence: I joined the army. A desire to defend Her Majesty wasn't really the motivation. I was still heavily under the influence of photojournalism books full of war-zone images when a recruiting poster on a bus shelter caught my eye. The picture showed soldiers patrolling through a pine forest and I thought to myself, that forest looks nice, I'd like to see that forest. Plus everyone in the recruiting office was really pleasant and seemed to think the army could do with my photographic skills. With hand on heart and facing the Queen, I made my pledge and signed on the dotted line. It's then the yelling started and it didn't stop for three years.

For starters we were treated to eleven weeks of midwinter bastardisation at Kapooka Army Recruit Training Centre near

Wagga Wagga in New South Wales. The corporals there thought it was hilarious when I said I was going to be a photographer. 'They didn't tell you that, did they?' was all they could manage between guffaws.

The army's simple strategy involves tearing you down to nothing then rebuilding you. They take everything you arrive with, even your hair. Then they start taking away everything they gave you when you arrived, like pillows, blankets, ashtrays and towels, and little by little, like lab rats, you learnt that if you pushed the wrong button you got a zap, and the right button got you a pellet of corn. I could accept that. In return they had to accept just one thing: they couldn't have my sense of humour and there was much to laugh at, unannounced locker inspections for one.

Any single item out of place resulted in the contents of your locker being ripped out and tossed onto the floor. This gave you the 'opportunity' to start afresh. I actually like being neat and tidy and ordered. Mine was a model locker, faultless to a point, or so I thought. For this character trait I expected praise but I was wrong. It infuriated them and they were ready to pounce, waiting for me to slip up. My undoing was socks. Done carefully, socks that are folded with the ends rolled back over have a neat, curved line. Knowing they were gunning for me I even ironed the socks. I was way ahead of these amateurs, or so I thought.

My platoon commander had so much starch in his shirt that he crackled like a broadsheet newspaper on a crowded commuter train. The smell of leather polish, Brasso and Brut 33 rushed up my nostrils as he invaded my personal space and began to hiss.

'You don't have smiley socks, Private Mather.'

'Sir?' I was honestly puzzled.

'The curved bits on your socks are pointing down, they look like unhappy socks. This is a happy platoon, Private Mather. In this platoon socks need to curve up. In this platoon we have smiley socks!'

I uttered a curt 'Sir' in confirmation and he gave himself a self-congratulatory nod. His attendant henchman had a wire hook to hand and gravity on his side. He stepped forward and disgorged my locker contents. To this day I am compelled to correct socks into a smiling attitude.

Graduating from basic training was another opportunity to remind them that I had been earmarked for photography with army public relations. More guffawing in the background. No, no, Private Mather, we've reserved a special place for you over here in the infantry, you'll be much happier as cannon fodder. Hence I became intimate with blisters and guns. It's also where I encountered one of the two scariest moments of my life, both of which started with me sleeping.

Still only nineteen, I was really just a babe and unaware that different social tribes have different rules. I naively and somewhat arrogantly thought most people would think along the same lines as me. I was a half-decent bloke with a bit of nous. Turns out not everyone shared my assumptions. When the army recruits it gets a broad cross-section of character types. It's a big organisation. It needs someone to lead, someone to clean dishes and someone to do the nasty jobs. My section had a few of the latter.

Every group has one, the person who constantly gets picked on. We had Private Eggleton. He plain got up people's noses but was always harmless and well meaning. Bigotry was alive and well in my section and differences were not tolerated. As the army would say, individuality is fine, as long as we do it together. Two other guys, self-styled homogeneity enforcers, thought they'd set Private Eggleton straight. Knowing he would have received a slapping from these two goons I checked on him. His room was empty and blood was splattered everywhere, up the walls, across the floor … He wasn't in the hospital either. I asked an orderly who said he was there and pointed to a face bloated and closed over. I hadn't even recognised him.

I wasn't the only person who thought this retribution unreasonable. So did Geoff Waldron. Geoff was a boy from Gippsland sheep country. He had a triangular face and one of his front teeth splayed out slightly. He was the original two pick-handles across the shoulders that tapered to a tiny waist, all upon a frame that stood an easy six foot two inches tall. He had a tough country way about him; if it needed doing, you did it. He was intelligent with an endearing smile. He also had an incredibly strong sense of natural justice that earned him the nickname 'the Fixer'.

You didn't want to mess up around Geoff. He would take it upon himself to talk the guilty party through the error of their ways with genuine avuncular concern. He would even put a comforting arm across their shoulder but finish by saying, 'You've got to take your punishment now,' and, like I'm guessing his father did to him, he'd proceed to beat the living crap out of the recipient of the chat. With more genuine concern he'd help them off to lick their wounds. This is exactly the scene that played out with Private Eggleton's two attackers. I had never seen and didn't understand this sort of justice but plenty around me did. Geoff unsettled me but to my surprise we became mates, which was much better than being on his bad side. We would while away an hour with a beer and some homespun philosophy.

One night while I was dreaming of cameras and girls, in that order, I woke to the sound of metal lockers crashing to the floor and lots of swearing. It was coming from the next barrack block. A voice called out, 'It's Barney and Geoff Waldron – Geoff's going to kill him.'

Barney was the group's other country behemoth. He lumbered around like a tree with legs and was pretty dumb. He had also just ironed a cat. In a drunken state he'd thought it a laugh to take one of the strays that cowered around our barracks and give it a good steam and press. It was Saturday night and Geoff was well plastered because that's what you did on Saturday nights. Barney had transgressed the unwritten law and the Fixer was bent on seeing justice was done. The screaming and thundering faded off into the dark as the fight grew legs and the chase was on. I thought, I don't want any part of this and went back to sleep.

You know how it is that sometimes when you're asleep you sense something and wake bolt upright? That's how I came to be looking straight into Geoff's maniacal eyes. Beads of sweat were growing from his pores, eventually losing the fight to gravity and plipping onto my sheets. He was sitting on the edge of my bed, a folding shovel clenched in his fist. 'Barney, that sick bastard, he ironed a kitten. That sick bastard, I'm gunna kill him. You're gonna help me, aren't you, Jules?' I went stone cold. Not only had I just had my first and only invitation to kill someone, I knew what was coming next. 'You know, Jules, it's times like these that you're either with me or against me.'

He was becoming increasingly agitated and I knew that my punishment would be forthcoming, so I'm not sure where this came from, but I leaned over and hugged him and said into his ear, 'Geoff, I'm not against you but I can't do that.' Surely the next sound would be the splintering of at least one of my bones but there was nothing. He just said 'OK' and left with a sense of purpose. The fight raged on and unfortunately for the world they didn't kill each other. I lay there the rest of the night wondering where my photographic quest had gone wrong. Daylight came and I resumed working with these guys. Now more than ever I was acutely aware that my co-workers were slightly unhinged people with loaded weapons in their hands. Relaxed I wasn't.

My yearning for photography took a back seat as I got caught up in a world of new experiences and adventures with the 2nd/4th Battalion of the Royal Australian Regiment. I was too busy learning and travelling. I learnt that I've got a bit of mongrel in me and that at times I can be lured by pedigree but I'm most comfortable with the less refined. I learnt that I must have challenge in my life, for without it I become intolerable to be around. I learnt through two good thumpings that I was very self-centred and this manifested itself as indifference to others. And I learnt that self-determination was not one of the key points on my job description.

To regain some small amount of control over my destiny I needed to get out of the chain of command that had me reporting to lance corporals who delighted in wringing every last drop out of the small amount of power they exercised. I went through officer training selection but they saw right through me. They wanted a team player. I've been a lot of things in my forty-seven years but never one of those. I nosed around and found something that took out a few unnecessary links in the chain of command.

My next job descripton read (and this is verbatim from the job description in the manual): must have above average powers of endurance. Must have a personality that allows him to kill calmly and deliberately under all conditions. Must be able to stalk, night or day, then lie in wait unseen and kill with one shot.

I became a sniper, a job tailor-made for me if ever there was one. Not that I had any desire to kill anyone and thank goodness I never had to. Not that I had any affinity with guns apart from my game-hunter Uncle Mickey in India, and father and Uncle Andy, and that was just photos in the family album. I could, however, blissfully indulge in my miserable antisocial behaviours and not have to talk to anyone for days on end. I could get back to nature by crawling on my belly through it, kilometres at a time. Often I would set up in a concealed position called a 'hide' and lie motionless from first light to dark. Small birds would hop along the length of my Parker Hale sniper rifle convinced I was nothing more than a log. Once, a harmless python coiled alongside me for hours enjoying the free heating.

Sleeping rough, on the ground, in what I was wearing, became a way of life. In 1981 I spent over two hundred nights like this. It was a wonderful time of finding out 'who' I was. Being alone in remote areas with a map and a compass and no one to blame but myself gave me insight into what we are all capable of but rarely get the chance to try. Fortress Independence was in good shape and I enjoyed hiding inside, ignoring the responsibilities of real life beyond the walls. And the cherry on the cake was my secret companion, my telescopic sight. Essentially it was half a camera, the more important half, the lens. Using my memory as film, I spent hundreds upon hundreds of hours honing an eye for artistic composition. It was here that I felt the first inklings of an interest in filmmaking.

Part of sniping involves going in under darkness and putting up windage indicators. These were generally small strips of camouflaged cloth we tied to branches 100, 300 and 600 metres away from the hide. This is necessary because a bullet is unstable as it leaves the barrel and steadies up later in flight. The flying deadly lump of lead is affected differently by wind at different stages of its journey. To add extra confusion, the wind can easily blow in three directions over a distance of hundreds of metres. Through the telescopic sight these secret wind vanes let you adjust the shot accordingly. It's this attention to detail that enables you to shoot dead accurate up to 600 metres. These little strips of cloth also became characters in little imaginary dramas I would pretend to film through the telescopic sight. Though uncomfortable, it was a poor man's film school heaven.

The filmmaking bug bit and I bought my first Super 8 camera. I 'permanently borrowed' from the library a book called *The Ten Golden Rules of Cinematography*. With this powerful combination in hand I set about making mini documentaries about army life. I had a little problem with Rule 2. It described the cutaway, a technique as vital and basic to filmmaking as verbs are to writing or incisions are to surgeons. Briefly, if the main focus of what you are filming is, say, a street parade, a cutaway for that would be a shot of the faces of the flag-waving onlookers. It's usually a reaction to the main action. More often than not the cutaway is a tighter shot, like a close-up. Somehow in my reading I had skipped over everything about a cutaway bar it being a close-up shot.

My mini documentary had a scene in which a soldier abseiled down a rock face for the first time. Scared, he took forever to go over the edge. This was just what I had been waiting for, a textbook place to use a cutaway if ever there was one. On screen it should have looked like this: a soldier on top of a cliff followed by a shot of onlookers going, 'Jump, you gutless wonder, jump,' again returning to the shot of the soldier, this time already over the edge and going down the cliff. My overlooking everything about a cutaway except that it was a close-up shot rendered my film thus: soldier on top of cliff, cigarette being stubbed out in ashtray, soldier going down the cliff.

Yes, you read that correctly. You and everyone else who saw the film wanted to know what's with the cameo appearance of the ashtray? Someone even tried to explain to me it was as ridiculous as having the Queen of England walking down the stairway of an aircraft and putting in a shot of a yawning walrus to shorten it. But I wouldn't hear of it.

With an exasperated sigh I would explain to each successive questioner the merits of Rule 2, the cutaway, and berate them for not understanding filmmaking. It is embarrassing to admit but I perpetuated this gross error for a few years into my professional career. I've decided I wasn't born with the cutaway gene.

Sniping gave me the ear of higher ranking officers. Enthusiastically I would argue my case to be transferred to army public relations. No immediate positions were available – ever, it seemed – but a true gentleman of a battalion commander encouraged me by providing me with opportunities to cover and report on battalion events. I began popping up all over the place with camera and notebook in hand. This new-found exposure had caught the eye of someone, as I was deemed the perfect candidate for an upcoming SAS counter-terrorism exercise. Someone was going to try and blow up the Comalco mining facility at Weipa and I was to be the 'mole' on the inside. Why me? It was thought I had what it took to fit seamlessly into Comalco as a new photographer in their industrial photography section.

I was schooled up with undercover training, given a false Comalco ID and sent to work in their photography unit for a fortnight. It was from here that I would send out my feelers and gather intelligence to save the country in this make-believe scenario. Are you kidding me? I had just been dropped, like a kid in a lolly shop, bang into a photography playground, and play is what I did. I had finally become a photographer, sort of. I would rendezvous via telephone with military intelligence every other day, making up whatever they needed to hear to secure my new-found lifestyle.

The crashing end to my fairytale moment came in two instalments. One night, in a mining camp somewhere on Weipa's outskirts, I passed out drunk after being led astray by hard-drinking miners. In the moonless black of early morning I stumbled along a bauxite superhighway, one of the large, w-i-d-e, smooth dirt roads used by the giant yellow mining trucks to transport bauxite. All I had to do was get back to Weipa before light and sneak in unnoticed. How hard could that be? Thwack! I was on the ground, flashlights in my face and a commotion of voices above. As part of the army's operational plan they had converted this section of road into an airstrip. I had just walked full tilt into the wing of a Pilatus Porter reconnaissance aircraft. This plane has unusually low-slung wings, the height of my forehead to be exact. To cut a long story short, I was unceremoniously relieved of my undercover status and recommissioned to assist an army photographer. It's here the second part of the crashing end comes.

There was to be a public relations photo shoot to highlight the cooperation between the army and Comalco during this 1981 exercise. Two really big yellow mining trucks were positioned in the centre of a bauxite mining pan. This is a multi-football-field size area with crumbly red blocks of dirt the size of loaves of bread, a surface very loose and difficult to walk on. Between these stage-set trucks an army Kiowa helicopter was to fly and, with a few presses of the shutter button, the front-page photo of the Comalco newsletter would be born.

Still skulking in disgrace I was relegated to carrying bags for the army photographer assigned to cover the event. His name was Quasi. I never knew his real name, but that applied to many of the people I worked with in the army. There was Robbo, Cowboy, Weeds, Carrot, Two Names (his I remember from his surname Breadingham-Moore). Mine was Big Julie. Then there was Quasi. Quasi was named because of his unfortunate and quite uncanny resemblance to the Hunchback of Notre Dame. In an organisation with demanding physical benchmarks it was always a mystery how Quasi got in. I relate this with the greatest of respect because he was a lovely bloke, but he was very short, had a hunchback and you couldn't help but notice disfigurement in his face, as one of his eyes was dramatically lower than the other. The culture in the military is to confront things head on, so before even stepping off the bus he had already been christened Quasi.

Quasi went in the chopper for the ride and the Comalco photographer (now fully aware of my duplicity) set up for the shot. A large crowd of Comalco workers gathered to witness the spectacle alongside a handful of army types. It looked spectacular alright, the helicopter zooming along just metres above the red bauxite. Orange smoke trailed from a strategically placed smoke flare strapped to the skids. Like threading a needle, the chopper navigated the narrow gap between the yellow machines. Click. Click. The photographer's work was done.

The camouflaged Kiowa helicopter roared skyward in a steep climb and banked sharply, way too sharply. With its blades no longer chopping air for lift it fell, like a brick, the seventy metres to earth. Looks of wide-eyed disbelief were traded. As if the starter's gun had been fired at a marathon, our hundred strong crowd sprinted across the loose ankle-snapping blocks of bauxite. Our discomfort was their saving. Like a shattered eggshell, the helicopter had broken into a handful of pieces. The loose, blocky ground had acted as an impact absorber. In the middle of this aviation junkyard were, intact and alive, the pilot and Quasi. The pilot's legs looked to be broken but he was lucid and talking. The focus shifted to Quasi, now the centre of much concern. Never before having laid eyes on Quasi, the Comalco staff whispered in hushed and grave tones, 'He's pretty bad' … 'His face, look, it's all broken up' … 'He may have broken his back.' Turned out Quasi was absolutely fine apart from one mighty big shock. His protests of good health fell on the deaf ears of a growing medical team convinced his misshapen form was the result of massive crash trauma.

The army tempted me to sign on for another three years but with no firm offer to make a photographer out of me I left. Adventure and testosterone oozed from my every pore, photography always on the brain. There was much talk in the army of offshore drilling rigs employing ex-army personnel so I applied to a dozen or so. But it was just talk. The only skill I had that counted for anything with them was being a strong swimmer and that alone wasn't going to win them over. If I couldn't find a challenge I'd make one. An approach to the World Wildlife Fund to charity walk from Perth to Sydney was met with deafening silence. Reality reared its annoying head and I took a job printing photos at an inner city photo lab. Nights I spent studying in a cinematography course and by day, in between endless out-of-focus baby photos, I approached the commercial television networks on Brisbane's Mt Coot-tha to take me on as a cameraman. Like the oil rig companies, they put little value on enthusiasm alone.

I didn't know how I would become a cameraman, all I knew was that I had a single-minded determination to be one. I'm sure a lot of that focus came from my mother, who at the time was midway through a twelve-year stint running a charity shop. She had set her sights on making a difference to the lives of children in a Thai orphanage. This was her passion. Sometimes, though, passion is a polite term for obsession; a number of times my mother sold all of her furniture to raise needed funds. I saw these obsessive tendencies in myself and made mental notes about keeping myself in check. Try as I did, there were times when it felt as though I was a train with no brakes, but so what? The track seemed never-ending from where I stood.

One Friday night, closing up the lab, I was shown a newspaper ad for upcoming ABC TV traineeships. The closing date for applications was the coming Monday morning post. It took a mad scramble over the weekend but I made it onto the list of seven hundred applicants for the five available positions. I thought I had no chance. I was wrong. In March 1983 the ABC welcomed me with open arms, sort of.

# 3

Knock knock.
Who's there?
Opportunity.
Don't be silly, opportunity never knocks twice.

Louise Kennedy smiled warmly. She was the ABC personnel officer given the task of inducting me into the system and, like everyone else that morning, she was cheerful and inviting. I liked the place already. On the desk separating the two of us was a tall pile of forms that needed signing before I could become an employee of Australia's national broadcaster. My life as a world-travelling cameraman was imminent.

'A long career is built upon solid foundations,' chirped Louise as she tidied the pile of paperwork. There was a copy of the Official Secrets Act for me to sign, a Code of Conduct outlining the behaviour expected of a public servant, and all the usual superannuation bumf and other bits and bobs.

'Let's get the important ones signed first,' Louise suggested as she extended form and pen to me.

'What's this for?' All I could make out was $1.85 in the total box.

'This is the authority to deduct one dollar and eighty-five cents from your pay for the tea fund. Mrs Smith the tea lady comes around at morning and afternoon tea, and she serves sandwiches at lunch but they are extra,' Louise set me straight.

Alright then, where are the cameras? I had, in my opinion, been selected from the seven hundred applicants into one of the five production operator traineeships (POTs to everyone) on the strength of my passion for, and experience in, photography. Little did I know that they had different plans for me. Even way back in 1983 the ABC was beginning to see the merits of a multiskilled workforce and we were to be the first of a new breed. Cameras to the right, you'll be turning left, Mr Mather. They didn't share my desperate need to be a cameraman, instead they began an amazing tutorial into the nuts and bolts of broadcast television. And so the racehorse was hobbled. The dash out of the photojournalistic gates became a canter at best. The ABC does lots of wonderful things but, I was to learn, it does them at its own pace.

The ABC is a collection of departments that don't talk to each other. They never have and likely never will. All departments share one common trait: a deeply held belief that if it wasn't for them the ABC wouldn't exist. I and the other four new POTs were in the production operations department. These are the people who physically make programs. Like wide-eyed kids in a toyshop, we rode the lift up to level 5 of Broadcast House, our home for the next sixteen weeks and a battleground set for a clash of ideals.

Level 5 was ABC training central for Queensland. It was run by the engineering department, as it was known then, the undisputed heavyweight interdepartmental champion of the ABC. Knitted walk socks to the knee, sensible shoes, pocket pen organisers and cardigans were the dress of the day. Our sartorially challenged supervisors were ABC technicians, or 'termites' as we lovingly called them. Theirs was a world of ordered systems, of fault dockets and ergs, ohms and other things electrical.

Individually all decent people, collectively they leveraged their ability to hold TV programs to ransom. It was simple: no working equipment, no program. They jealously held the reins.

There is one other factor that helped raise them to dominance in the early 1980s. Back in the 1950s when television started in Australia, there were no cameramen, editors, sound recordists or the like. TV was staffed by technicians from the PMG, a forerunner of Telstra. The call of 'Hands up who wants to be a cameraman? Who wants to be an editor?' must have seemed like a pleasurable career distraction from the tedium of test patterns and solder joints. This wave of unlikely program makers enjoyed their new-found life. As they matured in their career, many returned to the technical nest. Growing numbers of these came to be heads of department and the ABC had a distinct bent to things technical. So the arrival of the five new production trainees – one a punk rocker with spiked hair and an 'I Vomit on Your Grave' T-shirt, one a ruddy-cheeked, hyperactive would-be successor to Steven Spielberg, another a highly intelligent but slightly mad genius and two Joe Publics, myself one of them – was an affront to this conservative public service enclave. So began a three-year battle of ideas and ideals.

Our initial sixteen weeks were spent in a classroom separate from the Brisbane Toowong studios. In their zealousness to whip us into line and have us embrace their need for measured routine, we were subjected daily to lame attempts at management psychology. Zero tolerance of late arrival was the order of the day. Signing the roll book was mandatory. At the prescribed hour an enthusiastic instructor gleefully ruled a red line under the last name in the book. Latecomers signed under the line. Other technicians would titter and tsk! tsk! as the book of shame was paraded throughout the offices. Somehow they thought this ritual humiliation would break us but of course it merely strengthened our resolve to remain apart. We came from a different planet and our strength lay in a creative unity that needed to be expressed. We were far from anarchic but we were ready to fly and this Basic Electronics prison was not going to clip our wings.

Like assuring us Santa would come if we were good boys, our ageing instructors, when they hadn't fallen asleep mid-sentence (it happened) promised the land of TV milk and honey was within our grasp. On our fourth day, like preschoolers on a museum outing, we were chaperoned on a five-minute walk to the TV studios, though only after everyone had been to the toilet.

A long corridor ran the length of the main building. Midway along this was a temple of electronic worship called Master Control, home to the heartbeat of the station. As we moved towards it, every step a step closer to unlocking the secrets of Television, our cardigan-clad minders seemed overly eager that we avoid looking into one particular doorway. We of course developed an overly eager need to do the opposite. It was nothing more than a heavy-set man with a moustache, ironing. Granted he was wearing a yellow feather boa at the time. What's all the fuss, we thought? Only later would we realise what part he played in an enormously eccentric circus of characters that was the Brisbane ABC.

Our small band parked outside the wide doors to Master Control. We were instructed to look away lest we unwittingly memorise the security keypad entry digits. Ah, now I understood why I had been required to sign the Official Secrets Act. As we averted our gaze we eyed a figure coming from the unexplored end of the hallway. A veil of blue smoke from his cigar lifted and we were staring at the Fat Controller from *Thomas the Tank Engine*, a rotund gentleman in a three-piece suit and a pork pie hat, a silver fob chain stretching from breast to hip pocket.

'Welcome, welcome to the ABC at Toowong,' he enthused. 'You must be the new trainees. We've been expecting you and what a fine choice they've made. You will no doubt enjoy your long careers here, for the ABC is a *wonderful, w-o-n-d-e-r-f-u-l* establishment. I'm always here to answer any questions you may have. Well ... good luck, gentlemen.' For over a year I took this effusive and generous person to be the manager of the ABC in Queensland. I was later to learn it was Ricky Adams, a colleague only a few rungs higher than us on the career ladder and liked by all. He was a dedicated trainspotter, a collector of railway timetables and our conductor for the moment. This was indeed my station. It was Eccentric Central on the photography line. A long journey so far and I knew I wasn't there yet but this was the change of trains I was after. I could sense energy, a pulse. I could smell the cameras close by. But I was about to be derailed; my train was headed for the edge of a cliff.

It is my wont to throw myself whole-heartedly into anything I do and climbing was no exception. Climbing and the ABC were two areas in which I had little experience, but I was keen to learn. After a week of electronic confusion I set myself the weekend challenge of learning to lead climb. To this point my five-month-old climbing career had relied on the security of a rope always supporting me from above in case I fell. This is called top-roping and limits you to climbing on cliffs of twenty metres in height. The next step is lead climbing and mastering its basics means the world is now your vertical oyster. The trade-off is falling, and while relatively safe, falling is about a hundred times scarier. Well within my capabilities, I thought, and besides, I needed to clear my head of resistors, capacitors and all things electronic.

Buoyed in spirit from five days with the ABC, this new challenge of climbing seemed a natural addition to my bright future. With confidence and bravado masking the fact that I was shit-scared, I began the vertical moves up a beginner level climb named Iron Butterfly. I'll spare you the technical details here save to say that I didn't really know what I was doing. A slight bulge in the rock signposted the fifteen metre mark and the point where I lost my nerve to continue. With my knees shaking wildly, my free hand jammed a wonderful piece of equipment called a friend into a fist-size crack at waist level. I managed to clip my rope to the friend and I called out 'resting' to Bruce, my climbing partner below.

Happy to relieve the weight from my arms, I relaxed my panicked grip on the rock and let the rope take my weight – my trusty new friend would hold me secure. It didn't. Blurring streaks of lichen on the rock gave way to an eyeful of blue sky followed by a confusion of leaves and tree branches. Exactly what was happening I wasn't sure but I knew it was bad. I was falling, somehow rotating end over end on the way down. Inexperience was about to teach me a lesson. I had completely messed up my system of safety ropes and was truly flying. Two large rocks footed the cliff, one the size of a TV set, the other the size of a microwave oven, and spanning them was a head-size gap. My head speared into the hole and my shoulders took all the impact. Painlessly I blacked out and, I think, came to seconds later.

Just like in the cartoons, green stars fizzed and swirled around my head. I was sitting on an angled slope with warm blood running down my face. Instinctively my right hand found its way to the moist matted clump of hair and prodded. Hmm. My left arm was slowly making its way back into the shoulder socket from where it had been torn only a minute earlier. Clunk! It popped back in of its own accord. My right collarbone was detached and sat proud in an unsightly lump under my T-shirt. Save for a collection of other sprains and bruises I was alright.

My ABC career had come very close to lasting just one week. Against all medical advice I rolled up to ABC Training School the next morning. Painkillers left me vague in attempting to explain the ridiculous number of bandages and splints covering my body. With an assurance that I wouldn't get left behind I retired sick to count my blessings and reflect upon how I nearly ended my dream of being a cameraman. I made a silent pact to be more circumspect in putting recreation ahead of my career. Well that lasted about five minutes, didn't it?

My traineeship continued and was remarkable on two counts: that a scheme like this even existed and the sheer breadth of subjects it covered – thirty course modules including camera, editing, sound and all things televisual over the course of three years. But that's not all. ABC Radio, which shared the same site, took us under its wing and gave us a grounding there. So, too, the symphony orchestra – this was in the heady days when the ABC had its own. We were attached to them to learn multi-track recording and how to read music scores. Should I have needed to direct an orchestral broadcast, I was set to go.

Though liked on a personal level, we quickly became the grain of sand in the ABC oyster. We irritated so many supervisors and managers. In selecting us the ABC had unwittingly hired a basic production team. I flourished in camerawork, Lee Faulkner excelled in sound, Tim Wilson had an innate rhythm for editing, Bruce Redman wheeled and dealed as a producer and Roger Bradbury pulled it all together as director. I'm sure we signed something, somewhere, that said our primary role was to look, learn and listen. We, however, saw the ABC as a goldmine of training budgets, auxiliary program funds and local production purses all waiting to be mined for our own projects. So started a series of small films, many centred around climbing. Of those, a fifteen-minute mini documentary following a father-and-son climb of a spectacularly overhanging cliff became one of the ABC's most cost-effective programs. The father-and-son relationship had an element of cooperation that made it a hit with the educational programmers. Its short length made it perfect for filling gaps in the TV schedule and it was shown dozens of times.

No matter how hard we tried to elevate our individual strengths and break from our training schedule, the ABC was steadfast in their plans for our future. We were regularly banished to late-night shifts in the videotape and continuity areas. Videotape is where programs are recorded and replayed to air. Continuity is the place that controls the final product that goes to air – the ABC that you know on your TV emanates from here. The promos, upcoming programs and what's-on-next spots are smoothly inserted in between the programs. For us the work was repetitive and it should have been the dullest of areas to work in, but it wasn't. It was manned, and I use that term loosely, by sometimes flamboyant, often promiscuous, but never boring gay men. The heavy-set moustachioed man with the yellow feather boa we had seen on our first visit to the studio was a regular performer in an out-of-hours drag revue. It was a dress he'd been ironing. He was a big guy and often popped a few sequins in his Marlene Dietrich spectacular.

Videotape, on the other side of the hall, was even crazier. It was hilariously staffed by right-wing fundamentalist Christians and a sleaze of swingers. If you devised a sitcom around this premise it would be howled down as overly contrived, yet there it was and we were part of it. We, of course, sided with the swingers because they were more fun. It wasn't long before we were used as ammunition in this Christian–Pagan war. It was like being thrown to the lions. One side would give us a job that we had no idea how to do in an attempt to sabotage the career of someone from the other side. It was a bit of the old 'Well, you weren't here to do it when you were supposed to. I had no option but to get Julian to cover for you.' More often than not it ended in tears; tears of laughter for us, as we really weren't responsible for anything. 'Hey! I'm just the trainee,' was our ready mantra.

One time I was thrown into operating a telecine machine that converts a roll of movie film into TV pictures. It was playing a half-hour education program live to air. That meant it was a 400-metre roll of film. In the thirty-second 'do this, this and this' training session, the nuttiest fundamentalist of them all, who displayed a distinct lack of brotherly love, neglected to tell me a most important point – open the machine door every few minutes to check the film is going onto the take-up spool correctly. Half an hour later, feeling pretty chuffed with my new-found skill to drive one of these chattering machines, I opened the door to remove the used spool. Like a washing machine overflowing with suds, a wave of 16mm film washed around my body and spilled a few metres across the floor. Most of it was smeared with oil because this was the 'one' machine that had the oil leak. That oversight earned me a few shifts on the most boring of the boring: overseeing the test pattern go to air.

For anyone unfamiliar with the test pattern, there was a time when TV channels didn't run twenty-four hours. Programs often finished at midnight and started again at seven the next morning. Anytime a program wasn't scheduled a pattern of black and white lines, coloured bars and patches of varying grey were the only things you saw on your TV. It could just as well have been a black screen but this 'test pattern' was useful for TV repair people to make technical adjustments, so as a courtesy it was left up. Our one and only job, every thirty minutes, was to change the reel of classical music that accompanied the test pattern.

An idle mind is the devil's playground so we devised a really fun game. Without going into the technical details, we could make up a tiny black dot, about the size of a match head, that we would superimpose onto the test pattern broadcasting across Queensland, hiding it in the black patches until mischievously needed. Our little black dot was under our control via a joystick. When the tedium became too much to bear we would bring our little black dot out from hiding and whiz it around the screen in fly-like movements. After a fifteen-second outing it was parked back in hiding. We were regularly summoned and handed a record of the switchboard complaints. Usually they went something along the lines of, 'Look,

I've been repairing TVs for twenty years and I *KNOW* that this is technically impossible *BUT* you've got an insect in your system.'

Nearly two and a half years passed before I finally got closer to being a cameraman. Like so many lucky breaks, it was just about being in the right place at the right time. Brisbane's garbage contractors were on strike and had been for some months. Mountains of fetid rubbish were rising at the locked gates to the city's rubbish tips and all the real cameramen were on jobs elsewhere. Instructions to me were brief: grab a camera and go and get some shots. Like a flash I was in the car with a smile across my face that plastic surgery couldn't have removed.

Arriving at the tip was like entering an apocalyptic movie set: front-end loaders waltzed in ghastly silhouettes among the steaming mounds. With a swagger I had rehearsed many times in my head I set to work. The low winter light had created a bit too much mood. I was excited but unsure. I guessed and re-guessed my exposure setting about a dozen times before committing and began filming. The CP16 purred its soft chatter in my right ear telling me sprockets and holes were meshing as they should. I was in sync with the camera and it with me. Without much effort I shot five minutes of film – that's half a roll. I wanted to keep going, and going, but already the financial imperative of filmmaking had been drummed into me: it is a costly business.

Time was getting away. First the film had to go to the lab for processing. The hour-and-a-half wait back at the ABC for the viewable film to be delivered was nerve-racking. I saw the courier van arrive and tracked the journey of the silver film can. It went straight to our long-time chief of staff, Albert Asbury, a very experienced TV news man. As far as I was concerned this was a make or break moment for me. Either I can do this job or I can't. Albert threaded the film onto a Steenbeck editing machine and spooled quickly through the vision. Without even looking up he cast a general question across the busy newsroom: 'Who shot this rubbish?' About to spring from my discreet watching place and claim ownership I began to double guess his inflection on the word 'rubbish'. Was it literal or derogatory? I lingered in self-doubt too long and the moment that was rightfully mine dissolved. Regretting my weakness I slunk away unnoticed.

That night I watched, angst-ridden, as the story went to air. To my relief it looked good. Next day I nonchalantly sidled up to Albert's desk and got what I had been waiting for for so long: 'You shot that rubbish yesterday, didn't you? Nice stuff.' And with those words a cameraman was born ... almost.

I had cameraman stamped all over me. Every time I looked in the mirror I could see it. Why couldn't anyone else? Three years of training ended and my camera career nose-dived. I had been earmarked to be a vision switcher, something I had little aptitude for. Slowly it dawned on me that the ABC wasn't here to serve me but quite the opposite. I also happily married Vicky, my partner of three years. This wasn't part of the plan either. My longstanding proclamation had it that marriage was not an option until at least thirty, but I had fallen deeply in love despite all the arbitrary restrictions I'd devised for myself.

Reluctantly I did my time in the studio. In hindsight the experience was invaluable. Vision mixing involved sitting in the studio control room, a large panel with about a gazillion buttons, knobs and levers at your fingertips from which you 'mixed' together all the cameras, videotapes and other picture sources to make a smooth-looking program.

At the time a controversial strip show was touring Queensland and featured regularly on the news. One of the strippers, Fifi the French Maid, was showing much more of herself than Queensland legislation allowed at the time. Police raided the revue and carted Fifi, feather duster in hand, off to the watch-house. This was an ongoing story and needed lots of fresh vision, as television devours pictures. Cameramen would normally moan when given the job of shooting a bit of overlay but on this story there was a willingness rarely seen. The vision mixing desk was the hub of the station at the time. Everything that came in or went out passed through the desk so you saw it all. The fresh pictures of Fifi came through and were duly stored. Some of the more compromising ones that were unsuitable for broadcast were stored to the side.

Later that week I began my shift as usual, cleaning out the previous night's pictures from the picture storage unit. Like touch typing, you could blindly tap away at the keyboard all the while keeping your eyes focused on last night's paperwork. Midway through this routine housekeeping the first of the day's clients entered the control room. A religious unit producer was accompanied by two senior Catholic clergy. They had a booking to put the finishing touches to a religious documentary. Without breaking from my job at hand I acknowledged them and did what I did for any visitor to the studio control room, I put up the image of what I was doing onto the bank of TV screens in front of me, thirty-four to be exact. They chatted, I tapped.

I'm not sure how long it was before I tuned into their silence. I glanced at them and traced their stony-faced stares to the thirty-four pictures of Fifi beaming out. The previous night's shift had obviously had a private viewing session not recorded on the sheet. The more I tapped, the worse the photos got. There was nothing we didn't know about Fifi by the end. The whole episode ended with me getting one enormous reprimand from my superiors. In my defence I noted that at no time did the clergy avert their gaze.

But miracles do happen. The next studio roster came out and I wasn't on it. I flicked to the field roster and there was my name with camera next to it. I asked no questions. I just punched the air.

# 4

## You can't polish a turd but you can always roll it in glitter.

The next five years from 1988 to 1992 provided my real grounding in television. I did two things: I put my nose to the grindstone and immersed myself in cinematography, and when I wasn't doing that I climbed. Where I could I combined the two. By now I was writing freelance articles for outdoor and photography magazines. Life was busy, very busy. An unsolicited phone call came from senior ABC management telling me I was to represent the ABC on the upcoming 1988 Australian Bicentennial Mt Everest Expedition. Wow, they were going to pay me to go to Mt Everest. The ABC oozed opportunity and I also started a sideline business called Highly Strung, hiring myself out as a climbing cameraman to outside productions. I had purchased my own gear except the camera which I would rent. Strangely enough, this was sanctioned by the ABC. I asked no questions. Nothing else mattered except this hedonistic dream of filming and climbing.

What I was blind to at the time was the richness of the everyday jobs that were the bread and butter of my working week. Truly, no other job could ever come close to providing the eclectic variety of experiences you get as a cameraman. From prince to pauper, you meet them all, the good and the bad, the beautiful and the ugly. Sometimes you're welcome, many times not. The camera is your ticket, a backstage pass to people's lives. Something struck me as unusual way back then and it's played itself out hundreds of times since. Never has its meaning been lost on me to this day, and that's something, because I'm pretty jaded by most things now. I have this quiet out-of-body experience every time I find myself sitting on someone's couch, staring at their family photos, them offering me a cup of tea or a cold drink. Often this is at either the saddest or happiest point in their life. My face numbs and I get a rush of blood to the head. I'm thinking I've done nothing to earn the right to be here in the bosom of this family. That privilege belongs to the people in the photos I'm staring at; they've done the hard yards in this person's life. I'm an impostor.

Only because television demands pictures, for without them it's radio, do I end up there. Its appetite is voracious. I've never been able to shake the feeling that I'm just part of a process that uses these people, that we use their emotions as grease to keep TV rolling along. There are times when our being there is beneficial, but mostly it's because we've got half an hour of TV to fill. It's for this reason that early on I found myself wanting to work on longer forms of work, like documentaries. It seemed there was a more justified reason for intruding in documentaries and there were more opportunities to shoot demanding and complex scenes. The work seemed more thoughtful, considered and purposeful.

That said, I, like, resolved my idealistic fantasies with the next breath and got on with the job of pumping out stories. Shooting news I would usually cover three or four stories daily, current-affairs programs like *The 7.30 Report* and *Landline*, one, maybe two. A quarter of these were really worthy stories, another quarter had some merit, the rest were filler that we had to somehow make look interesting. Over the years it adds up to a lot of stories, and a lot of new people you meet, some more memorable than others.

At one stage the national UFO convention was being hosted at Brisbane's Hilton Hotel. Journalist Peter Greer and I thought this would be a story we could have a bit of fun with. Half an hour after arriving I learnt one of my first professional lessons: never take a camera and a microphone into a room full of people with conspiracy theories. Like iron filings to a magnet we drew them in. (Cameramen often refer to cameras as 'loony magnets'.) Nothing gathers a crowd like a crowd and we were soon swamped. The crush around us had two things in common: no fashion sense and everyone clutched a tattered manila folder bursting with well-thumbed photocopies of official documents. Three actually. They all prefaced their argument with 'No one will listen to what I'm saying'. An event manager rescued us then made an announcement over the PA system to suggest that attendees leave us alone.

Our main talent (an industry term for a main character in a story) was articulate and refreshingly normal. He had been measuring UFO activity around Brisbane for a decade and he wanted to tell us we weren't alone. The description of his UFO detector, its complexity, his qualifications for building it and his normality lured us to his suburban home. Bad move. His was the only house in the street with knee-high grass, a year's worth of uncollected newspapers and blacked-out windows. Inside I took in the surroundings starting with his green velour couch book-ended by lamps with red lace shades. It was like a set from an Oscar Wilde play and also an island of style in a room dull with function. Piles of dusty paperwork and stacked cardboard cartons lined the walls, top to bottom. These contained the data he had collected from the UFO detector. Inside this sealed-up house the temperature was high and rising.

'Could you show us the room with the detector?' Peter asked.

'You're looking at it.'

In front of us on the coffee table was a lump covered by a hand towel. He whipped off the cover. Voilà! His cloak of normality was slipping and his true colours were starting to shine through. I had never seen a UFO detector and it's not what I would have imagined anyway. Straight-faced he took us through the workings, how it measured the gravitational interference caused when a plasma pulsing craft came near. He had spent a decade recording the data from this machinery. In his hand he held a twenty-centimetre length of sawn-off fence paling. On one end a D-cell battery was secured by bent-over nails. Sticky-taped to the battery terminals were wires which ran to the opposite end of the plank. There they were attached to a swinging needle compass, much like you'd find in a boy's-own adventure set. That's it. If a spacecraft were to cruise by the needle would flutter. We watched for flutter but it proved a flutter-free day. Apparently we should have been there the day before. Like ET, it was time for us to return home.

Now I was on the road full time, new experiences were my staple diet. I loved that I was learning so much but there were times I felt out of my depth. Jeni Edgley's couch was a lot more comfortable than the UFO man's and she, as a former Miss Australia, was much nicer to look at. Once married to showbiz promoter Michael Edgley and at the time running an exclusive health resort in the Gold Coast hinterland, she was rating well on the credibility-o-meter. Lunch was being prepared by her chefs so we took a cool drink while we waited and recovered from filming in the high humidity. The setting gave no hint that I was about to get one of the oddest suggestions ever put to me.

She began to quiz me about my health routine. I just said I was an outdoors sort of bloke and climbed and ran whenever I could.

'Health farms are for everyone and you look like you need one,' she said.

'Not me.' I was fit and knew it.

'Not on the outside, on the inside,' Jeni cut in. She had large eyes that stared into you and right then they were making me really uncomfortable. 'I want you to come to one of our colonic irrigation sessions. You can do the enema yourself or we can help you. You collect your contents in a large jar which you bring with you to the following group session. We all examine and discuss our contents and learn from it.'

I got embarrassed and blundered out a no thank you.

'Oh, you're just shy,' she said. 'Maybe a men's-only retreat would suit you better. It runs over a few days and culminates in a tribal outdoor ceremony. We build an American Indian sweat tent and you go in until you start hallucinating. Then you all dance around an open fire, chanting, getting back to your inner animal self.'

I'm thinking nuh-uh, no way, and I'm sure my face telegraphed this message. Apparently not.

'And the best part,' she continued, 'you all get naked and you start howling and you get down on all fours and' – time may have jumbled my memories slightly but these next four words are etched in my mind forever … 'sniff each other's bums.'

By this time I was glowing red with embarrassment. I didn't know what to say but I knew what I wanted to say: 'It seems all very un-Australian to me.' I wished I had said it but I just didn't have the confidence. I still regarded myself as a kid and far from having grown up. I was in my late twenties and suffered from regular bouts of low self-esteem, but never self-doubt. I had a total belief that I could achieve any realistic goal I set myself, but upon reaching it I would never feel worthy of the accompanying accolades. So at this point I was a person confident of my abilities but with low self-confidence. This was in part made worse by working daily alongside reporters with loads of confidence, sometimes more than was good for them.

Despite some exceptions the industry was full of decent people. One of the nice guys was Michael Beatty. He had an air of showmanship on camera, a slight stutter off camera and single-handedly kept tobacco companies afloat. One day he called to ask me if I'd like to go to prison. (Though I've never stayed for more than a day I've been into prisons in five countries.) This was to do a story on a corporate motivational/bonding workshop with a difference: it was for hardcore prisoners.

We visited the kitchen first to get some general vision of one of the workshop inmates doing his daily work. This was not by chance but deliberately structured by us. And here's a handy tip: it's always a good idea to do a little PR work, to show the prisoners in the kitchen that you're an OK sort of person so they don't add a little bodily fluid that wasn't in the recipe to the food you will likely be eating later. A prisoner in Brisbane's Boggo Road Jail once told me, 'You seem a good bloke. Take it from me, don't eat the custard.'

The workshop itself was surprising in that the inmates were taking it very seriously and opening up and being very touchy-feely. It seemed incongruous when a meaty hand with *hate* and *kill* home-tattooed across the knuckles offered some comfort to a teary-eyed hard man confessing this or that to the group. Throughout the day we would take individual inmates to one side and do short interviews with them. Michael would start by asking, 'What are you in for?' The answers came back: murder ... rape ... rape ... murder ... rape ... I made a mental note to make sure I paid my parking tickets.

By the second day we were on first-name terms with everyone. This was the day for the physical bonding exercises that helped build trust in their fellow man. The room was awash with positive energy and much goodwill towards us. Hmm. My antennae went up. They were in the last moments of a group exercise in which one person stands on the edge of a table, closes their eyes and falls backwards to be caught in the arms of their trusted comrades. Then it came. I knew it. 'Not *everyone* in the group has had a turn,' announced the saccharine workshop convener. All eyes turned to us and the tattooed and scarred faces softened and beamed an angelic invitation to us. These guys had been drugged with positive thoughts. I used every excuse in the book – can't leave the camera unattended, bad cameraman's back – but they weren't having any of it. Like the condemned walking to the gallows I slowly climbed the chair to the table top, turned my back to the crowd, folded my arms across my chest, closed my eyes and fell into the arms of murderers and rapists.

Unsettling as it was, it was a soft landing. Many times, though, the cameraman's job is marked by discomfort. There's often a lot of waiting in awkward locations. I was well trained for that. In my army sniping days we would build covered holes in the ground called hides, just deep enough to roll over in. There we would stay for two days. Quite often they would flood in heavy rain. We were tasked to do a job so we stayed in a cold, muddy, wading pool of water with the toads. It should have followed that sitting in the cramped back of a van during a stakeout would come easy to me, but it didn't.

*The Investigators* was a forerunner of consumer-affairs programs on Australian TV. The commercial networks have now made an art form of them with programs like *Today Tonight* and *A Current Affair*. Essentially you chased shonky business people with the camera to publicly shame them where the law had often failed. It's the modern electronic version of the stocks. Brisbane crews were kept very busy on the program because of the Gold Coast. As far as dodgy dealings went, this sandy city was the gift that kept on giving.

A pastor from a charismatic Church of Christ had strayed and was keeping a few coins from the collection plate for himself. Thus far he had avoided the angry congregation's attempts to bring him to justice. That always amused me, as I assumed they would be happy in the knowledge that the big guy upstairs would eventually sort him out. However, no, *The Investigators* were called in. They used the services of a private investigator whose job it was to set up surveillance on the shady shyster and set a trap for him. Our PI worked from a small Mazda van that was cleverly disguised as the 'A1 Electrical' van. It had signage and windows with false boxes of connectors and bits of conduit that were used as peepholes.

Unlike the Tardis on *Dr Who*, inside this didn't expand into a spacious secret lab, it just remained the inside of a small Mazda van. Central to the storage area was a swivel chair, around that was a video camera, still camera, police scanner, two-way radio and other PI bits and bobs. The remaining space ... that was for us: an adrenaline filled producer twitching at every little sound, a yawning sound recordist complete with big microphone in a fluffy windsock on the end of a cumbersome boom pole, and last of all me, with a camera and a mountain of batteries. A few blocks from the rogue rector's place we squeezed into the van and with the PI at the wheel we crunched through the gears in the now overladen van to park across the street from his house.

It was sort of fun for the first ten minutes. Four hours later the novelty had worn off. Every part of my body had gone to sleep and everyone was busting to go to the toilet, most of all the soundo. The producer had slipped into the most annoying of modes for a crew, the *my career depends on this one story* mode, and was having none of it. The soundo made it clear that he was getting to a toilet or peeing in the van right then. It was a quiet street with spacious modern low-set brick homes, tidy lawns and little action. The soundo opened the sliding door and scuttled to the house nearest us. He knocked and was greeted by an elderly lady who listened intently and soon gestured him in. A few minutes on and he returned much happier.

'Who did you say you were?' was everyone's question.

'I just told her exactly what we were doing and she said *The Investigators* is her favourite program. I was her best friend from then on.'

Well, now the floodgates were opened, everyone had to go, so one by one we made the journey from the innocuous A1 Electrical van to her house and back. Relieved and stretched, we settled back in and listened to the producer angst about whether or not we'd blown our cover. All was well, we reassured him. His anxiety levels subsided until the knocking started on the outside of the van. We all looked at each other and did the old let's not breathe for a moment and maybe they'll go away. The knocking continued. We had no option but to open the door. There was the lady from the house with a tray of teacups, teapot and sliced cake. 'I thought you'd probably be hungry by now so I whipped you up a little something,' she said as she started pouring the tea.

The producer was beginning to freak so I thanked her and kindly suggested she leave the tray with us. 'Of course, of course,' she nodded and hurried back to her house.

Six hours passed before the rascally reverend arrived home. The exercise of chasing him down his driveway and confronting him was welcome. It ended as these chases normally do with a door being slammed in our faces and the journalist continuing to ask probing questions through the wood. That way the audience could see that their ABC gave that cagey cleric a bit of the old 'what for'.

Mind you, I didn't really have to leave the station to witness conflict. *The 7.30 Report* at the time bristled with incompatible personalities. One producer worked on the principle that anything was possible as long as he wasn't the one doing it. Queensland organised crime identities were still sore from the walloping they received at the Fitzgerald Inquiry. Their cosy relationship with a corrupt police force was terminated and they weren't happy, least of all with the ABC, a major player in bringing on the inquiry. The producer's idea of having one of the crew members wear a hidden microphone, enter a club *undercover* then try to get one of the club owners to admit that they still ran illegal casinos and brothels was met with the contempt it deserved. He and his personality disorder put a black mark against the name of everyone who refused: well, that was everybody.

Another person on the program was worse. She was a tyrant. It wasn't just me who thought that, the majority of the station signed a petition refusing to work with her. I saw her leave one of the incumbent government's senior headkickers, a minister known for his street-fighting tactics, open-mouthed. We set up a two-camera interview in his office. Normal practice was to set up lights and cameras and the minister would come in when we were ready. Against our wishes this person demanded the minister stay for the set-up. He was perplexed but agreed. The journo was incapable of making small talk so it was the stoniest of silences.

We rolled for the interview. With no warning she went for the jugular and ambushed him with a topic that was not agreed upon prior to starting. It was very tense and I couldn't wait to get out of there but we still had to get our noddies and two-shots. These are the shots you see where the journalist is seen to be nodding and a wider shot that shows the interviewer and the interviewee, usually taken from over the journalist's shoulder. If you return without these shots the editor will eat you alive as they are essential for trimming down an interview to fit a given timeslot.

I started to set up for those. It'd take an extra five to ten minutes at the most. She said, 'No, I need make-up and I need the make-up artist to do it. You'll have to drive me back to the ABC, I'll get it done and we'll drive back here to finish off the shots.' Before I could protest she turned to the minister and said, 'You, be back here in an hour and a half. We'll leave everything set up. Get your people to look after it.' It was one shell-shocked, slack-jawed minister we passed on the way out.

By the time we got back to the station a very unhappy government had been on the phone to complain. It was on. I was asked for my version of events and as she was standing nearby and could have easily spat venom and vaporised me at any moment I wisely declined and left senior management to do the patch-up. I hated working with her because she sought conflict on a daily basis – it seemed to fuel her. I was the opposite, I avoided confrontation. Somewhere in the middle was a healthy mix that was necessary to survive in this job. But I didn't want to learn it from this place. The *7.30* office, known as the viper pit, was cloaked with tension on a daily basis. I took any chance going not to work on the program, so much so it was becoming a bit obvious. I was so desperate I went to my mate, a dentist, and asked if there was anything in there I could do without. He told me two wisdom teeth weren't doing me any favours so I said, 'Great, whip them out.' A few minutes later I had a plastic bag with two gnarly bloodied teeth and a doctor's certificate for five days off. I stapled the teeth and certificate to a sick leave form, dropped them in front of the executive producer and escaped for a week.

On the whole, working for the ABC was terrific and the opportunities for meeting people were many. I would often meet someone of an age similar to mine and quietly wonder what we'd both be doing in twenty years' time. Sitting on a young Eddy Groves's couch, long before the failed entrepreneur was the owner of the world's biggest child-care organisation, ABC Learning, which he left with a multi-billion-dollar debt, I was quite intrigued, by two things. This guy was younger than me by five years but wealthier beyond compare. What was this secret quality that many seemed to have and I didn't? Part of it had to be confidence. I had some confidence but obviously not the sort these guys had. Not only was I working in an industry full of confident people, I was having daily forays with high achievers. I wanted some of it to rub off on me.

The other thing that intrigued me was his interior decorating. It took me a while to put my finger on it. Everything came from a franchised store in a shopping mall except they were all the most expensive items, as if you had walked into Copper Art, Granny

Mays, the sports memorabilia shop and the store that sells leaping aqua blue ceramic dolphins and said, 'Give me your best.' He had worked hard as a milkman in outlying new suburbs where the cultural centre was the mall. Was this a reflection of the world that had produced him? He had money and confidence but at least I had taste.

# 5

## What did the snail say when it jumped on the turtle's back? Wheee!!

I made it a rule to stay out of the office as much as possible, so much so that I was always about a year behind any gossip. A juicy piece of info would come my way and I'd knowingly relay it only to be told, 'You're kidding, aren't you? That happened last year.' None of that mattered to me as I was out doing and learning. Not just technique, but from the people I came across.

I've got to say back then I was arrogant. Not nastily, not openly, but quietly to myself. I thought that climbing, the outdoors and fitness were the mark of a satisfied person. I simply thought that if you weren't outside, challenging yourself against Mother Nature, you weren't really living and were frankly wasting your life. At the same time as I was quietly passing judgement on my fellow man I was wallowing in low self-esteem. I'm guessing this was my way of keeping the lid tightly shut on something that was embarrassing to me and could only translate as weakness in a fairly competitive industry. Logically I should have been able to read a self-help book, follow a few guidelines and voilà, I'd be oozing confidence. But it's not like that, it's completely irrational.

No matter how much I achieved, any accompanying kudos would be turned around in my own mind as hollow platitudes. I had such a low opinion of myself I couldn't see why anyone would bother saying something good about me. Obviously they were just nice people and felt sorry for me is how I rationalised it. I found myself mired in negative thoughts and I hated it. I wanted to move beyond this but I was continually viewing the world through my own perceived limitations. It was like I was going through life with the handbrake on. The crazy thing was that it all played out only in my head, alone. Being male I talked to no one, because that's the way we do things.

It took a climbing trip to Nepal for me to start to shake off these self-imposed shackles. My good mate Chris Hawthorne and I had climbed a small mountain named Imja Tse in the Everest region. We were to fly out of the mountain airstrip at Lukla. As often happens, the weather clapped out and flights were cancelled. Missing your flight relegated you to the bottom of the list and slowly, as the flights resumed, you clawed your way back to the top. The weather closed in for three days so our names weren't even physically on the board anymore. Sir Edmund Hillary was also flying out after building yet another school for the local Sherpa people. So magnanimous were his building efforts and so great his love for the Sherpas, the Nepalese treated him like their king. When the weather cleared he would be the first out. By some quirk of fate, so would my mate Chris and I. As we scrabbled our gear together I was elated about being on the plane going home, let alone sharing it with Big Ed.

Things quickly soured. I saw through the plane window only one bag not being loaded – mine. As the Twin Otter bounced its way through the majesty of the Himalayan scenery I fumed and cursed and sulked. I had become so attached to my climbing gear that the possibility of losing it meant more to me than this once-in-a-lifetime opportunity. We landed in Kathmandu and as I walked from the plane to the terminal building, a small, frail old beggar approached, extended his hand and gently uttered, 'Rupee.' I glared daggers at him and bellowed, 'FUCK OFF.' Bad timing. Before I could suck the words back into my mouth I sensed the presence of someone behind me. I turned to see the lofty bulk of Sir Edmund Hillary, one of my life's idols, looking down on me. He said nothing. He had a look of pity in his eyes directed at me, an angry young man who needed to get a few priorities straight.

It didn't happen overnight but I started feeling better about myself. I think embarrassing myself in front of Big Ed was a sort of personality low point for me. I didn't like who I had become. Outwardly I had a reasonably likeable persona but inwardly I was battling. Whatever was going on in my head, I thought, there's no one but me who's going to sort this out. I don't know what I did but I just thought enough is enough. One thing I did do was get rid of my pious notion that being an outdoors hard man was the be-all and end-all. I started to listen to people's stories more and, lo and behold, they seemed to have a pretty good reason for most things they did. What a revelation.

So it was that I didn't look twice at the dining suite and sideboard that hogged more than their fair share of floor space in this modestly small but clean and tidy house. I did, however, notice the dulled scuffing of the paint on the narrow hallway walls as we followed our host inside. Only because she had to twist herself slightly to keep her hips from making contact with the walls was I drawn to them. She was a big woman. So too was her daughter, who was licking the mixing spoon when I caught her eye. They were the reigning cake-making champions of the Ekka, Brisbane's yearly agricultural show, and they were preparing for a battle of the cake batter.

My initial concern about avoiding stereotyping obese people gave way to worry about how I would physically accomplish shooting the scene. The kitchen was small, long and narrow, with a servery window at chest height down one side. The opposite wall was all cupboard and fridge. That left a doorway at either end, one of which had a bedsheet immaculately thumb-tacked over the opening. It was taut and perfect but it was still an oddly out-of-place bedsheet that robbed me of a much-needed angle. A flurry of aprons and sifting of flour was already in full swing. These women were on a mission to defend their sponge cake's honour yet there was no room for me in there with them. I had a problem.

'What's with the bedsheet?' I asked.

'We aren't going to talk about that,' Mum put to me in a matter-of-fact way without lifting her gaze from the Mixmaster.

I gently suggested it would have to go.

Breaking from cake making they turned to one another and loudly sucked air in, engaging each other in silent dialogue with their eyes, before joining in a combined exhalation of defeat and slump of the shoulders.

'We didn't want to have to tell you so you wouldn't be burdened with conflicting thoughts. The temptation might prove too much ... and if the people at home know we have them it's only a matter of time before we'll be robbed!' Mum blurted out.

'Excuse me?'

More deflated huffing and puffing, then off came the aprons and we squeezed our way out and around to the other side of the bedsheet.

'These!' They gestured at the sideboard and table. 'If people see we have these they will break in and rob us.' Mum was near tears and Daughter bit her lip while quietly pleading with her eyes.

All I saw was a pile of chipboard covered in faux wood-grain veneer held together with staples but they obviously saw something much different. This concern about being robbed by viewer and camera crew alike had obviously consumed their thinking for many days. It was all unravelling for them now and so too our story. Yet again I ended up on the confessional couch. We reassured them society had come a long way since Adam and the apple incident and we were happy enough with our own furniture. We ended up moving their furniture into an adjoining bedroom and promised to forget we ever laid eyes on it. They returned to their quest for the perfect sponge with the weight of the world lifted from their shoulders. A year earlier I'd have thought to myself: stop piling cakes down your gobs, get out of the house and get a life. It wasn't that I'd suddenly discovered empathy, it was more that now I could be bothered making the effort to listen and take on board their anguish. I was slowly climbing out of my own personal depths. It felt like I was moving onwards and upwards in more ways than one.

In 1991, prospects for joining climbing expeditions as the cameraman were promising. Australia's ancient landscape, worn smooth over millennia, provided limited opportunities for the sort of climbing experience I was after. Selfishly I left Vicky at home while I headed to the US for a seven-week climbing holiday. I would have loved to take a movie camera but I had to settle on my stills camera. Unlike today when you can get broadcast-quality video from a camera no larger than your fist, then it was a cumbersome and weighty business.

My climbing partners were Trevor Gynther and Ken Cox, our transport a yellow Hertz removalist's van with a big roller door on the back. It was a basic hotel room on wheels. Looking like the old Three Stooges, we sat shoulder to shoulder across the van's bench seat and headed east from Los Angeles for the big rock walls of the Nevada desert. Three hours later at Barstow we pulled into the White Horse Truck Stop for a late-night feed. It was eleven pm. This was the sort of place where a waitress poured you coffee the moment you sat down, whether you wanted it or not. It gave no hint that I was about to receive one of the most liberating insights of my life.

Let me tell you a bit about Trevor 'the Revver' Gynther, a name given to him in his old rally-driving days. Climber, surfer, seagoing kayaker, helicopter pilot, adventurer, botanical savant, Trevor has the enthusiastic outlook that belongs to a twelve year old on Christmas Day and every day is like Christmas Day to him. Trevor is eternally inquisitive and is never afraid to ask what's on his mind. In a misguided way I sometimes thought I knew better, that he needed protecting from himself and I should be the arbiter of when and where this happened. I think there is a name for this sort of person: sanctimonious, self-righteous prick comes to mind.

As the pancake stacks were served, in walked two highway patrolmen on a break. Their polished leather utility belts creaked and their starched uniforms rustled as they took the vacant seats alongside us at the diner. As police in Queensland didn't wear guns then, the gleaming machined-metal finish of the Smith and Wesson sidearms had Trevor's gaze fixed upon it. Trevor turned towards Ken and me and whispered, 'I'm going to ask if I can hold one of their guns.'

'Are you flippin' crazy?' I had visions of Trevor being spread-eagled over the diner floor, guns pointed at his head and officers radioing for backup. 'You can't do that,' I implored.

'Why not?'

'Because,' I said, 'you just *don't do* that sort of thing.'

It took all of a second for Trevor to digest that lame answer before he turned and disarmed them with an enthusiasm offensive. His outstretched and welcoming handshake led the charge. 'Gidday, I'm Trevor from Australia. How ya goin'?'

Caught completely off guard, the patrolman nearest him hurried to swallow and wiped his lips with a napkin like he'd been caught mid-chew by a presidential visit. Stunned, he offered back, 'Hibberts ... Sergeant Arthur E. Hibberts,' and accepted the handshake.

It took but thirty seconds and Trevor had already asked them to let him hold the gun and have his photo taken. I was cringing in disbelief and distancing myself with a look that said 'I'm not with him'. But when they said, 'Sure, come outside,' I was with him. Trevor had just got us tickets on the experience express and I was boarding at hippo critic station. We got photos of them with the gun, us with the gun, them and us with the gun. They gave us a tour of the patrol car and insisted we take a ride. They were very proud that they could hold their own in a pursuit and keen as mustard to show us. Lights flashing and sirens wailing, our limited view from the caged back seat with no inside door handles gave no hint we were travelling at 150 mph, and he still had 'a bit more up my sleeve'.

'Let me show you Barstow and I'll introduce you around,' Sarge yelled above the road and engine noise.

At an intersection with traffic lights but no cars, Sarge summoned over one of the local hookers. A black girl whom he introduced as Dani peered through the wire cage at us. I'm sure all she saw were our huge Cheshire cat grins.

'These boys are from Down Under and we're showing them around. If you come across them, you treat 'em good.' I wanted to wind the window down but the window winders were gone as well. If I'd had a tail I would have wagged it.

The police station was next. 'You boys wanted to see guns?' He appeared with an overstuffed keyring and opened the walk-in armoury. It was a terrorist's playground. Most of the weapons had been confiscated from drug and gang raids: belt-fed machine guns, Uzis, handguns with BIG barrels. Then it was the police dogs. I never found out exactly what they were supposed to do but they were very good at scaring people. We were instructed to walk to the far corner of a gravel compound and wait. An officer unknown to us appeared at the opposite corner and let two German Shepherds off the leash. One curt command from him and two bounding fur balls of canine tooth and gum were heading for us. Fang and Klaus corralled us into the corner of a chain-wire security fence. A cluster of officers chortled from a distance. This was obviously their favourite party trick. With the dogs called off and back on the leash, the handler started into doggy talk: 'Who's a boot-i-ful boy, aw, who's a good boy, they're just big boot-i-ful puppies.' Yeah, right.

Back inside Sarge seemed suitably impressed that we hadn't started blubbering and called an impromptu meeting where he made us honorary deputies of the Barstow Police Department. Small badges were pinned to our shirts and we were driven back to our van. Our yellow removal van made him laugh out loud.

'A parting gift for you.' He leaned against the van window and handed us each a business card with his name. 'Anyone pulls you over while you're in California, just get them to call me and I'll sort things.'

Trevor showed me that there's no such thing as a dumb question. The realisation didn't happen overnight but I was becoming open to the idea that the worst thing anyone could say back to you was 'no'. Had it been left to me I would have censored Trevor and none of the above would have happened. The best I could have written now was 'the pancakes were nice'.

Packaged with my low self-esteem came a fear of rejection. Yep, I was a walking catalogue of fears. Over the years I have come to see that being afraid to ask questions is like walking around with your hands tied behind your back. Understanding and overcoming this is truly like casting off manacles. Professionally it's a must. I also wondered if my father, along with his passion for photography, had passed on something else to me. I had plenty of confidence in my camerawork but still lacked confidence with people. I was reading up on self-esteem and kept coming across a symptom: *not looking someone in the eye when you talk*. Who did that remind me of? Dad and me. I'd never noticed it before because, if you think about it, how could two people who never look people in the eye know the other was doing it? It was only after I started trying to improve my own lot that I realised this.

Don't get me wrong, all this self-esteem guff was not a major part of my life, it was just a constant nagging twinge that I'd had enough of and was determined to fix.

A month later, still in the US, the second-scariest thing in my life occurred. Like waking with the maniacal Geoff Waldron staring at me, this too started while asleep. Yosemite Valley is a world mecca for big walling – that's climbing talk for routes ten to thirty pitches long, a pitch being fifty metres, the length of most climbing ropes. As far as big cliffs go, El Capitan is the granddaddy of them all at over a kilometre high. It is the Mt Everest of the rock-climbing world and a very popular trade route.

Preparations for our planned three-day ascent took place at the cheap climbers' campsite known as Camp 4. Almost every campsite hosts climbers of different nationalities, united in the language of climbing and a lack of money. On the opposite side of a large pine tree to me was a German climber, Skinny Hilby, as he became known. During our month-long stay we never saw him climb once. His passion, it seemed, was for beer. Long night-time drinking sessions usually had him rising at around 11 am. Scrunching his eyes towards the almost noon light he would proclaim, 'Ze hour ist too late for ze climbing. I zink I vill rest.'

A big wall team consists of three: you, your partner and the pig. The pig is a heavy-duty bag designed to be hauled up the cliff as you go. Enough water, food, sleeping bags and storm gear for two people for three days adds up to a lot of weight. It's a pig of a thing to haul up behind you, hence the name. Good weather was forecast and we were fired up. All my climbing gear, including the pig, was set neatly outside the entrance to my small two-person dome tent for a quick and quiet pre-dawn getaway.

Sleep was hard to come by and fitful at best. A gnawing sound outside my tent woke me: bloody squirrels. Camp 4 is over-run by them and they are masterful at sneaking into food supplies. They were trying to get into the pig. Still cocooned in my sleeping bag, I slipped on my head torch and rolled onto an elbow. My sandshoes would serve as missiles to launch at the little buggers. I was pissed off. Unzipping the tent entrance and propped on my elbows, I swung the torch's beam looking for critters. I caught a yellow eye in the light. A hand span to the right was another yellow eye. Central and a bit lower down was a wet black nose. These sat atop a beach-ball-sized head covered in deep-chocolate-brown fur. I was looking directly at a bear less than a body length away.

Yaaaah! I suddenly understood the saying 'your heart's in your mouth' – that's exactly where mine was. Blood surged upwards to my temples and deafened me. It felt like someone was giving my ears a good beating between two frypans. I froze and clearly remember thinking I had no idea what to do. Spiders, snakes and the like don't worry me. I know the drill with them. Save for crocodiles, Australia doesn't have big animals that eat you. I was mightily underprepared for this.

Our stare-off lasted, I'm guessing here, fifteen seconds. I could feel his warm moist breath as it rolled across my closest hand. Of more interest to the bear was the food-laden pig, its contents now spilled out for his perusal. Each day's food was separated into individual drawstring bags. The bear used his worryingly sharp claws, the size of a five year old's fingers, to easily slice through the nylon fabric of each one. He knew what he wanted: Pemmican Bars, a high-energy food bar popular in North America. The cameraman in me returned and my first rational thought was to take a photo, maybe my last. Nope, no photo tonight; my camera was on the ground in front of the bear. I'd packed it snug as a bug in a rug amongst the food bags for protection.

My thoughts turned to putting some distance between us. I looked towards the back entrance to the tent but it was padlocked. I'd locked it in a futile attempt to stop falling victim to the rampant daytime thievery when Camp 4 was vacant, the climbers having hit the rock. Bugger, where was the key? I'm always putting things in clever places for safekeeping and promptly forgetting where. Now was no different. Like the bear only a few metres away, I created a scatter of camping gear as I scrabbled to find the key. Awful slurping sounds reminded me he was hungry. The key! Without fuss the lock opened. Now there was only a zip between me and freedom, but it still had to be opened. In the still of the night the noise was like a machine gun letting loose. The bear glanced up. I froze. Thank goodness he had a penchant for Pemmican Bars and went back to dining.

My way was clear, apart from a chasm of ignorance about how to deal with the situation. Did I slither out slowly or spring out and take my chances? At this stage my springs were tightly sprung so I chose the latter and commando-rolled out, still in my sleeping bag, onto a soft layer of pine needles. Things were looking up. Now at least I had the psychological comfort of a piece of nylon, a waft of flyscreen and a loose knot of lightweight aluminium poles between me and the 200-kilogram bear. I rose from my crouch to peek over the top of the tent to check on things. The bear mirrored my move, rising from four paws to two, sniffing the air. I vividly remember looking at his mouth and seeing the glooping strands of saliva falling from his jaw. He sniffed the air a bit then resumed dinner and I continued wobbling like jelly.

In a millisecond of bravado I bolted to wake Trevor, hoping he would like to share a bit of the fear. I was dismissed as mad. A quick peek out of his tent and he pronounced me sane. With backup on hand, I puffed up my chest. It came to mind that the noise of pots and pans banging would scare a bear off, and it did, with one small hitch: the bear ran straight over the top of Skinny Hilby's tent. No noise came from the disfigured nylon mess so he must have been out knocking back the lagers.

The gentle snore from Ken's tent prompted Trevor and me, still ripped with adrenaline, to set a trail of apples to his tent. 'Nothing beats first-hand experience,' Ken was fond of saying. Next morning, our climb postponed, we recounted the tale to anyone who would listen. The morning passed and on cue, at about 11am, Hilby the skinny German boy emerged from his tent with a whopping big bruise across his torso. 'Oooww ... Duss anybody know, vas I in ze fight last night?' Under gathering clouds and plummeting temperatures we updated Hilby on his new medical condition.

Snow transformed the shabby campground into a magically pretty place but also halted climbing. Not given to idle time, I taught myself to juggle. What I found so hard to master others around me took to with ease. I thought, what's the point, when will I ever need to juggle?

Four days later, with good weather on the horizon, Ken and I were back on for El Capitan. I was finally on a climb I'd dreamed about for the best part of a decade. About a third of the way up, while tied to the wall and slowly feeding out the rope to Ken, who was leading above me, I heard laughter and voices floating up from the meadow below. The acoustics were terrific. Even though they were just match-head-size dots I could hear them clearly. It was a family. They'd parked their car at a place popular for climber spotting. Mum and Dad looked skywards while the kids ran around. I watched and watched and all of a sudden my drive for climbing stated to wane. I didn't want to be where I was, I wanted to be down there with them. I started to think about kids. It was like a switch in me had been flicked. That night while tied to our little ledge and both mentally spent from seven weeks of full-on climbing, Ken and I pulled the pin on El Capitan and began the long series of abseils down. A few days later I began the journey home to start a family.

# 6

## Extended on a leaf, a caterpillar hesitates – which way?

Documentaries and, more to the point, shooting them, consumed my thinking. I read about, watched, videotaped and deconstructed documentaries. I've always subscribed to the idea that chance favours the prepared man. When the offers from ABC documentary producers started coming in 1992 I was ready for the challenge. This is what I had been working towards for a decade and career-wise it was everything. The downside to this was that it meant travel away from home. I could say that Vicky being pregnant with our first child complicated matters but the truth is it didn't. Cameraman and travel are said in the same breath. We were both aware of the deal but now three- to four-day trips would turn into three- to four-week trips. What did complicate things was the due date for our baby: 16 August.

Glenn Singleman was a climber, Nic Feteris a BASE jumper, meaning he parachuted from buildings, cliffs, bridges and such things. They came up with the idea of teaching each other their respective skills and testing the practicality of this novel idea by finding the highest cliff in the world, climbing it, then jumping off.

If they lived they'd consider it a success. The Pakistan part of the Himalayas had just the right sort of cliff. It was named the Trango Tower. Their planning was almost complete. They had *National Geographic* on board and I was asked to film their story. Are you kidding? My lust for climbing may have been tempered on El Capitan but it hadn't just vanished. I flicked through the schedule and saw 'Proposed jump date: 16 August'. I had a dilemma.

Vicky and I had met nine years earlier at a rock concert where I was filming. No one was more surprised than me when she showed interest. I quickly charmed her with my total lack of style and converted her to climbing. Nearly killing her with a falling microwave-size rock was my way of saying I love you and it was my idea to honeymoon in a snow cave ... that she would have to dig; the all-important photos weren't going to take themselves, were they? Next morning during a white-out, the winds were so strong that Vicky was pushed uphill on skis. But take away the tears and the terror and the discomfort and I think she enjoyed herself.

Her greatest strength is that of a friend. You're a very lucky person if you have Vicky as a friend. Once she takes one on, that person gets a life sentence. Opposites attract and that is the case here. I'm not a good friend to people. It would be easy for me to paint myself in a better light but as a large part of my career has been spent perpetuating the myths and false façades of many public identities, I don't want to add to that. I've spent time with many people of public note who are put forth as superachievers of the family/work balancing act. On the surface their lives appear pretty damn good. Spend enough time, get behind their PR machines, and you see the cracks and the behind-the-scenes turmoil that is remarkably similar to every other family.

Invariably they have a pillar of strength at home or they can finance a healthy support team or their home life is really a shambles. Often they are keen for this to remain hidden. I understand that many times the image they present is their livelihood and of course their families have the right to privacy. I don't want any confusion about me. The whole reason I've been able to have so many experiences stems from two things: my focus (translation: selfish mindset) and the unending way Vicky gives of herself to others, especially supporting my ambitions. I'd like for that to be otherwise but it's not. I don't pretend that it's going to miraculously change any day soon, either.

I dealt with the climbing versus fatherhood issue by temporarily ignoring it. A flood of opportunities rose around me. I was ready. I'd been industriously building my ark of ambition. I was also lucky to work for the Production Operations department of the ABC. As such I was never under the control of one program. They just hired my services from the department. It was like being a freelance cameraman within the ABC but I had a guaranteed pay cheque. There was a rotating roster that moved me around programs but often my services were asked for by a competing program and I would be reassigned. Spiritual callings were in the wind. Actually it was a phone call asking me aboard an ABC series *Temples – What Do They Do In There?* We spent a week each with the Buddhist, Sikh, Hare Krishna and Taoist communities in Australia. It was a fascinating insight that showed me that, despite the physical differences of their facial features, the clothes they wore, the God they worshipped and how that manifested itself, they were, above all, uniquely Australian in their outlook and humour.

Frank, the shopping-centre builder, was about as Australian as they come: red hair, ruddy Irish complexion, a construction hard hat with 'Frank' written on the front and a roll of architect's plans clutched underarm. He had been contracted to build the largest Taoist temple – at that time – outside mainland China. Everything was ready for the big machines to move in and convert the mudflats next to the Brisbane motorway into a place of spiritual tranquillity. Taoist protocol required the site to be aligned in harmony between the mountains and the sea. Frank, armed with a theodolite, charts and engineering know-how, met on site with the Taoist 'big guys', specially flown in from China. 'Thanks but no thanks,' they said to Frank and his technology. A quick glance east and west and skywards and it was all but done. Two sticks were driven into the mud, a string connecting them. 'Align the axis of the temple to this,' and they were gone. Frank rolled his eyes and recorded the bearing.

Back in the office Frank got curious and dusted off the protractors and set squares for a late-night workout. Bugger me, thought Frank, it's just what they said it would be. It was a mathematical fit. Well, Frank started gazing down the rabbit hole and just got *curiouser and curiouser*. A few years on, the bloke who probably built your local Kmart became a Taoist monk.

Eastern religions have a great marketing advantage: their cuisine. The food was fantastic and so too the mixed entrée of philosophies that we picked on. It stimulated my thinking. The experience was enriching but it wasn't here that I found most nourishment, it was from the ABC producer on the series, Jack King. You can say many things about Jack and many people have, but he is about the most honest person I know. Sure, he tells his share of white lies but Jack doesn't roll over on his principles. He's honest with himself and is prepared to argue a point. I was so impressed because I don't like confrontation and knew I needed to work on this shortcoming. Jack just takes it in his stride. Like a leech, I silently attached myself and fed on his strength of character and his doggedness to achieve an outcome. I appreciated the philosophical underpinnings of the eastern beliefs but Jack's actions made the greatest impression on me.

The temples series was well received by the ABC audience. Cash for program making was in good supply and creative thinkers were respected. Jack had chanced upon a great story about a former world champion rodeo rider named Tim Kelly. Tim had cracked the world circuit and spent a few eye-opening years in North America. Apart from a shiny big cowboy buckle with 'WORLD CHAMPION' on it, Tim brought back with him a belief in God. The cowboy ministries had given Tim new meaning in his life and like many a neophyte Christian, he was keen to tell people about it. In his big cowboy hat and driving his trusty '74 V8 Ford, the rodeo preacher spread the word. We first caught up with him in a little town on the Queensland–New South Wales border called Wallangarra, where he lived with his ex-bikie barmaid wife Lesley. Only months earlier I had been in Wallangarra but for a different reason, one that caused me to question my suitability for this job.

The biggest visitors to Wallangarra in the 1950s were beef cattle but they only had a one-way ticket; it was the abattoir they had come to see. This was a tick-free zone and remained so by dipping all the arriving cattle in chemical baths called cattle dips. The work was messy and wet. Forty years later and a growing number of workers from the cattle dips were dying premature and awful deaths. Our story centred on the chemicals used. Were they responsible?

Getting people to talk on these stories can be difficult. Grief is intensely personal. To open up to strangers, even if they are sitting on your couch, is difficult. We were doing a delicate interview with the widow of one such worker who had died just a month earlier. She didn't want to be there, and nor did I. Her small house was right next to a sharp ninety-degree corner on the highway. Trucks outnumbered cars that day and each one had to wind back up through the gears after negotiating the tight turn on the highway outside. Normally a sound recordist will interrupt an interview to silence a ticking clock or because a fly burped; they hear every little noise. In sensitive or non-repeatable interviews good soundos exercise restraint and allow for less than perfection but this was ridiculous. Our interviewee would quiver and cry her way through an answer only to be asked to repeat it over and over as each time a roaring exhaust or gearbox crunch would splinter the moment. I felt terrible imposing upon this poor woman and actively suggested we just drop the interview. The journalist was of a different mind. She insisted we continue. There was no option but to move location, but where?

We drove to Wallangarra Cemetery, resting place of her recently deceased husband. There on the hillside, far from the noise of the road, we could continue in silence. We could also film some emotive scenes of her visiting the grave for the first time. Back rolling the camera again and halfway through one of her teary answers: vaaaar roooom! A crop duster had begun spraying a field on the opposite side of the hill to us. It would end each pass with a tight turn above us. This pattern continued for some time. Our poor woman was at breaking point and I stepped aside with the journalist, a person senior to me, and aired our differences. She told me if I didn't see that this was part of the story, I needed to rethink what I was doing in the job.

The plane eventually finished and we resumed. Finally all the questions were asked and the woman was now spent but we still needed to do the graveside scene and coaxed her on. Just as we began a yellow council truck towing an industrial air compressor squealed to a stop next to us. Two knockabout blokes stained by sweat and dirt jumped down and set to work checking some figures and measurements. They agreed on the dimensions and one sprayed a coffin outline onto the hard ground. The other started up the generator, attached a jackhammer, and they busied themselves with digging a grave.

My only thought was to whisk the woman away from this horrible reminder of her husband's death. I moved to put the camera away but was begged by the journalist to film the digging and the woman's uncomfortable reaction to it. Reluctantly I did. The journalist's instincts proved right. The new grave was for another local, also a former cattle-dip worker. The powerful sequence, when it aired, went a long way in communicating the plight of a growing number of widows. As long as we were professional, respectful and all our requests were within the context of the story, I was out of line to try to filter what this woman should or shouldn't be exposed to. Looking back, I was probably using her condition as a shield for my own inability to deal with people's emotions. I'm sure, too, that she was a lot tougher than I was giving her credit for. I was wrong and the journalist was right; I would have to stop being so thin-skinned.

Back in Wallangarra with the rodeo preacher, the only things thin-skinned were the sausages. Tim was a butcher and a nice bloke. Our story followed him as he temporarily left his wife Lesley, the kids and his job to drive the two-thousand kilometre journey to Mt Isa in northwest Queensland for Australia's biggest rodeo. I knew he was a nice bloke. The day before setting out on the long drive, I was with him in his butcher's shop as he carved up the meat for our evening meal. Tim asked me what cut of meat I would prefer, the choice was mine. 'Er, I'm a vegetarian.' The poor guy went silent, a look of panic written across his face. I don't think he'd ever met one before. He wiped his hands and disappeared for a few minutes. I could hear him on the phone to Leslie. He returned but he wasn't happy.

'Leslie says she can whip you up a lasagne ... without ... meat.' I could see he was trying to figure out how *that* would work. It was an oxymoron to him. If I'd just told him I was homosexual I think he would have been a lot more comfortable, but vegetarian? Conversation was sparse and he eyed me suspiciously. In between thwacks of the cleaver he hedged around to asking me why.

I told him that a lot of my work had been with the rural department which was run out of Brisbane. *Countrywide* was the original program that evolved into *Landline* which is still broadcast today. You film about every animal process known to mankind if you spend a few years with the show. I've filmed on the killing floor of many types of abattoir and the killing of animals doesn't affect me. I would often go pig and roo shooting in my army days. What started to affect me was intensive animal farming, all those practices that get meat onto our tables at a price we are willing to pay. I saw a lot of suffering up to the point of death and it got me thinking.

The tipping point came when I was at the Kilcoy abattoir and, after another charming half-hour on the killing floor, I wandered down to the holding yards where the cattle entered the single-file chute like families queuing for a theme park ride. Though in no physical distress at the moment, it was really obvious to me that the cattle knew where they were going. It wasn't in their eyes but in the sounds they made. (I've since spoken to quite a few abattoir workers who concur.) I held my own moratorium on eating meat while I processed my thoughts. Doing it as a symbolic gesture wasn't enough for me; it had to achieve something or it was futile. What I found was when people asked the inevitable 'why?', it gave me a platform to briefly highlight the issue. In a way I'd found a means to make a difference through education, so I continued not to eat meat.

The two-thousand kilometre drive would normally have taken Tim two days except for one thing: he had a film crew in tow. This was what the industry prosaically calls a road movie where the journey is the story. Road movies are very tiresome to make – stop the car, get the gear out, shoot, put the gear back in the car, drive a kilometre further, stop the car … A large part of the problem is that I failed mind-reading at school. Because you don't know if a better location is coming up or what the weather will be like when you get there, you take the opportunity when it presents. Of course there's always a better location just around the corner. That's what happened en route to the small town of Barcaldine.

It was late afternoon and golden rays of sun put me on alert. The magic hour was upon us, the half-hour before and after sunset when the light is at its most dramatic and flattering. Flickering fingers of shadow from the brigalow trees were making driving annoying so any opportunity to stop was welcome. We rounded a long curve and came upon Tim stopped on the road, for good reason. Sheep were being moved across the road in big numbers. It was noisy, dusty, the sun had caught a glint in Tim's eye under the brim of his big hat and it was *so* Australian. Photographically it was no challenge, just point the camera in any direction and all the shots were winners. Just as I started, the last of the sheep crossed the bitumen.

'You are kidding me. That would have been a sensational sequence,' I moaned to Jack.

'Do you want me to get them to bring them back again?' he asked.

'Are you flippin' crazy? You can't do that.'

'Why not?'

''Cause you just don't do that sort of thing out here,' was my lame reply. At the time it went unnoticed that history was repeating itself on me.

Before I could continue Jack was bounding through the trees to the stockmen on horses bringing up the rear. Through the dust I saw Jack gesticulating from us to the sun. Then Jack started running back.

As soon as he was within earshot I yelled, 'You flippin' idiot. I bet they told you to piss off, didn't they?'

'Nope, they said no worries.'

Back across the road went the horses and riders, dogs and sheep … lots of sheep. Then they turned around and went back again to continue their original journey. In all there were fourteen thousand sheep. The sequence earned me a cinematography award and a huge piece of humble pie. My fear of rejection had reared its ugly head again. I had apparently gained little ground, if any, after Trevor and the Barstow police. We had plenty of hours of driving ahead in which I could finish my slice of pie. I still wasn't the confident person that I wanted to be.

Tim warmed to me when he realised I wasn't going to pull some animal welfare stunt and bring adverse publicity to the rodeo circuit. We hit it off pretty well for a slightly odd couple: the God-fearing butcher and the vegetarian atheist – I gave him time to process the meat thing before I hit him with that one.

It was late 1992 and my experience was steadily growing, as was Vicky's bump, and so too was the pressure on me to respond to the offer to join the BASE-jumping team in Pakistan. Glenn Singleman had invited me to go to New Zealand to film a warm-up climb and jump before the Himalayas. Accepting this made me feel I would be obliging myself to take on the longer project. But I'd cross that bridge when I came to it. I could put off my decision just a little bit longer. We were headed for the Kaipo Wall, one end of the little visited Kaipo Valley. In New Zealand vernacular it's just up the road from Milford Sound but that's the thing, there are no roads.

The last ice age put a stop to that by carving glacial valleys with walls so steep it's pointless to try. This is remote country unless you've got a helicopter. If you want to be a cameraman you'd better like helicopters. Including army helicopters, I'd already clocked up about a hundred flying hours in my so-far short career and in a vast array of them. So when Glenn, Nic, Simon Wyatt, Geoff Gabbites and I pulled up at the helicopter company in Milford Sound, it was me who first blurted out, 'That's not our helicopter.' In front of us was a Hughes 300. It looked like a toy.

'It fuckin' well is.' The voice belonged to our pilot, Jeff Shanks. He stood there in a multicoloured flight suit that was splattered in … blood? More colourful, though, was his language. He constructed every sentence around expletives. I had never before heard someone swear so consistently and never have since.

'You're fuckin' late. Weather can change in the hour. How much fuckin' gear have you got?'

Leaving the hellos till later we stacked the climbing, parachuting, camping and camera gear into a pile that quickly grew as large as the helicopter. Jeff tested the weight of a few boxes and wasn't fazed by it, though I'm guessing that 'What have you got in these fuckin' things?' meant they were classed as heavy. He sorted the boxes into three new piles and looked at the five of us. 'Who's the fuckin' heaviest then?' Simon stepped forward.

'You go last. I'll fly three sorties, two, two and one and split the fuckin' gear between them.' He directed us to drive the gear to a flat landing area that was on the edge of a twenty-metre-high slope.

With Jack and the sheep still fresh in my mind I spoke up. 'There's no way that tiny thing is going to fly with us and all the gear.'

'You fuckin' watch then.'

A cargo net with our gear was readied. Jeff and one passenger would lift off and hover into position above the cargo net that had a long strap secured to it. The person on the ground would attach the loaded net and climb up, onto the skids of the hovering chopper, and onto the tightly crowded bench seat (one bum cheek short of a true three-seater). Giving the machine the entire available throttle, the tiny buzzing mechanical insect would shoot skywards until the slack in the cargo strap took up. The load was jerked off the ground as the engine and blades audibly strained and slowed like a lawnmower hitting a patch of thick grass. The chopper tipped sideways and seemed to fall before picking up speed and heading up.

For the first time Jeff Shanks smiled. 'That's trans-fuckin'-lation, boys, that's physics changing horizontal speed into vertical lift for ya.' Fear evaporated as the majesty of Milford Sound unfolded all around. Below a lone kayaker was paddling hard with a pack of dolphins alongside, like he was taking the dogs for a morning run. Our path zig-zagged up the mountainside, flying very close to the steep walls of rock and tussock grass. The little bubble of glass was buffeted violently. 'Why so close to the sides, Jeff?'

'So we're at least in with a fuckin' chance if we go down. I reckon that cable to the net might snag and hold us ... if we're alive.'

The higher we went the slower we went; wind of increasing speed caused us to slew and buck. We hit the snowline and snuck through a gap in the ridge. Snow-covered rock walls rose either side and the wind pushed us around more than before. Popping out the other side we were in the Kaipo Valley, ahead of us New Zealand's biggest wall, the thirteen-hundred-metre-high Kaipo Wall. It was bigger than Yosemite's El Capitan and shrouded in mist. This was not going to be easy.

We went to put down about a kilometre back from the wall. Strong winds made the tussock grass shimmy. Jeff misjudged releasing the cargo strap and my camera gear dropped the last few metres to the ground. 'I do that every fuckin' now and then,' Jeff apologised. As he went back to collect the next group, Glenn searched for a campsite and I checked on my gear. The heavy duty aluminium camera case had blown out on one corner. I was able to hammer it back into shape with an ice axe. Inside the camera was intact but a quick peek through the viewfinder confirmed my suspicions: the jolt had whacked the lens out of alignment. No matter how I focused, the picture was blurred. I eventually remedied the problem, so I thought, by cutting makeshift packing rings from a Milo can. I slipped these behind the lens to bit by bit bring the image back into focus.

Our camp was set back from the vertical kilometre of rock. Some exploratory climbing up the lowest sections of the wall reinforced that it was wet, mossy and BIG. I was used to climbing warm, dry rock and even Geoff Gabbites, our New Zealand climbing guide who had grown up on this sort of stuff, looked less than enthusiastic. Added to that there would be an extra fifteen kilograms of camera gear on my back and the decision was made: it wasn't going to happen. Everyone agreed. Plan B was to get Jeff Shanks to fly the jumpers to the top. Getting the jump right was important.

'Not anytime soon. This weather's coming in and I'm fuckin' outta here. I'll come back as soon as I can.' And with that Jeff was gone.

Sub-zero temperatures sent us into hibernation. Snow covered everything. We had plenty of food and did what all climbers do best: sat out bad weather. As there was no couch, I found myself sitting on a sleeping bag chatting to Glenn about the seriousness of what he was doing. He produced an updated version of his will and asked me to witness his signature. Fingers crossed that it all went well, as I'd be one of the ones picking up the pieces afterwards if it ended badly.

Our entertainment consisted of eight keas who became our base camp companions. These mischievous green mountain parrots comically rock from leg to leg in a show of mocking defiance. Their sole purpose on this planet is to destroy anything man-made. Any item misplaced would *never* be found intact again.

Jeff and the flying lawnmower returned on the fourth day. A deer hung lifelessly from beneath the skids. Jeff was unshaven, dishevelled and covered in more blood than previously.

'I didn't make it back through the fuckin' pass when I left. The fuckin' weather got me. No problems. I love me huntin' so I went and shot me some fuckin' deer.'

'For three days? Where'd you sleep?'

'I know a rock that's pretty dry. I had plenty of fuel to keep a fire going and I found half a loaf of old bread under the seat from the last hunting trip so I had deer sandwiches for three days. Fuckin' delicious they were too. I could go a cuppa though.'

Over a few cups we got to know this tough New Zealander better. He was a professional deer hunter who got his helicopter licence simply so he didn't have to walk into these areas to hunt. Helicopters are expensive so he built his business to support his hunting needs. He's not the sort of guy you want to get on the wrong side of – as the owners of the *Star Lauro*, formerly the

*Achille Lauro*, came close to finding out. This cruise ship made headlines when it was hijacked by the PLO in 1985. In 1991 it was sailing off New Zealand's west coast when all its engines died. The ageing ship floundered for a few days then an onboard emergency arose. An elderly passenger had acute appendicitis and needed immediate evacuation. Jeff flew out to the ship bobbing around on the rough seas. He contacted the ship's captain to issue instructions: remove all deck chairs, clear anything that could get blown into the blades, get everybody back inside. Choosing his landing site was easy; there was only one option, next to the pool. He landed, strapped the patient in and increased the throttle. Carefully lifting off he constantly monitored everywhere for any debris that could end up in his rotors. That would be bad for everyone. He looked everywhere except up. He reasoned he had just landed from that direction so the passage should have been clear.

Unbeknown to him and contrary to his requests, passengers had surged out onto the promenade deck above and crushed forward to get a view of the unfolding action. A pole holding a string of festoon lights had snapped in the push and this string was now flapping wildly in the wind. As he lifted off, the string wrapped around the rotor blades and he immediately lost power. In the 'translation' manoeuvre he used with us, he dropped the helicopter over the edge of the ship and was able to keep up enough speed to stay a few metres above the waves and head directly to nearby land. He said the old lady's eyes were out on stalks like a crab by then. He put down on a black stony beach and escorted the lady to a safe spot, then returned to shut the helicopter down.

This was the bad part because with the wire wrapped around them, the blades were out of balance. Like a washing machine that has an uneven load, it became violent when it slowed down. The helicopter bucked wildly but didn't break up. The resulting repair bill for new blades was many tens of thousands which the cruise company refused to pay. Jeff prepared his revenge by welding up a large drum of sump oil that he had rigged and waiting in his shed. The next time the ship returned he was going to drop the black gloop over the lovely white pool decks and those sunbaking upon it. The ship sank in 1994 off the coast of Somalia before Jeff could ever exact his revenge.

This and more stories left us uncertain as to whether Jeff was a really good pilot or just a maverick with a lot of luck. Either way, if you had to be flying around these mountains, he was the man you needed at the controls. The weather cleared enough for one jump, which I skilfully shot as an unrecognisable blur. My repairs to the camera had not solved the problem. From everyone's point of view, the exercise was invaluable as a training run for the problems the Himalayas would present. Those, though, were not to be my problems. I made the call not to go and thankfully so. To have missed the birth of my daughter Georgia would have been unthinkable. I was so moved by it that for years afterwards anytime I heard a crying baby my eyes immediately glassed over.

If it did feel like I'd had my wings clipped professionally, what I didn't realise at the time was that it expanded my horizons emotionally, which in turn made me a better documentary cameraman. Having empathy for people's situations is obviously an important part of the job. Again this didn't happen overnight but I could feel myself heading in a different direction, away from actively pursuing the climbing work. With my propensity to focus to the exclusion of everything else around me, climbing might have led me down a narrow professional and personal canyon from which I'd eventually find it very hard to extract myself. Remote locations, however, and a sense of adventure stayed with me.

# 7

## Failure is not the falling down, but the staying down.

For me, '93–'94 was the time of discovering for myself that the great Australian character, the quintessential Aussie, was alive and well, contrary to reports emanating from the bastions of cultural myopia, the capital cities. To me northern Australia was still the frontier land: Cape York, across the Northern Territory and west to the Kimberleys and the Pilbara. Lanky characters from Russell Drysdale paintings went about their work under the burning sun but away from the burning gaze of society. Almost every dirt road we followed led to people living extraordinary lives in a landscape where the outstanding geographical feature is the horizon and the unit of measure for hail is a golf ball, for huntsman spiders a dinner plate and not forgetting the country mile – 'it's just down the road, mate'. This reduction of vast distances and areas of land into manageable terms that you can drop into a conversation often had us come unstuck.

Two days after leaving the Kaipo Wall I was on a government jet flying to Miles to cover the opening of the 100th Land Care group in Queensland. I was with journalist Harry Williams. Harry's dead now but his spirit lives on.

Everybody has a Harry story. He was genuine, dependable, caring, and had a way of making everyone feel that their story really mattered. One day, a local farmer had me nodding off as he chattered on about his water-efficient irrigation techniques, but not Harry. He was all ears and the farmer was enthusiastic he had found an audience. Not only was Harry a great ABC ambassador, he was a conduit between the ABC and the taxpayers who funded it.

My eyes were glazing over until the farmer said something that put a spark of interest back in them. He had just talked about the nearby high ground. What high ground? To my eye it was dead flat.

'No, there's good fall there, it drops one metre over the kilometre,' he said as he pointed.

The contrast between here and the Kaipo Valley was mind-boggling and I'd experienced it all within three days. The uniqueness of my job was starting to dawn on me.

We were herded onto a minibus to visit another property.

Robin was our driver for the day. 'Where's your property, Robin?' Harry threw in to start conversation.

'Oh, I don't own a property, I'm the local butcher. I've got a shop in town but I've got a few acres out back of the shop that I can hold a few cattle on occasionally if need be.'

'How much land is that?'

'Oh, seven hundred acres,' he said without missing a beat. The country mile was something that could get you into trouble if you didn't recalibrate your brain before heading west.

Within the month I was back in the Northern Territory. The driving directions given to us couldn't have been clearer. There's only one road into King's Canyon. It's impossible to be on the wrong road as the next road north is one hundred kilometres away and about the same south. Clearly written on the fax sheet was 'the entrance to the King's Creek Station is at the end of the bitumen'. Then how come we couldn't find it? A few hundred metres onto the dirt we started to double back, sure that we had driven past the entrance gate. No, there was the end of the bitumen but no gate, no tyre tracks leading anywhere. We drove on, peering left and right for a hard-to-see entrance. Five kilometres along we turned and headed back to the bitumen then, for a third time, headed out along the dirt again. The odometer kept ticking over until, to our left, appeared the large floodlit entrance to King's Creek Station. It was twenty-three kilometres past the bitumen. We pointed this out to station owner Ian Conway, who said, 'Yeah, just like I said, at the end of the bitumen.'

The camel industry was growing in the Northern Territory in the early nineties. After a century and a bit of breeding (since first being imported into Australia for the ill-fated Burke and Wills expedition) wild camels in the Territory now numbered about half a million. Good camels attracted handsome dollars from the Arab states as racing camels, though most likely they were destined to be camel burgers with chips on the side. Regardless of their final destination they had to be caught first. We were going camel mustering.

By his own admission Ian Conway applied a fairly unscientific method to catching camels. It consisted mainly of four-wheel drives, helicopters and a lot of adrenaline. Our pilot was a young gun named Craig who could throw the tiny Robinson R22 helicopter around like he was playing a video game. I often have dreams where I can fly, where I swoop with ease and confidence through trees and I always make it through the narrowest of gaps. This was that dream, except it was a lot noisier. Whooshing along through the trees – and I mean through the trees – Craig rotated the chopper one hundred and eighty degrees as though pivoting on an imaginary pole, and at the same time he dropped the nose and sort of skidded to a backwards midair stop. As we were only three metres off the ground and in front of the camels, we looked them directly in the eye. The tallest males turned the herd and pounded a new course through the mulga.

The plan was to run and tire them. This took longer than I expected as camels have blood pumps in their hooves: the more they run the faster they run, though only to a point. Thwoomp thwoomp thwoomp – the blades groaned and the engine screamed. The little machine crabbed and hopped in front of the herd, countering their moves, steering them towards the catch vehicles. All the time I felt safe in the hands of this pimply faced kid. The chopper moved as though it was an extension of his thinking. We put down in a clearing and I transferred to one of the catch vehicles.

Crash thud thud bang – Nick was my driver who was throwing this clapped-out Toyota over the mulga. Standing on the trayback behind, hanging on tight with his shins behind my head and armed with a noose dangling from the end of a pole, was the catcher, whose name I never got – introductions proved awkward. We were into the herd, right in amongst them. A brown woolly rump bulged through my glassless window opening and I got a nostril-clearing waft of camel. You could hear the thundering of the hooves above the painful screaming of the engine stressing at high revs in third gear.

The camels pulled away to the left and we momentarily lost them. Nick spun the steering wheel into full left lock with not even the slightest hint of backing off the accelerator. The wheels dug into the red sand, and myself and the twelve kilograms of glass and electronics I was trying to hold ended up in Nick's lap. Nick didn't bat an eyelid; I was just another waste-of-space passenger to him. He went back onto a couple of young bulls split from the herd. Within seconds the Toyota was alongside and the nameless man up back easily slipped the noose over the camel's neck. Nick's foot came off the accelerator for the first time and the gearbox and the soft desert sand pulled the vehicle to a smart stop. There you have it, one camel.

This smelly catch was compliant and quiet so we obliged his good nature and tied him to a tree as a backdrop for the main interview with Ian Conway. During the lengthy interview no one, particularly me, noticed the camel slowly drop out of shot. Eventually I did remark on its disappearance. The rope had tightened around its neck and strangled the beast. A government vet named Taffy ran over and used the camel as a trampoline – this apparently was the way you delivered CPR to a large beast – but its camel-racing days were cut short and it never even got a chance to be served up with chips on the side.

Quite often, the further you go into the deep north, the harder it becomes to understand people. Many grew up on stations alongside Aboriginal children. The Aboriginal voice when speaking English is very distinct and its influence on station hands and ringers is common. The local story, as it is told, is that people have learnt to talk through their teeth so the flies don't get in. I was in Kununurra and the reason I couldn't understand this particular bloke's name was because he had *no* teeth and as I was suffering from a wickedly infected ear I had little hearing. He'd launched himself upon me as I was minding my own business under the shade of a tree to escape the intense afternoon sun and Blair's snoring.

Three of us were sharing a single motel room (not by choice): rural journalist sans pareil Blair Roots, sound recordist Mike Charman and I. We weren't happy. Three rooms had been booked but the blank stare from the motel owner telegraphed that he disagreed. So too did the hire car company when we suggested we would *never* have booked an open ute to carry twenty cases of camera and sound gear around one of the harshest parts of Australia. All twenty cases of gear had to be brought into our shared motel room. While Mike and I were doing this Blair had decided to slip into something a little more comfortable as evening wear. He emerged from the bathroom wearing just a pair of Stubbie shorts that were way too small. They disappeared under his considerable girth, rendering him ostensibly naked. Mike and I shot uncomfortable glances at one another. Our new roommate produced a chilled six-pack of VB beer and chugged down three of them in under three minutes. He lay back on the faded chenille bedspread, pulled his trademark felt hat over his eyes and said, 'Night, lads.' The sibilance from the last 's' was still hanging as the snoring began.

The room was hardly a place to relax so Mike and I escaped to the shade of the tree, only to be press-ganged into listening to our toothless friend's story. He claimed to be the first person in Australia to single-handedly catch bulls, aided only by Whiskey the dog. He wanted to demonstrate the technique 'on us' but settled on 'for us'. They'd chase the hapless bull on horse, then on foot. He'd get one almighty headlock on the beast, which was Whiskey the dog's cue to bite the bull on the nose and not let go. He swooped his battered face in close to us and said, 'You don't get scars like this from running away.' His nose looked like two cauliflower florets that were spread across a mass of scar tissue that passed for a face. His tongue poked in and out like a lizard's as he relived the moments. He was also very proud that he had never worn shoes in his life. His broad wads of torn, tattered and calloused skin verified that.

A Labor Party man straight from the womb, he boasted of his handiwork for the good of the party. At one election soon after Aboriginal people had been given the right to vote, the Liberal Party was wooing the new Aboriginal constituency with all sorts of claims and promises. He snuck out to the Aboriginal reserve the night before voting day with a forty-four-gallon drum of booze. He got the Aborigines so drunk that they passed out, unable to even tick a ballot box. Single-handedly he destroyed the conservative vote for the area. Is any of this true? I don't know. Whoever he was, he *had* lived the toughest of lives. Toughness and resilience, though, come packaged in many ways.

Diminutive in size but large of heart would be one way to describe Sister Anne Maree Jensen. Working in a Catholic nursing home on the Gold Coast was how she dutifully served her calling. A notice in the Catholic newsletter caught her eye: the local priest-cum-pilot at Longreach was leaving. Was this what God had in mind for her? With no flying experience, Sister Anne Maree amused fellow nuns by practising her flight calls as she peeled potatoes in the convent. Within months she was airborne. If ever there was an inescapable moniker, it was hers: the Flying Nun. She called herself a reluctant pilot, never really that comfortable in the air let alone in remote areas. Her two dioceses were the size of Germany: west to the borders of South Australia and the Northern Territory and south to the New South Wales border. Germany has seventy million people, her patch has fifteen hundred. This made crshing one thing but actually being found another. She was happy for our company on board the flight to Sunnyside Station, one hundred and twenty kilometres southwest of Longreach. Sister Anne Maree had been named an Australian of the Year and we were doing her profile for an upcoming awards broadcast.

Her little Cessna 172 sat at the end of the Longreach runway. The aviation headset overwhelmed her small face. A quick sign of the cross then above the engine she yelled, 'Lord bless us and get us all safely to Sunnyside.' She pushed forward on the throttle and pulled back on the controls. Up we went, closer to her God and further away from the red earth below. It's from the air that you can appreciate what she had taken on. The vastness of this country never ceases to amaze me. My immediate work of filming her at the controls was done so I secretly stared at her past the viewfinder. I can't help but marvel at these people I meet every time I go outback, where the sound of the Cessna is a call to put the kettle on. There is a real quality about them that I admire so much. Just being in their presence enriches me.

The owners of Sunnyside Station were Jim and Leonie Nunn, a tough no-nonsense pair with four boys aged from thirteen to three. Leonie was the only female within hundreds of square kilometres of blokes' world. She had no one to confide in, no one's ear to bend, no one to gloat to about the children. Sister Anne Maree listens a lot – it's the biggest part of her job – but if there's work to be done, she mucks in. A freak accident while helping to lay irrigation pipes a year earlier ended with Sister Anne Maree requiring major surgery to repair broken bones in her face. She was such a positive person that a few scars would never conceal the look of hope on her face.

The faces I really love to film are Aboriginal. Photographically their deep black, almost blue skin reflects light in a way that makes their expressions pop from the frame. Something else I've noticed is that Aborigines don't laugh, they giggle. It's a conspiratorial sharing of something funny. And they don't laugh alone; young or old, they always look for a pair of eyes to share the moment.

I, like most big-city Australians, had only minimal contact with Aboriginal people as I grew up. My travels in the army gave me my first exposure to the original Australians but most of these were very negative experiences involving drunken whites calling drunken blacks 'drunken bastards'. Meeting Aborigines on my ABC travels has established a whole new relationship for me. All in all I've visited a few dozen communities. Fast repartee has never been one of my strong points so I particularly like chatting with Aborigines because their responses are thoughtful and considered ones. Silence on their part doesn't mean they don't understand, it often means they are thinking about their answer. I naturally fit in with this relaxed conversational pace. Early on I humiliated myself by slowing down to almost childlike speech so I could be understood, only to find out that the person I was speaking to held a university degree.

In television where time is money, it can be difficult. I recently watched some of the Super 8 film I had shot in Cooktown when I was a cameraman in waiting, back in my army days. Men with the shiny black skin I so loved to film filled the frames. In 2008 I shot a similar ceremony. Again it was back in Cooktown. The difference was striking. Gone was that really dark skin, light brown in its place along with lots of rolls of fat. Of course this is purely anecdotal, and in any case, the strength of Aboriginal culture doesn't rest with skin colour alone, but I've certainly witnessed a physical change over the years.

I was getting established in documentaries and starting to build contacts with documentary producers within and outside the ABC. I was a big fan of the *Bush Tucker Man* and quietly dreamed of shooting a series like that. In 1994 that opportunity came along. It was a six-part show about a vet named Peter Trembath who flew his own plane to attend to the cockatoos, buffalo, crocodiles, snakes and kangaroos of the remote Top End of Australia. The PBS network in America was on board as well as the BBC. I wanted to be on board too but it was a Sydney-based production and that essentially excluded anyone but Sydney cameramen. I lobbied where necessary, luck stepped in and I landed the gig. The irony that this show about animals would prove to be a wolf in sheep's clothing that would bite me wasn't apparent until much later.

The twelve-week shooting schedule was broken into two six-week blocks. The sound recordist assigned to the shoot was the cheery and dependable Mel Radford. Julie Hornsey was signed on as camera assistant. We got on well together and she was more than capable of taking over the filming if needed, as she did many times. We even had a producer's assistant, the teaspoon-collecting Lana Ruckley. Fresh from the Sydney studios where time was measured in seconds, she was going to need serious reprogramming, as NT (or Northern Territory) time was diametrically different from what she was used to and just waiting to give her grief. NT stands for not today, not tomorrow, not Tuesday, not Thursday. Two directors were assigned with a few episodes apiece that they would be responsible for. First up was Jack King. Everyone was keen and the schedule spelt adventure. The problem for me was that I was armed with a little knowledge and that became a dangerous thing.

Documentary making consumed me. I even took my own VHS player along to study docos that I had taped. I had concocted a style of shooting in my head that was slavishly tied to spontaneity; nothing could be set up as far as I was concerned, we had to shoot every scene with no intervention. It was achievable but it was a naive purist's viewpoint that completely ignored the fact that we were there on somebody else's time, using somebody else's money, and they were expecting a predictable result. For the first few weeks all I did was frustrate Jack, Julie and Mel, who, to their credit, put up with me. Everything was working, we were getting good material, but I was making everybody do it the hard way. It was like being made to do long division when a calculator was at your fingertips. A few weeks in and Jack took me aside to give me some attitudinal panel beating. After that I was as good as new and we launched into doing what we had come to do: capture on film that most unique of all characters, the Territorian.

Kid Eager was the nickname we gave to Peter Trembath, who was always halfway out the door before you'd even decided to leave. His energy and his plane were necessary to cover the vast distances. We're not talking luxury here. His serviceable but knocked-about Cessna 182 was like the old family Kingswood station wagon. They take a hammering from the dirt airstrips that dot the landscape, none rougher than the one at Bloodwood Downs. The loose dusty finger of dirt had been bulldozed the day before especially for our visit. By the locals' reckoning, it was a small place at only five hundred square kilometres and hard to find by air. The station's owner, Tony McFarlane, said he would light a fire as a navigational aid. By the time we located the airstrip a bushfire was burning across about a kilometre front. Below, Tony was swinging a mattock, grubbing out a few remaining stumps, as we made an inspection pass prior to landing.

The plane pulled up in a swirl of dust and Tony chugged up in his clapped-out Land Cruiser. It was like central casting had arranged a leading man. Six foot two and a good pick-handle across the shoulders, lanky with piercing eyes, a crooked smile, barefoot and clothes with an attached ton of dirt: that was Tony. Every part of his truck squeaked and it had more rattles than a millionaire's baby. And it wouldn't start. Peter had to help with the hotwiring but that produced only sparks and twelve unwanted volts up Peter's arm. Push! The old girl roared into life and Julie and I were up back on the open tray with the dog. As we banged past the anthills I busied myself with getting the necessary travelling shots. I thought I'd better check back to see that no gear had bounced off. I wish I hadn't. The dog, with a very sheepish look, was marking his territory by crapping on my tripod. I would have preferred not to see that.

We made the house in good time except that it was not a house, it was a shed. Well, technically a shed has walls; this one consisted of metal posts and a metal roof. It served as workshop, kitchen, place to put your swag and, now, surgery. A section on the table was cleared by pushing the salt, peanut butter and other condiment jars to one side. A bull terrier was about to face Peter and 'a cutlass that would render him nutless', so he wasn't going under without a fight. Peter had to give him what seemed like a horse's dose of anaesthetic to get him to sleep. Speaking of horse doses, it was the dog's equine workmate who farewelled his manhood next. The horse was too big for the kitchen bench so he was 'cut' under the shade of a tree to the sounds of Tony cracking his stockwhip to keep the dogs away. Nothing goes to waste here and the dogs each got a testicular treat.

Finding safety in numbers, fellow vegetarian Julie and I formed our wagons into a circle. There were times we found ourselves in hostile territory, none more so than with Lorraine, the cook at the muster on Willaroo Station. Before our encounter with her Julie was a bit shaken and, come to think of it, so was I. We had approached a bloke driving a road grader to ask him to create some dust to add atmosphere to our late-afternoon shots. He opened the door of the grader, which is about two metres off the ground, and swung sideways to address us. Inertia, then gravity, had dislodged his unspeakable bits and in the apparent absence of undergarments, they swung to an obvious stop at our eye level. Oblivious to his dress code indiscretion, he saw this as an opportunity for a chat. I mean, where do you look? What do you say? How do you broach it?

We were off our food by now but still needed to announce our meat-free status to the blood-lusting camp of station hands, stockmen and jackeroos. We approached the solid redheaded Lorraine and before we could say anything she said, 'We knew youse were coming so we killed another beast for youse. He's hangin' up to bleed now.'

'Gee thanks, but you know, Lorraine, thought we'd better tell you, Julie and I are vegetarian, but p-l-e-a-s-e don't go to a-n-y trouble on our behalf.'

It stopped her dead in her tracks. Only her eyes darted around as the cogs turned trying to process that last sentence. Finally she spoke: 'That's good, 'cause youse can eat cow shit and grass.' With that the conversation terminated. We thought this was good ol' country humour until the meal was served. It was steak, liver, or steak and liver. Julie grabbed a loaf of the super-size white sandwich bread and I found the tomato sauce. Alone we had tomato sauce sandwiches for tea. By now word had spread throughout the ringers and younger jackeroos. They stared at their food as they ate and would shoot glances at us then laugh under their breath. One voice drifted over to our table: 'He's a vegetarian. Obviously didn't get enough of his mumma's milk growing up. And he's got a girl's name – how's about that for bad luck?' It was harmless enough but you could tell they were happy to have an outsider to kick for a change. The law of inverse proportions was alive and well for Julie and me, or Jules and Jules as we became known. It seemed the less meat we ingested, the more cows that were killed on our behalf, even if it wasn't dinner time.

Rowlands Dairy is the only dairy in the Northern Territory. Any sick cows have to be quickly put down and autopsied to make sure they're not carrying any disease that might infect the entire stock. Peter was called in and a hapless, scrawny cow was led over to the back of Peter's truck. He gave her snout a gentle rub then put the muzzle of the .22 calibre rifle directly above her eye and pulled the trigger. The loud bang startled me and the camera jumped momentarily. It also startled the cow. She looked up from her cud chewing to see what the fuss was about, gazed left and right, then resumed chewing. Peter unloaded the rifle to check that a freshly spent shell popped out. It did. He looked down the barrel to check the lead slug hadn't lodged there. It hadn't. He leaned close to inspect the hole in the cow's head and poked his finger in up to the first joint. Somehow the bullet hadn't connected with anything of importance to the cow's well-being.

A second bullet, this time at a different angle, and the cow dropped to the ground completely unaware. With just a pair of gumboots, a white apron and a big knife, Peter turned the three-dimensional carcass into a spread of organs in quick time. His work was done, as was Jack King's. This was Jack's last day. His first two episodes were complete and the editors in Sydney needed his presence as they started to turn hundreds of hours of footage into half-hour episodes. He would return to us a month later to begin shooting a new episode. Our relationship with Peter and his team was standing strong. The bumps I had caused at the start of the shoot had smoothed themselves out and, as a team, we were on fire.

In twenty-five years with hundreds of directors, I've only ever had serious working problems with two of them. One I will call 'Rodger'. My first impressions were positive. Organised people like other organised people, and I'm organised. Rodger came on the scene with schedules, sub-schedules, scripts, lists, ring binders, spreadsheets ... I welcomed this intrusion of order. Jack, for all his many strengths, had a very relaxed approach to scheduling and frustrated everyone with his lateness. The need to be on time is out of my control. I was born with the punctuality gene. I work by the axiom 'if you're not early you're late'. Even if they can't find anything else to write on my headstone it can say *At least he was punctual*. I went to sleep full of excitement about the coming weeks.

One morning I answered my door. It was Lana, the producer's assistant. She was looking good. She had used the opportunity of a few months in the Northern Territory as a launching pad for a healthier lifestyle: she'd stopped smoking, was eating good food, had slimmed down and was obviously happy within herself. Then why was she looking glum?

'Rodger has asked me to pass on these requests: no more sharing the vehicles. From now on he will have one car which will be known as the director's car and the four of us and all the gear share the other. Julian, you'll need to move out of your room so Rodger can have it. It's the biggest and, as director, Rodger says it should be his.'

Inside, my egalitarian sensibilities were enraged but I remained composed and negotiated a practical outcome. He got the car but the room was needed as a base for the mountain of camera equipment.

Late morning came and we readied to hit the road. Assembled at the car our collective jaws almost hit the ground. Rodger appeared dressed in a beige adventure outfit replete with zippers and cargo pockets. From shoulder to opposite hip hung a leather map case and encircling his wrist was a watch with a swing needle compass attached to the band. Turned-wood pens poked proudly from the pocket of his hunter's vest and complemented the spotted yellow cravat that was knotted around his neck just so. All that was missing was a pith helmet. From here it went downhill.

We couldn't have cared less what Rodger wore, but the locals did. Territorians have an inbuilt bullshit radar that is activated from about a kilometre away. Whenever we arrived at a new location with new people, they treated Rodger as a carnival oddity and promptly ignored him, preferring to deal with us. This infuriated Rodger. Our attempts to counter this and direct questions to Rodger were futile. The locals were having none of it. Rodger was from the old school of BBC filmmaking where the system is hierarchical, like the military; directors were like officers and the crew were the enlisted soldiers. Collaboration was the strength in our team, as in any successful documentary team.

Rodger grew steadily more dictatorial in an attempt to regain power but every new location made matters worse. As a team we were working poorly and great cinematic moments were being lost.

As this was my first big series I was aware that many eyes were upon me. I resolved to rise above this and deliver nothing but solid work. Being professional and dealing with the problems was the course I had charted for myself. Boy, was I naive because conflict is never a one-sided event. Distance myself as I tried, I was getting sucked in to a point from which there would be no getting out.

We all prepared to fly to Minjilang, an Aboriginal settlement on Croker Island, a few hundred kilometres northeast of Darwin, where Peter was running a dog desexing clinic. Two hundred people in forty houses and about five hundred dogs lived there. Some houses had up to fifteen dogs, all in appalling condition: open sores, scabies and skin disease that result in dogs with no hair, which are known as leather dogs. Abuse and neglect are common but the reasons are complex. If there are fifteen dogs in a house with little kids running around, they can't allow the dogs to be aggressive and assertive so they kick and throw things at them to keep them submissive. The culture of dog dreaming links the dogs with the spirits of their ancestors so they are very reluctant for any dogs to be put down. Grocery prices are exorbitant in these remote settlements, meaning little money is left over to feed dogs. Most importantly, without desexing the cycle of misery continues.

A nine-seater plane was chartered for the trip. We removed two seats to accommodate the gear. We were weighed, our gear was weighed. Something had to go. I culled much of my equipment such as lights and extra videotapes. Still we came in overweight. No one was happy to do so, but Julie, Mel and I removed a few sets of clothing from our personal bags. Our target met, we loaded the plane. Amongst everything was a cardboard box I just assumed belonged to the pilot. I loaded it without another thought.

It was a Saturday and despite weeks of planning, no one seemed to know we were coming. We hired two vehicles from the locals: an open-backed ute that Peter used as his mobile surgery and a beat-up Troop Carrier that was empty of fuel when it was given to us and, as it was Saturday, the diesel pump was closed. 'If you're not using it then …' They took it back even though we had booked and pre-paid. Not only was the diesel pump closed, so was the store. It was about half past two in the afternoon and we hadn't eaten since breakfast. Julie had half a packet of peanuts that she shared around. Rodger passed on his handful and went off to see what could be done. He seemed to have our best interests at heart. This was a first.

There was no accommodation for us so we began setting up our camp in the local park. On Peter's advice we had brought tents and sleeping bags. We wandered aimlessly until Rodger returned with the news that the shop wouldn't be opening anytime soon. It was now 4pm and we hadn't eaten since 6am. Rodger was acting strangely and disappeared again. We followed and, from a discreet distance, watched. He went to a bench outside the community hall where his gear was stored. First he checked that no one was around, then slid out a box from under his gear. It was the cardboard box I had found while loading the plane. He quickly inventoried the contents: fresh rolls, pastrami, pesto, water chestnuts, chocolates, cheeses. (We knew because we checked later.) He made up a pastrami roll and, lickety-split, polished it off, always on the lookout for anyone coming. A sparkling mineral water washed it all down followed by a dusting away of the crumbs. The box was returned into hiding and Rodger headed back.

We were stunned. Julie and I initially thought we were unwittingly part of a candid-camera-type reality show. This was such bizarre behaviour. The first rule of the road is to look out for each other, not to mention that I had left behind camera gear that was important to the success of the series. We stuck to our guns, remained professional and chose not to challenge him and see how it played out. Sometime later that evening the store opened and we had a dinner of canned food.

Peter had so many dogs to desex that we took turns at being the anaesthetist to speed things along. At times Peter had been criticised for his veterinary techniques by vets from the polite surgeries of the southern cities. This was Peter's reality: his operating table was the tailgate of a ute and the recovery room was the sand under his feet. His patients had the toughest and saddest of lives. A great north–south cultural divide existed in his profession. Dirty work like this had to be done and I respected Peter for doing it.

We finished at Minjilang and I flew with Peter across the top of Arnhem Land to Gove. The Cessna 204 flew smoothly through the canyons of clouds. The coastline was a jigsaw of estuaries, islands, inlets, snaking rivers and vast tracts of deep green roadless forests. Just like pulling the car up on the side of the road, we landed on a remote beach for a toilet stop. No application forms in triplicate, no permit fees, no allowing time for seeking public objection: I could see the appeal of life up here. If you could put up with the toughness there was so much freedom to be had.

The working relationship between Rodger and me was deteriorating by the day. Good camerawork on documentaries is all about intuition and pre-empting situations. You get this by building a relationship of trust with the people you are filming. Any attempts by us to do so were seen by Rodger as a direct threat to his status as director. No one was in any doubt that this was important to him and we tried to allow for it but, just in trying to do my job well, I infuriated Rodger. It had become a catch-22. As his behaviour became more erratic, my resolve to maintain a professional approach strengthened and strengthened.

Our friction was detrimental to a successful program so someone was going to go. I knew that. As a new kid on the block, I had to be careful. Head office in Sydney was aware of the problems but the logistics of time and distance prevented anyone being replaced. I wanted to be able to say that I had done my job well and, importantly for all of us, we had to make sure the ABC was well represented, so we just soldiered on in this farcical situation. Besides, there were only a few days left before we headed home for the mid-series break – things couldn't get worse, could they?

Gove was rich in characters but rather than getting out amongst them, we were in our rooms. Rodger had taken to driving off for hours to find stories and demanded we be on 'standby' at the motel. As frustrating as this was, Julie felt it most, as outside her room was a caged cockatoo that screeched obscenities: 'You're all a bunch of bastards' and 'Stop staring at me and let me out of here, you bastard'. Lana had been reduced to tears. She was back smoking again and the stress had caused her to break out in terrible spots. Peter the vet was talking about pulling out of the series if Rodger stayed on. By now Rodger was punching bare-fisted: 'You do not roll the camera unless I say "Roll". I'M THE DIRECTOR!' And so it was that great scenes and characters were never captured, like Peter and the nuggety 'local' fishing on the beach. Peter noticed that this bloke's pit-bull had no ears. 'Skin cancer got your dog's ears, huh?' The guy ashed his cigarette and said, 'Nope, I ran out of bait one day.' The days and the opportunities slid by. Our last day promised to be a beauty. We were going fishing to one of the 'best barra fishing spots on the planet'. It would be a long day so we needed to buy supplies and told Rodger so, continually. But it was to be 'standby' for us. The cicadas thrummed their deafening evening song and the stores closed their doors. We hadn't shot a thing and we had no food for the trip.

Rick and Cheryl were the owners of the Gove Vet Clinic. They and their kids guided us along the sixteen kilometres of track. It was slow and rough through pure stands of Darwin stringybark with an understorey of livistonia palms, cycads and anthills. The day on the river was long and hot and plagued by two-stroke engine problems. Peter, Rick, Mel, Julie and I were on the river for the best part of the day. Curiously, Rodger stayed back with Rick's family and picnicked by the water's edge. In a complete turnaround it was left to me to direct and film the day's action. Unbeknown to us, Peter and Rick had eaten before going in the boat. That stuffed our plans to sponge a bit of food from them. We returned hot, sunburnt and hungry. Without going into detail with her, I quietly asked Cheryl if she had any food to spare as we hadn't eaten.

'Well, of course. I don't have much left but you're welcome to it.' She pointed me to the Esky that was in the back of the boat, now on the trailer and ready for the trip home. 'Ours is the old battered Esky. Rodger's is the nice new one.'

What?

Next to theirs, half-hidden, was a shiny, soft-sided, zippered blue Esky. Inside were rolls, cheeses and all sorts of delicacies. The gloves were well and truly off now. I grabbed handfuls of Rodger's food and gave them to Julie and Mel. Then, without a moment's hesitation, I uncapped a nearby bottle of two-stroke oil and poured the best part of it onto, into, over and around Rodger's food. Then I zipped it back up nice and snug. Julie was livid and wanted to confront him but this was not a fight to be had in front of our hosts. Besides, I wanted to see him open his Esky.

We began the return journey and it quickly turned dark. As had happened a few times on the way in, we became bogged. This was a stretch of wetlands and the classic territory where you'd expect to find taipans. Rick and Kid Eager were on to it. They were experts at getting out of bogs. Peter chopped lengths of saplings while Rick jacked the rear of the car high then Peter slipped the branches under the wheels as traction pads. With little for me to do, I held a torch. From nowhere Rodger snatched the torch from my hand and said, 'I hold the torches around here.' Julie and I laughed. Was there anything else we could do to undermine Rodger's authority? As it transpired, that was left to Julie.

Rick told everyone to push. Obviously Rodger was unaware that the worst place to be when getting out of a bog is directly behind a back wheel but no one, not even Rick, could be bothered telling him to move. As the engine revved and the tyres spun looking for grip, a huge rooster tail of mud covered Rodger. The car got out but now Rodger was momentarily bogged. His feet were stuck in place. He teetered as he tried to clear the mud from his eyes. We all walked past without lending a hand except for Julie, who, acting on our behalf, extended her arm and pushed him. Like a tree felled in the forest, Rodger went down and we walked on.

Along with our return home came a string of complaints against Rodger and a show of support for us. I went into a fortnight of days off confident that was all behind me. I was looking forward to more time shooting with Jack. Suddenly an urgent meeting was called. The executive producer of the series was flying up from Sydney to attend. As we gathered in the room, the talk was convivial. Once the door closed, that all stopped. Rodger, it was explained, had been reassigned. I was then made to watch three scenes that didn't quite scrub up to the expectations of the production. So? They can't all be winners. What about the other hundred that were terrific? It took a moment for it to register. It wasn't just Rodger, I was off the shoot as well. A whole lot of politics was going on and removing me was the easiest solution. Fighting was pointless.

I maintained the professional manner I'd adopted the whole way through this saga and took it on the chin, just like all those hardworking men and women I'd met in Australia's north would have taken it. But it still hurt. Underneath I was gutted. Being removed from a shoot was bad for your career. It didn't happen often and when it did the gossip mill ramped up. It was the worst possible outcome. At that point it seemed to me that everything I'd aimed for since shooting that first street march all those years back had just slipped away. I just didn't get it or how I'd managed to do it to myself. It was a lesson in something I'd never been good at: politics. It's never enough to keep your nose to the grindstone and just do your best. You've got to keep your eyes and ears wide open all the time.

Fortunately Vicky didn't have to put up with my wallowing in self-pity for too long. My time in the professional wilderness was short: about a week. A groundswell of support came my way, including a phone call that was the start of going places I would never have dreamed of.

# 8

**A thimble full of water
Holds a thousand lives or more
Tiny minute creatures
In an ocean
With no shore.**

AJ BRADLEY

At school I liked science, particularly physics and biology. They were my strong subjects, the ones I just managed to pass, unlike chemistry, for which I once got a token one out of a hundred for merely writing my name on the paper. Clearly, science didn't like me, which is sort of sad because I championed its cause for a long time. 'A scientist' was my stock reply to that often-asked question 'What are you going to be when you grow up?' I used to draw pictures of myself wearing a white lab coat surrounded by glass tubes. It almost became a reality, but as that was at the bottle factory on nightshift, I guess that didn't count. When a phone call came from the ABC science program *Quantum*, I felt that flame inside of me splutter back to life.

A considered, well-modulated and almost whimsical voice asked if I was available to do a shoot over the coming fortnight. It was

Richard Corfield, a producer with the science unit. We had previously worked together on a kangaroo-culling story. He probably remembered me from the incident where forty kilometres down the road from leaving Idalia National Park, I insisted we turn around and go back as it was pretty important to do so. We retraced our steps through the bush and there, in the long grass where we had previously been, was the camera. At least we established that I didn't bandy the term 'important' around loosely. That aside, we had quickly developed a mutual respect for one another, something that is a key to being on the road with someone.

Richard's appearance was striking: with his shock of wiry grey hair and bushy moustache he looked like an elongated version of Albert Einstein. Turtleneck sweaters were his trademark. He had a wonderful way with people and loved making programs about the human face of science that focused on the scientists as much as the science itself. His style of program dispelled the myth that all scientists wear lab coats and subscribe to *Pipette Monthly*. He asked me to accompany him to one of Australia's best-kept secrets. At eighteen kilometres long and three hundred metres high, it is a rock face roughly ten times the size of Uluru. Despite being referred to as the Ayers Rock of the north, for some reason this rock remains virtually unknown. Being an early explorer must have been exhausting work as there seemed little energy left over for coming up with creative names. The best they could do was the very pedestrian Mt Mulligan.

The sandstone bluff is Queensland's oldest Aboriginal site and is owned by the KuKu Djungan people. Between the First and Second World Wars the KuKu Djungan were forcibly removed from their land. With the assistance of government grants the remaining descendants were able to buy back the land. They wanted to start an eco-tourism venture to showcase their Aboriginal culture. As much of their traditional knowledge had disappeared with their displaced and massacred elders, many of the mountain's secrets were just that: secret. In an attempt to reunite with this lost knowledge they employed an enquiry of scientists – botanists, zoologists, archaeologists, social anthropologists, pollen experts, bat experts and at least a half-dozen other '-ologists' whose precise expertise I can't recall – to help find the missing pieces of their cultural puzzle. It was a hard but rewarding time.

Most places on the broad flat-topped mountain were only accessible on foot but that gave us more time to enjoy getting to know our trail mates. We were in the company of some fascinating characters. It was uplifting to hear the passion and unrestrained excitement in Dr Glen Ingram's voice. A large, jovial zoologist from the Queensland Museum, he would wax lyrical over a tiny snail, the size of a match head, but then why wouldn't he when it was a new species? Over the two weeks we were there, the scientists managed to discover one new species a day.

Richard and I were hitting it off well, the group was welcoming of our presence but I was feeling homesick. Vicky was pregnant with our second daughter and my time away from home was growing to around one hundred nights a year. I was beginning to feel nomadic, like I didn't belong anywhere. I'd found myself falling into a habit of never bothering to commit to any social engagements or join any clubs as three out of four times my work bookings would change and I couldn't make it. Consequently my social life dropped off and Vicky was getting used to the words 'Jules is away'. I know plenty of cameramen whose marriages didn't survive the rigours of this lifestyle. I was very lucky to have met Vicky. She has always unflinchingly supported my need to achieve goals. She would write and say she felt abandoned but always end the letter on a note of support for me. This was a situation of my own making and I was at any time able to reverse it and spend less time away but I didn't because I'd found my perfect job. I'd slip on my tunnel-vision glasses and get back to the work at hand.

The highlight of this trip was the once-in-a-lifetime opportunity to discover new Aboriginal cave art. A potential art site had been identified but it was strictly off limits until Sammy, our KuKu Djungan representative, had cleared it with the spirits. Igoo is the spirit of the mountain and Sammy and he would regularly confer. These one-sided conversations became commonplace. Boy, did Igoo wield some power. A scientific expedition costing thousands of dollars a day was stopped in its tracks if Igoo had cracked a wobbly. The scientists respected this but every moment spent waiting was not so much thought of in dollars but in lost discoveries. It was a bit touch-and-go for a while but Igoo eventually gave us the green light to visit.

Imagine rounding a corner and laying eyes upon artwork, possibly being the first person to do so in thousands of years? It sends shivers up your spine. It's a perk of the job. Five small hand-stencils graced the overhanging wall. One of these had only four and a half fingers. Was this a child who had undergone some initiation ritual? Was it a bit of bad luck in the bush? Was it done all those years ago with a mischievous glint in the eye? These scientists had worked hard for this moment. Then an impostor, a freeloader like me, just walked in. I had queue-jumped again with my access-all-areas pass: the camera. The guilt lasted all of a second and I resumed marvelling.

Cameras are much more powerful than many people realise. Modern lens optics allow the camera to see farther into the distance than ever before. As useful as this is, it's not the camera's greatest optical triumph: selective focus is. That ability to frame out all of life's distracting clutter and concentrate on a scene, an individual, an object, a face and, in particular, eyes. I know eyes. They are my stock in trade. Bulgy ones, deepset ones, shifty, shiny, glassy ones. Through the hyper-real world of the viewfinder you can see deeper into people than you can ever hope to face to face. This lets you catch a moment, an emotion, a feeling ahead of those not looking through the lens. It might only be a split second faster but I'm first through the door when it opens. This is exactly what happened when we interviewed Sammy.

We were seated on the rocky ground at the opening to a shallow cave. It was a place of his ancestors. An archaeological dig was unearthing tens of thousands of years of prior occupancy. Richard concluded what was a revealing interview but I kept the camera rolling as he moved to stand. I was kneeling directly behind him and placed my hand on his shoulder to stop him and maintained the pressure. Richard wasn't sure what I was on about but he trusted me enough to go with it. An awkward ten seconds of silence passed then Sammy's eyes glassed over and tears rolled down his cheeks. He gave a heartfelt summation of the importance of this site. I had seen this coming in Sammy's eyes. It's not that Richard isn't perceptive, he is, very much so. He just didn't have the powerful set of glasses I did.

After two weeks there were only two things left that we needed to do. One was to visit the old Mt Mulligan coal mine, the scene of Queensland's worst mine disaster. In 1921 a massive explosion killed at least seventy-five men. Despite efforts to seal off the mine, industrious visitors had penetrated the barrier. Squeezing through a small hole, we entered another world. It was like we had chanced upon an *Indiana Jones* movie set. Rough-sawn posts propped up chunky timber roof supports. Every third or fourth post had collapsed. There was little holding the carved tunnel in place. Curtains of fine tree roots hung from the crumbling ceiling. The humidity was so high, so oppressive, that the finest of water droplets clung to the roots, creating a veil of lace in the dead still air. Tiny bats hung from the ceiling and others darted in and out of the torch beams.

The consensus was to explore deeper but my instinct was telling me otherwise. Climbing had given me a good appreciation of unstable rock when I saw it. Thanks to Japanese technology I had the perfect out. The humidity warning on my camera sounded its alarm. It's a funny thing – people seem to have an innate respect for television cameras and they are often far more protective of the equipment than I am. It was the scientists' suggestion that the camera needed some fresh air, not mine. I happily turned and headed back for the greying daylight, a sign that we wouldn't be shooting aerials the next day. I would have to return in a fortnight's time for those. In the meantime I traded hiking boots and broadbrimmed hats for some finer attire. I was off to the art gallery.

As the ABC is heavily into the arts, we knew most galleries and their staff reasonably well. One gallery had an upcoming exhibition of Jeffrey Smart paintings and *The 7.30 Report* wanted me to shoot the works to cover thirty seconds of screen time – easy enough, especially as I liked his work. I met the gallery manager and she directed me to a hall where the works were being hung. Many were stacked against a high-topped bench waiting their turn. It was lunchtime, everyone was on their break and, as the ABC was a familiar face here, I was left to my own devices.

Shooting paintings is dull but essential camerawork. A half-dozen or so paintings later, I felt hunger pangs myself and made a quick visit to get a takeaway black coffee. Back in the gallery I placed my coffee on the bench, or so I thought. The cup tipped and a black waterfall of steaming coffee went straight over and onto the outermost painting in the stack below. Oh shit! Had anyone walked in I was done for. The painting was still steaming, which was sort of a giveaway. Nothing was at hand to wipe it down so I used my shirt. Apart from what I considered to be an attractive brown wash it looked OK. Given the circumstances, I did the right thing: I hid it towards the back of the stack and got out of there. I've always wondered if this painting was fixed or it went out as one of Jeffrey's more unusual pieces.

The gallery's casual attitude of allowing me to work unsupervised surprised me. I wouldn't allow a TV crew into my place alone. Generally crews are respectful of property but that's not the issue. It's one of ever-tightening schedules and growing stylistic expectations; everyone wants tracking and crane shots nowadays. It's a case of more for less. The only way to achieve that is to work faster and that's when accidents start happening. I know of many ornaments in people's houses that are held together with gaffer tape. (We often call gaffer tape *the force* – it's got a light side, a dark side and it holds the universe together.)

As I had contributed enough towards the arts in Australia, there were still the Mt Mulligan aerials to attend to. Beautiful, smooth, soaring aerial shots cost money. The gyroscopic stabilisation camera mounts needed for these are very expensive to hire and our budget didn't extend to that. Another option was to use camera supports that dampen out but don't remove the bumps. The budget didn't extend to those either. The old fallback is a powerful helicopter with a good pilot. The budget couldn't manage that either. The best *Quantum* could do was an R22, the same type of helicopter I went camel mustering in, and no amount of jumping up and down on my part was going to change that.

The shots I would get from this tiny helicopter were not the shots that would do justice to the grandeur of this mountain. Stuff it, I thought, I'll build my own mount, which is what I did. Admittedly I didn't have the experience for this but I like being inventive. I measured up a similar helicopter in Brisbane and set to work. It took longer than I had planned but was near completion the day before the aerials were booked in. I was flying to Cairns that night ready for a six o'clock departure in the helicopter the next morning. I loaded up some equipment boxes with drills, electric grinders and vices and headed to the airport for the two-hour flight.

My hotel room in Cairns Central easily converted to a workshop and I drilled and ground away all night. Management rang numerous times with complaints about the noise. 'It must be someone else, you've got the wrong room, mate.' I flipped the two double beds on edge to form a cubicle with a wall as one side. The doonas and pillows completed the walls and roof of my soundproof workshop. A never-ending rooster tail of sparks from the grinder made it cosy in there and by three am my masterpiece was complete. Trying to nab some sleep was pointless and, besides, the room needed reassembling.

At the helicopter hangar the pilot was impressed with my handiwork and we took to the sky. The weather was kind and the mountain glowed spectacularly for the camera. My entire helicopter-mount-building experience had totalled just three days and this showed in the footage. Excessive vibration rendered ninety percent of it unusable *but* ten percent was stunning.

Stunning too was my new baby girl, Sophie. She made for matching bookends with her sister Georgia and we were happy to have two beautiful girls who were both healthy. Our family was complete as far as Vicky and I were concerned. Far from complete was our house, a rundown late-1800s Queenslander that with zero building experience I decided to restore. Dad's help was sought and a few times a year he made the bus trip from his home on Phillip Island in Victoria. Flying to Brisbane was not an option for my dad. His fear of flying saw to that. It also made his time as a paratrooper seem questionable but as a home-movie buff all of his life he had that time recorded on film, except the bit where he refused to leave the plane. So I think Private Shaun Mather was really a small 'p' paratrooper.

This fear of flying also frustrated Vicky and my attempts to get him to return to southern India, the place of his childhood. He talked about the little village of Gundlupet, his home, with such fondness that it gained mythical status in our house. Out came the photo albums every time he visited. We would get him talking about India, which only made Vicky and me more determined to go. I'm sure he was toying with us, seeing straight through our clumsy attempts. This went on for the better part of a decade. With him or without him Vicky and I had to go to Gundlupet and see for ourselves. It was without him.

When the overcrowded bus from Mysore pulled into the station I was anxiously scanning all the signs and posters to make sure we were in the right place and then finally saw the word Gundlupet on the grubby, faded turquoise walls. A magic word I had written many times in my life, a word few in the world knew or cared about, but to me it marked a pilgrimage of sorts. We were staying at my recently deceased Uncle Mickey's, the game hunter I had come to know through our family photos. From the crowd of confusion that is India a voice said, 'Michael.' A straggly looking man beckoned. I guessed he was talking to me and he was referring to my uncle, so we followed where he led. All eyes were upon us. We were expected. '*Kole-dore*' (pronounced collie-door-ray) came with the occasional whisper and pointing. Uncle Mickey had had about one hundred chickens that he had inherited from my grandfather and as this was a poor farming area, he was known as the *kole-dore*, or 'chicken king'.

We stayed at my Uncle Mickey's farm with his daughter, my cousin Veena, her husband Giri, and my Aunty Bibi, the tribal Indian woman my uncle had married many years ago. She was beautiful, with henna tattoos covering her arms. Though she spoke no English, the bond of family bridged the gap. A patchwork of cultivated red soil plots and small granite domes surrounded the simple white-walled mudbrick house that had only had running water installed a month earlier. The water cart and one very relieved-looking buffalo stood quietly to the side waiting to be reassigned.

The past hadn't completely disappeared and the photos in my family albums took on life; a leopard had been taking goats on the nights before our visit and was still around. As we were visiting, an urgency had been placed upon shooting it. Great! Another animal killed in the vegetarian's name. Snakes were common and everyone had a good snake story. My favourite is my Uncle Mickey being bitten on the big toe by a cobra and immediately shooting his toe off to stop the spread of the poison.

I would never shake the hand of the owner of these tales, as Uncle Mickey had died eleven months earlier. His death had hit everyone hard and emotions were raw. I'd missed someone pretty special. Even Sammy his dog was still in mourning, of sorts. When Mickey died Sammy didn't eat for three days; he lay on his grave and, for want of a better word, cried. Mickey had been buried in the front yard and when we arrived there was Sammy, on the gravestone, still loyally waiting. I wondered if he knew his master was really gone or a flicker of hope remained.

Vicky and I were quite the royal couple as we received visits from village people who wanted to pay their respects to this bloke and his missus from suburban Brisbane. An elderly man with a particularly beaming smile held and squeezed my hand for longer than usual. 'Shaun-apa, Shaun-apa,' he kept saying. Veena, my cousin, told me he had been waiting for this day; he was one of the men who had looked after my dad during my father's cherished childhood years. He had recognised my father in my face the moment he walked in. It was as though the old photos had come to life and I was a link in this chain that time couldn't break.

I wanted to hug him as though passing it on from my dad, but it seemed not right at the time. Immediately I wanted to search through all the old black and white photos to locate him as a young man. Disappointment and anger took turns at heading up my emotions over the next few days. Why hadn't Dad come with us? This was the India my father had always talked of, the simple farming life, the quiet rural atmosphere so far removed from the bustle of the cities, the welcoming people and their gentle smiles. Vicky and I both saw looks and little quirks of Dad's that were common to these village people.

Our time was way too short and there remained one important task, to visit my father's old family home 'Dharmacrag'. I knew it well from photographs and the imaginary tours, room by room, that my dad had taken us on. Time had been unkind and now about half a dozen families, one per room, squatted in the tumbling-down ruin. The cameraman in me took over and I shot off a whole roll of photos to document every aspect of its new form. I don't think it was possible for me to look at anything without having a view as to how I would photograph it. We couldn't get my father to return so I had done the next best thing and left no stone unturned. What I couldn't convey in words, the pictures would. It was very sad leaving India. I don't access my emotions much but the times I do they seem to run fairly deep. All my family there found it particularly hard as well. The Anglo side of the family had all but disappeared and it was as if my going there had for a brief moment returned things to the comfort of the old days. There was definitely a part of me rooted in Gundlupet and I was thankful for the opportunity to explore it.

Back in Brisbane, Dad returned for one of his forced-labour camp holidays, helping me with renovations at home. Question after question came about India. 'I said you should have come with us,' I berated him as I gave him the photos of his old family home. He put his glasses on and thumbed through a few, swore, dropped the photos and stormed off. I'd rarely seen my father angry or upset. He refused to look at any more photos and didn't want to speak further. In my eagerness to piece together parts of my make-up I had unwittingly shattered a part of his. His joyous memories of his childhood were of a time and place that had passed and he was wise enough to know that. He never wanted to return because he knew India could never live up to his expectations. The fear of flying was always a convenient excuse. Giving him those photos was the wrong thing to do but the damage was done. Images can be powerful; I should have known better.

Unlike a still photographer's ability to capture an individual moment in time, moving pictures are gregarious and need other moving pictures to assist in getting the message out. Each shot is bookended, or topped and tailed, with the previous and following shot. Once you have three shots in succession, you have the vehicle for storytelling: the beginning, middle and end. Understanding this or, more to the point, wanting to understand the powerful storytelling tool you have at your fingertips, isn't that common amongst cameramen. There are plenty of good shooters but many don't want the extra commitment of following the story – 'Just tell me what you want shot and I'll shoot it' is the ready mantra. There seemed to be an opening for shooters with a real interest in the narrative and I was happy to fill the gap. But TV is collaborative and there really is only room for one storyteller, and that is the director. A sure recipe for disaster is to let your ego take hold and think you can do a better job than the director; maybe you can but go and get your own program to prove yourself on.

I enjoyed the storytelling potential inherent in my job and people were starting to recognise this, people like Richard Corfield. This is how I found myself sitting next to him in the grubby airport departure lounge at Beijing airport. Richard's Mt Mulligan documentary had been well received and cemented our ability to work as a team. His next 'human face of science' doco was following Australians working in a sheep-research program in the remote Xinjiang province of northwest China. This was right up my alley, he thought. Completing our team was sound recordist Mike Charman.

Sound recordists are an interesting bunch. They suffer from a condition called Sound Recordists Disease, brilliantly named by a colleague of mine, Brett Ramsay. Cameramen are the ultimate authority on sound recordists. Don't ask us about other cameramen, we never work alongside them, but sound recordists, journalists and directors we are well placed to comment on. Sound Recordists

Disease manifests itself by magnifying the worst characteristics of these otherwise thoroughly likeable and talented people. Their mistake is to pursue a sound-based career in a visual industry; when was the last time you went to the cinema to *listen* to a movie?

If a budget needs to be trimmed, sound is usually first to go. These people work in an industry that pays lip service to their skills but doesn't respect what they do. Some soundos, the good ones, rise above this and make themselves invaluable by taking up the slack with all the other logistics associated with life on the road: car hire, excess baggage, navigation, finances. They are a joy to work with. Some don't. They become quietly bitter and find sneaky ways of holding the shoot to ransom by halting proceedings; only their skills and knowledge can fix the problem. Miraculously they solve the problem and the production is eternally grateful to them. It's very much like the arsonist who lights the fire so he can be seen as the hero who is first on the scene to put it out.

Mike's one of the good ones. Originally from England, he's a steady-as-you-go sort of bloke who, like a lot of soundos, has an interesting backstory. Mike started his career working on feature films and had a starring role in *The Shining* alongside Jack Nicholson. He was Jack's stand-in – more specifically, Jack's hand. In the scene where Jack Nicholson goes berserk and breaks the door down with an axe, it is Mike's hand, not Jack's, that comes through the splintered wood and grapples with the lock. Should anyone ever ask, I can always say that I've shaken Jack Nicholson's hand.

From my seat I could see a row of planes tethered to the long concourse, each with its tail signage painted over. The white paint wasn't thick enough to hide the ghosted letters spelling 'Aeroflot'. Handpainted over this was 'Xinjiang Airlines'. Rivers of red paint had bled from the lower corners of some letters. Garbled flight information in Cantonese was blaring out at a deafening volume from the threadbare speaker connected by a couple of unsafe wires. I guessed it was the boarding announcement as a one-hundred-person rugby scrum materialised and surged forward, pushing us down the air bridge.

Seat allocation hadn't been introduced on Xinjiang Airlines, nor had cabin baggage restrictions; many carried full-size suitcases on board, someone a TV set and one man in the crush had a large cardboard box dotted with crudely punched airholes. First one, then a second orange goose's bill popped out and the honking started. Trying to establish some order was a dishevelled, burly and very hairy pilot wearing gold chains who barked Russian orders into deaf ears. We were the only non-Chinese on the passenger list.

The old Russian Tupelov plane started down the runway under full throttle. The engines roared and crackled like an Apollo launch. With all the associated flexing of the aircraft the tray tables started to unlatch and drop down. Mine had graffiti carved into the plastic and refused to latch back up. As in-flight service wasn't optional this was quite handy; you were getting your one can of beer, salty pickled vegetables and steamy syrupy buns whether you liked it or not. Those passengers asleep when the meal cart came by had everything left precariously teetering in their lap.

Xinjiang province is a cultural melting pot that nestles between Mongolia to the east, Kazakhstan to the west, Siberia to the north and Tibet down south. It's rich in foods and nationalities – twenty-two – and it's home to many sheep with poor-quality wool. An Australian team of scientists led by Ken Roseby was trying to introduce Australian merino breeds to the local population whose sheep with poor wool quality collected a higher price at the abattoir. With the view that quantity trumped quality, the local sheep herders were seriously overgrazing. This had eroded the countryside, a countryside that, from a photographic point of view, was stunning: panoramas of vast desert basins fringed by snow-capped mountains, the foreground dotted with an eclectic jumble of people, faces, animals and modes of transport. It was a complete contrast to filming outside of Australia's urban centres where you point the camera in any direction and all you see is bush and more bush. As beautiful as it is, it does what bush does best: just sits there. This was like the pages of *National Geographic* magazine had unfolded before my eyes. Having spent an inordinate amount of time trawling through those magazines as a teenager I was now living the dream and it seemed so easy, the shots just came to me.

Through my viewfinder the stark, treeless mountain landscape looked perfect except in this instance there was nothing in the foreground of the shot. All I needed to do was wait, though, and it was never for very long. Clip clop clip clop ... a falconer atop a horse rode into frame. Falconer was possibly the wrong word, as he was holding an eagle the size of a dog. A leather hood spiked with an upstanding tassel covered the bird's eyes until it was time to hunt marmot and foxes for their pelts. On its talons it wore leather anklets studded with patterned brass. The man was elderly and the last of a dying breed; synthetic fibres had almost relegated falconers to the history books. His skin was beautifully smooth and taut except for the fine lines around his eyes and mouth. A wispy Genghis Khan moustache, a furry hat and deep blue coat completed the picture.

As I was sure this would be my only chance at filming this magnificent pair I rolled the camera over their every move. They tired of me first and went on their way and we thought about getting some lunch.

The bird was not the only one with eagle eyes. I was so attuned to what I was doing that the others hadn't seen what I had. As we were hungry and about to break for lunch no one shared my enthusiasm but they watched, mildly amused, as I urgently snapped the camera into the locking plate, making the camera and tripod one. Still no one had seen it. All they saw was bald snow-capped mountains. But there was something else: seven black dots, equally spaced and moving. I knew what they were. I'd seen them in a *National Geographic* magazine. Nomadic Kazakh sheep herders were bringing their flock to lower pastures as winter neared. They carried their cylindrical skin tents called yurts on camels. This tethered camel train was just about to disappear behind a ridge. I had one shot at this. The sniper in me was about to resurface. I sure-footed myself and zoomed in as tight as possible, took a few good breaths to oxygenate my blood, exhaled two-thirds of what my lungs would hold, relaxed every muscle and started to s-l-o-w-l-y zoom out. As the shot widened interest in the laden camels lost out to the sense of place. Ten seconds later they were pencil dots in the stark, white and brown vista. It was a winning shot and I was on a photographic high.

Even interior scenes, which required extra lighting, were going without a fight. It's strange, because visitors to Australia from the northern hemisphere always comment on the magic quality, the colour-enhancing clarity of harsh, high Australian light. I don't see it; it's just daytime to me. In a hemispherical shift, the opposite happened in China. The low, hazy winter light created a photographic playground for me, especially indoors. Long shafts of filtered brown sunlight punctured the dreary green and white office interiors. Pools of light formed eye-catching centres of interest to the compositions. Stray light bounced off surfaces creating blooms of lens flare. Almost every photographic how-to book will caution you about the problems of flare: always shoot with the sun behind you, they say. I say ignore those slavishly tied to technical propriety and embrace flare and the mood it brings to a shot. Like the sun that created my luminary shafts, I was on fire. Everything I had worked towards came together and it wasn't just me who thought that. My future was written in the dumplings: the number of dumplings you got by dipping the net into the steaming pot told of your prospects. At one restaurant I scooped three, which ensured I would have a long and prosperous career.

Everything we had filmed to date had been *establishing shots*, which are essentially pretty pictures to illustrate where the action takes place. Now we began the scenes of our scientists going about their work, the guts of the story. They did what they did and I just followed, interrupting only if I had to take control to ensure I had the shot I needed. Over the short time we'd been there I'd done my homework on the Australian scientists by studying their movements, mannerisms and hierarchy. This is an important part of the job as it helps you pre-empt the action when it happens. I was becoming quite good at this and when it worked, it was like dancing with a good partner. Well, when it came to filming the Chinese team, all of a sudden I'd grown two left feet. Everywhere I thought the action would lead, it went the other way. When I thought a group would tighten, it dispersed. When I sensed a congratulatory handshake was imminent, I'd let the camera drift down to catch it only to end up framed on a vacant shot of belts and crotches. After a while I worked it out: different cultural groups have different body language and I was unable to read theirs. What had seemed so easy and fluid with the characters of northern Australia was like honey in wintertime here. I hadn't realised how much I had built my work around those subtle cues and when I wasn't tuned into the right station, it all became distorted. Simply framing my shots wider and being conservative with my camera movements helped matters. It quickly slapped me out of a fleeting thought that I had developed some sort of photographic Midas touch.

The mountains were calling. So were the nomadic sheep herders we had seen earlier from a distance. Northwest we headed alongside the Tian Shan Mountains on the main road that leads to Kazakhstan and Russia, sharing the road with the overloaded coal trucks, the overloaded onion trucks and the overloaded buses. They worked by the maxim that if the axles ain't bowing there's no point going! The rules of the road were straightforward: whoever has more power has right of way, and don't use headlights at night. So we were on a black road under a black, moonless sky surrounded by sooty black coal trucks with no lights on. Many heavy transporters lay upturned on the road's edge. Two sooty black, bulging coal trucks had collided and formed one sooty black mess. Driving under these conditions scared me, more so, it seemed, than everyone else chatting and laughing away in the car.

I have an ambition not to die in a road smash and if I'm not at the wheel I can get very edgy. It's not that I'm afraid of death. I'm not. I've had a few goes at coming close to it and it wasn't that bad. There was the spearing head-first into the ground while climbing when I blacked out immediately, and I'm guessing that if I had never come to I would probably have been dead. There was no associated pain. It was all a rush. I think adrenaline anaesthetises you. When I was thirteen I raced around on motocross dirt bikes which ended with me having a head-on collision with my brother. The accident was fairly serious and a long titanium screw has held my arm together since. Again I blacked out with the impact and the moment was painless.

Surfing was the same. I should have known it would end badly. I wasn't very good. Getting washed onto the rocks went hand in hand with my surfing style. A powerful two-metre swell got the better of me and pushed me onto the rocks again. Somehow my leg rope became caught. The swell banged me around and kept me under. Tugging and panicking did nothing to get the leg rope off my ankle. I started to lose the fight and felt myself begin to relax with the movement of the water and it was then that my leg rope unhooked. My head popped above the surface and I sucked in air. More scars to add to my growing collection. Again the process, for me, involved no pain. It was full of sensations but nothing I would label pain. Consequently death itself doesn't worry me. I consider it to be like 1952. I was born in 1961. As I have no feelings for or recollections of 1952, it's not something I spend a lot of time worrying about.

The process of dying, however – well that's different. With all the things I've done I'm adamant I'm not going to die in a car smash. It seems so pointless and wasteful to end that way. This is why I am always uncomfortable driving with people I don't know, including the professional driver dodging the coal trucks who worked by the saying an inch is as good as a mile. Mind you, we're all going to die, some sooner than others. This part of the world seems to give you more opportunities to die young, like the men we saw earlier that day before we set out on the drive up the horror highway. We needed to visit the bank often, as Richard was forever handing over the 'special' payments required by government officials to expedite our filming. The foyer of this particular bank was having a new brass sign erected about three metres off the ground. The man drilling the holes for the bolts teetered on a metal bar which was supported on the shoulders of two men below him. From the drill ran two wires with bared ends that were held in the wall socket by a fourth man. A fifth man with a mop was not going to change his cleaning schedule so he threw bucketful after bucketful of water towards the man with the bare wires. I didn't want to witness a mass electrocution. 'I'll just wait in the car,' I told Richard.

The scary drive was worth it. We were closer to Kazakhstan and enjoyed the wonderful hospitality of the nomadic Kazakh families and they enjoyed that I knew about camels. Through our interpreter I told them about the camel mustering in the Northern Territory. I ended up inspecting their camels and slapping their rumps like I was kicking the tyre of a car in a car yard, in some way expecting this action would cement my new-found expert status. By day's end we were like family and were invited that evening to a party. 'And what sort of party is it?'

'A circumcision party!'

I almost didn't go, for no other reason than that I can be a bit over-earnest at times and I still had work to do. Richard demanded I see sense. Checking all the tapes of the day's shooting and cleaning the camera could wait. He steered me to the tractor and trailer that would take us there. We arrived at a small mudbrick house displaying the same architectural design as just about every other building in this part of China: the rectangular box. A beaming smile and welcoming arms greeted us as the door opened. 'Yes, yes, we are Kazakh, welcome to circumcision party.' Inside we were ushered to one side of a low bench-table and formal introductions followed. The honouree was a pint-size six-year-old boy who was shuffled forward and had a look of 'oh no, not again' on his face. A dozen motherly hands tugged this way and that at his clothing until he was bare from ribs to knee. The handiwork had been performed a few days earlier but the family was bursting with pride at the apparently fine job; all I saw was one sore and sorry-looking little pecker. A knowing nod transcends all languages so we nodded our approval.

Dinner was about to commence. Dozens of local breads were spread over the table. Upon them was a large metal tray holding a neatly arranged disassembled sheep. Topping it all was a steaming boiled sheep's head. An imposing man with dark leathery skin, massive hands, a furry hat and big moustache took his place at the head of the table. He opened a penknife and cut off the cheek, handing the slice to the first big nose – big noses are what they call westerners. Richard accepted the white meat and the crowd clapped. In a bit of biblical humour that was lost on the locals, the large man turned the other cheek and that went to me. The crowd cheered. An ear was sliced and held aloft. The crowd went quiet. Next in line was Mike. When I turned to smirk at him the colour was already draining from his normally rosy cheeks but it returned when the ear went to the young guest of honour. We all cheered.

Bowls of delicacies that seemed remarkably vegetarian-friendly soon covered the table; wrong again. Baby corn turned out to be chicken feet, potato was not potato but sheep's foot, and eggplant was cow's ear. I happily snacked on the multitude of breads. Everything was washed down with a rice wine called mao tai, which I think is Chinese for pure alcohol. A buzz was spreading across the room and my head. I knew what it was. Word had obviously got out that I was vegetarian. Pointing and giggling were directed my way so I countered by showing photos of my daughters. Dancing was mandatory. By some strange quirk of fate they could all waltz and jive and we, especially me, were clod-footed big noses with rhythm bypasses. Before leaving a quick speech was directed at me: they thought my daughters were lovely but hoped they would grow up to eat meat. They'd had a quick straw poll and the last person that anybody here could think of who didn't eat meat was Buddha.

Richard's China documentary was well received and at the annual National Awards Night I picked up an Australian Cinematographers Society Award for my work on it. The Australian Cinematographers Society is the industry body that recognises the work of cameramen across Australia. Winning an ACS Award was satisfying but I wanted more. To be recognised or 'accredited' by this society entitles you to use the letters ACS after your name. You submit a reel of your work and hope the panel finds something unique about it, that it shows a 'style'. It's hard to become accredited. Since its inception in 1963, about three hundred have earned the honour. I had set my sights on becoming accredited. It was a lofty target and I went about it quietly. I told no one, except Vicky. I could only have come across as conceited, but I wasn't. I was doing things the only way I knew how: setting a deadline.

One of my favourite sayings that I live by is 'a goal is a dream with a deadline'. All my life I've put deadlines on my plans and this was to be no different. Deadlines create results. By 1995 I felt I was on track with a solid show reel of my work. Another saying I use is 'chance favours the prepared man'. If any opportunity came up I was readying myself to jump at it. I was living and breathing cinematography. I subscribed to every magazine and read every line then reread them to wring the extra meaning from in between the lines. When the ABC budget couldn't afford gear, I made it. If I couldn't make, I'd buy it myself. If a problem came up I'd address it. Standing still was the only crime. Shooting was what was going to make my shooting better. Treading the boards, getting my hours up, paying my dues was so important. When you get in that mindset everything becomes an opportunity.

At that time I seemed to be one of the only ones who thought that way, so there were plenty of openings as I took on shoots that weren't popular. The ABC rural program *Landline* journeyed to the Tamworth Country Music Festival every January and made music video clips, one a day, for eight days. These music videos had a budget of about zero dollars and were made on the goodwill of a lot of people. There was never a queue of cameramen waiting to do this; a lot of the music was hokey and it was physically and mentally hard work. The gig was mine for five years. Forty music videos came out of that time and, of those, about half a dozen were ones I was proud of. Why no one wanted this golden opportunity was beyond me so I just shut up and got on with it. The thing about music videos is that nothing is really 'wrong'. If I messed the lighting up, if the framing was way off, if focus was dodgy, it all found a home in the video. Any bold idea or new technique I wanted to try out happened here. There was no consequence for failure; if it didn't work, we called it art.

Getting enough ideas to make the clips visually interesting was easy. Throughout the year if I was in a motel room I'd always scan the channels for music videos. I'd draw on ideas from these and add them to my collection of ideas I kept in a book that went with me everywhere. That's how I was able to do eight videos over eight days in Tamworth. It was like ordering from a Chinese menu: we'll have the forty-seven, two of the number twenty-two … With all this new knowledge came a confidence to steer my career where I wanted: that was where it was already going, with the science unit.

Working on science documentaries was sort of a natural progression for me. I related to scientists' sense of focus and I could live out my childhood ambitions vicariously through my job. Scientific research has few boundaries, especially geographic ones, and also progresses our understanding of the world. Through working with the science unit, science did both these things for me. While I was on a series called *What's Your Poison?* which looked at drugs and their effects on the body, I made my first trip to England and Europe. The rich history was new to me. When I first walked into St Paul's Cathedral in London I was gobsmacked. What struck me was the power the church must have wielded. If someone like me, working on a science program and with an assumed moderate level of intellect, could walk into a church as we approached the new millennium and be stopped dead in my tracks, what must a simple peasant have thought all those years ago? I can imagine there was only one answer: God *must* have built this place. I appreciated the opportunities the ABC was giving me, and I was growing as a person as well as a cameraman.

It seemed the science unit was taking note of my efforts. They approached me to shoot a fairly ambitious international co-production called *Black Holes*. Not surprisingly, it was about cosmic black holes that are thousands of light years away and invisible, so photographically I was up for a challenge. Most ABC programs are based in Sydney or, as we liked to call it, the SBC: the Sydney Broadcasting Corporation. There are many fantastic shooters in Sydney and the rule of thumb is that those crews get first dibs at Sydney-based productions. Enough feathers had been ruffled by the Flying Vet, Mt Mulligan and China shoots going to an interstate crew. It meant a Sydney-based cameraman and a soundo missed out on the work. On *Black Holes* it was only my services that were sought, so now the Brisbane soundos were miffed with me as well. I didn't like the idea of being unpopular with anybody so this didn't sit well with me, but all my best efforts and intentions to keep everyone happy always made matters worse. Over the years the term 'diplomatically retarded' had been levelled at me enough times for me to know it was best if I just shut up and let the system work it out for me.

The science unit was full of Richards at the time: the woolly-headed and insightful Richard Corfield, of course. Richard Campbell was the smart, funny and pragmatic executive producer at the time. The other Richard was Dr Richard Smith, probably the most tenacious and capable TV producer I've ever met, whom I'd be working with on *Black Holes*. Sound for the shoot was provided by Gunter Ericoli. We didn't know it then but this was the start of many shoots together. Everything we needed to know about black holes was to be found in the US, so we flew the fourteen hours across the Pacific: time enough to get to know people.

Richard Smith achieved his PhD in marine biology by studying marine worms, more specifically their eyes. It's similar to working on something the size of a nit on the nut of a gnat, only smaller. He decided that the work of a practising scientist was slow, painstaking and underfunded, so he moved to telling science stories at the ABC, which he eventually realised was also slow, painstaking and underfunded. Even on that first flight I knew he was a man of many talents. While chatting he drew the preliminary artwork for the computer-generated animation that would feature in the program. He was very good at a lot of things, except relaxing. I've never been one for sitting around but this was a whole new level. Richard's mind never stopped.

Gunter had already intrigued me. As I had found with many sound recordists, he had an interesting backstory. One of the first things he said to me was, 'You'll have to excuse me for being German.'

'OK, Gunter.' My impression of him so far had been very positive; he was thoroughly professional, good-natured and a real-people's person. After a good chat on the plane I added to that list: a big chip on the shoulder. He was full of self-deprecation and seemed hell-bent on being anything but German. Gunter resided in some psychological Teutonic prison I was yet to understand. To distance himself from his European beginnings he needed to deal with his strong accent; it was always going to give him away. The English language and its subsequent mastery was his ticket out, so he reasoned. He spoke thoughtfully and eloquently and loved using mellifluous words to counter the guttural attack of spoken German.

He illustrated this thirty-year quest with a story. One of his first jobs at the ABC was in the northern New South Wales town of Grafton. At day's end, the crew took the young Gunter to his first RSL for dinner. This was back in 1966, only two decades on from Australians fighting the Germans. The cameraman taught Gunter how to play the pokies, hang onto a schooner of Reschs correctly and reminded him not to speak too much 'bloody German English'. No one had thought to alert Gunter to the RSL's 6pm ritual of turning off the lights and standing silently and respectfully as the 'Last Post' was played. The second schooner was just hitting its mark and he was in mid-pull of the one-armed bandit when the lights went out and the room went silent. In a seamless segue Gunter yelled out in his best German accent, 'Shit'ze fuse has blown.' A hissing chorus came back at him: 'Shut up, you fucking kraut, shut up!' It was a bad start for Gunter's quest to be a small 'g' German and a big 'A' Australian. Regardless of what was going on in Gunter's head, I liked the guy a lot.

The collected idiosyncrasies of our crew were minor league compared to many of the scientists who lay in wait. We launched our shooting schedule at NASA's Marshall Space Flight Center in Huntsville, Alabama. As an eight-year-old, I had sat cross-legged on the floor with my Grade 3 classmates to watch, along with the rest of the world, the moon landing. Four letters filled the screen while we waited and waited for something to happen on the black and white TV set: NASA. I never really knew what it meant except it represented something amazing and bold. Like many of my generation, it became part of my lexicon. Now, as an adult, I felt chuffed getting a NASA visitor's pass with my name on it.

The facility looked the part; when you've got a few old rockets lying around you may as well put them to good use – here they made perfect garden ornaments to line the driveway. Part of our story was to examine what would happen if you were to visit a black hole. Apart from being uncomfortably stretched by space time you'd be feeling pretty tired: it'd take about a million years to get there. Here they were researching possible alternative propulsion systems hoping one day to travel faster than the speed of light. Conceptual thinking was paramount and NASA had recruited some creative minds. Our NASA public relations host was keen to introduce us to some of them.

'We'd like you to meet an anti-gravity theorist, but be warned – he may act a little strange.'

Inside a large lab with high ceilings and long benches, a red-haired man of about twenty-five was crudely sticky-taping lumps of timber, magnets and wire together. It wasn't how I had envisaged anti-gravity research; in fact it looked a lot like the home-made UFO detector I had seen in suburban Brisbane many years earlier. Our host quietly and proudly suggested we might be looking at the next Einstein. The best way to describe this unusual scientist was 'Rain Man'. He kept running away from us, literally. Mid-thought he would notice the camera and scurry off, sending chairs rolling and papers flying. Ten or so steps on he would completely forget why he was running as another piece of apparatus caught his attention and he lost himself in the possibilities it presented. This cat and mouse game repeated itself three or four times over ten minutes until we had enough footage.

Because black holes are black, they can't be seen with optical telescopes. A new approach was needed: gravity-wave telescopes like Gravity Probe B. Again these seemed to operate much the same way as the UFO detector I was unfortunate enough to witness many years earlier: they detected irregularities in wave patterns that came from space. Unlike the ten-dollar model in suburban Brisbane, these were international projects, very costly and for some scientists their life's work. Understandably, when a yawning film crew arrived they got a little edgy.

Gravity Probe B, which would fly around space looking for black holes, was being constructed in a Class 10 clean room; this is about as clean as it gets on earth – it would leave an obsessive compulsive bored. The chief scientist didn't want us there as one speck of dust could scuttle the project. He asked us to consider this: central to the telescope is a ping-pong-ball-size sphere. It is perfectly spherical to the tolerance of a human hair over twenty kilometres, which in lay terms means it's the same as the earth having mountains no more than one metre high. That would explain why he took one look at the scruffy Australian film crew and went into a panic. It took over two hours of cleaning, vacuuming our camera and sound gear and suiting up for us to get in there. The entire time we were inside he kept an eye on the digital particle counter. Mid-interview, panic registered on his face again. He propped his nose in the air and said, 'I smell dust.'

What surprised me early on was that Australia didn't have much clout with the big end of science. Often, after having travelled great distances at obvious expense, we were left waiting for hours as the precious minutes of shooting time slipped by. A four-hour schedule would shrink to one. Kip Thorne, one of astrophysics' big-hitters, delayed us for hours as having his photocopier fixed took priority. Generally, though, we were always welcomed. American crews, it seemed, were overly serious and uptight about the process of making TV and demanded a lot of time. Australians were seen as a breath of fresh air. Consistently, whenever shooting a program in the US, we would be told, 'You Aussies are so professional and quick and *so* much fun.'

In Chicago we attended a function at the International Black Holes Symposium. If ever there was a place where I found small talk a challenge, this was it. Stephen Hawking was a guest of honour and I watched with interest. Although he was the centre of all these orbiting scientists, the mystique surrounding this wheelchair-bound man, and an ignorance of how to deal with his physical condition, seemed to repel others. Wherever he was pushed the crowds parted; few made contact and though he was the centre of attention he cut a lonely figure. Our plan was to take him aside and shoot a high shot looking down on him in his wheelchair going around and around in decreasing circles. This shot would eventually be superimposed upon a space background as he described his theory of space time. It was never to be. Whether he was sucked into another galaxy through a wormhole we never found out, but he was gone and we couldn't find him. Richard was fast losing his hair over many things beyond his control.

We left to check in at the hotel and found we were at the Ramada Inn in a dodgy part of town. My room door was askew on its hinges and the jamb sported telltale scars where screwdrivers and jemmy bars had been used in preference to the doorknob. Outside temperatures were sub-zero and nearly the same inside. The heating in my room didn't work and the water had frozen in the pipes. Stuff this for a joke. A phone call or two later and we changed hotels to the grand and historic Palmer House Hilton in downtown Chicago. Spending someone else's money was easy, checking in wasn't. A queue of forty or so stretched between us and the desk. Richard was continually on the phone dealing with all sorts of problems. I think I saw steam coming from his ears at one stage. When we finally made it to the counter and the clerk matter-of-factly told us he was moving us to another hotel as they had overbooked, it wasn't good. In many years of working together I saw Richard lose it only twice; this was one of those times. He was not moving from the check-in desk until we had a room, call the police if you must. 'There's always the penthouse, you know,' was Richard's off-the-cuff last retort.

Ten minutes later we were loading our cases through the door of our new home for the coming days. The dining table for twelve was nice, so too the library; the convenience of two full kitchens was useful, and relaxing around the full-size Steinway grand piano after a sauna is the way film crews should finish every day. I stared at the bland industrial rooftops made pretty by blankets of pristine snow and wondered about the series of events throughout the day that had led to us being here. My moment of introspection was ended by the sound of gorgeous music filling the room. It came from the Steinway grand. I turned to see Gunter playing, so beautifully that tears welled in my eyes. 'Don't ask or I'll stop,' he demanded of his shell-shocked peers. Eventually I had to ask.

His father was a concert pianist and it was thought Gunter should follow that path. Having the piano lid slammed on his fingers for hitting wrong keys quashed any enthusiasm for the instrument. His real strength was his alto voice and his mother was keen to exploit that potential and live her ambitions vicariously through Gunter. She was aiming high and this little ten-year-old German boy was accepted into the Vienna Boys Choir. A lengthy train trip from his home town of Augsburg finally delivered him to the main door to the palatial residence of the famous choir. A quick peck on the cheek by mother dearest with the stern instruction to be a very good boy and she was gone. 'That hurt!' he said.

It lasted eleven months. Back then the choir was funded by the citizens of Vienna, who deemed supporting a German inappropriate. The foreigner was told to go. He moved to Germany's premier church choir, the Regensburger Domspatzen, freely translated: the Cathedral Sparrows of Regensburg, a city on

# I grew up marvelling at these pictures every time I opened the family photo albums. Do you think they might have influenced me?

My father, on left, crawling up to see a leopard shot by Uncle Mickey. This is at 'Dharmacrag', my grandparents' house in the village of Gundlupet, southern India.

My Uncle Mickey, the Indian Game Hunter.

My Uncle Andy (standing) in the Spanish Foreign Legion.

# Round one of my ringside view of life.

Anti-Bjelke-Petersen-government street march in 1977. My first attempt at photo-journalism. I was seventeen.

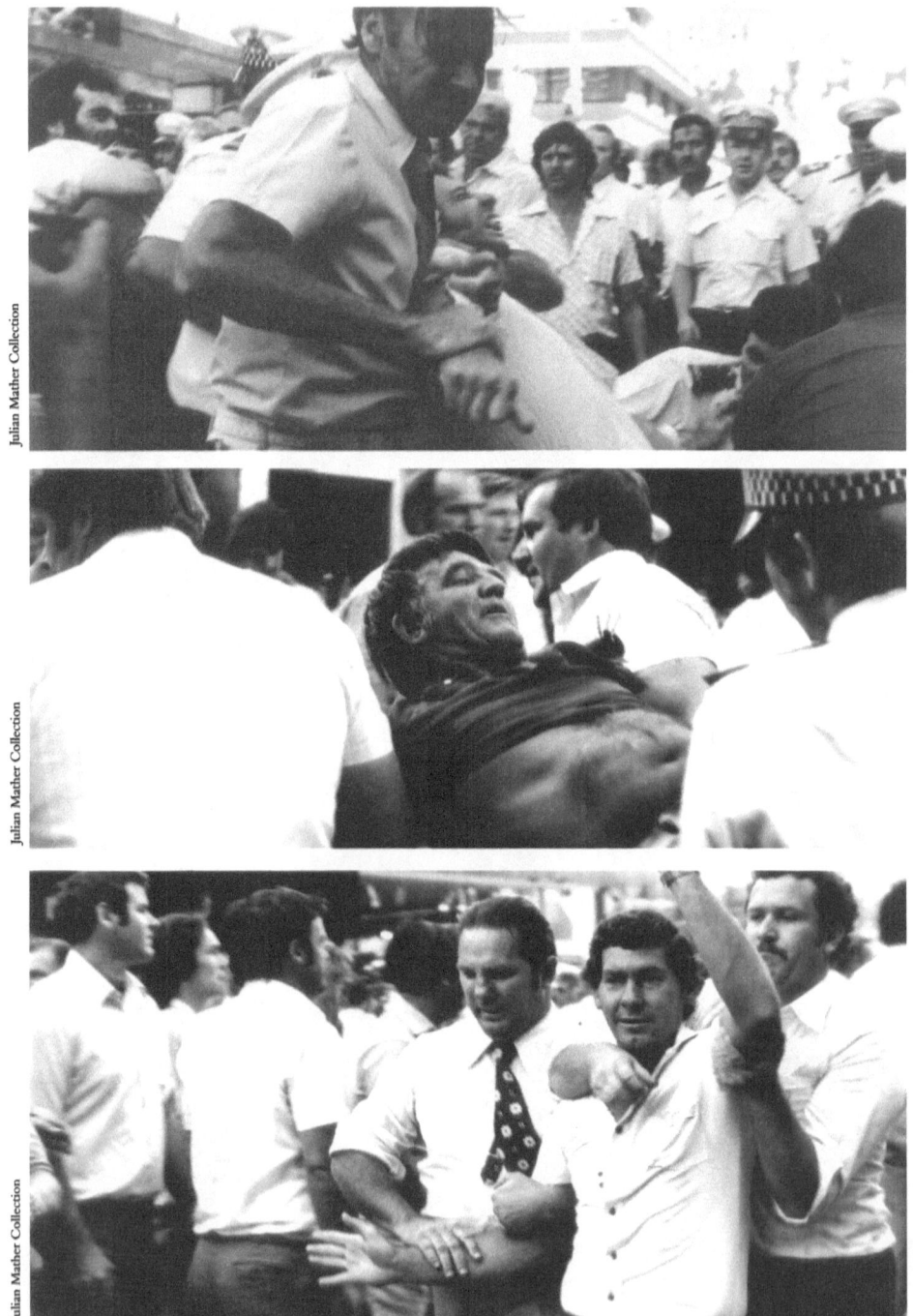

**Army service opened my eyes to a new world.**

My mug shot, taken on day one. I was eighteen. This is the benchmark photo I use to see how far my hair has receded over the years.

The army Kiowa helicopter that crashed in Weipa in 1981.

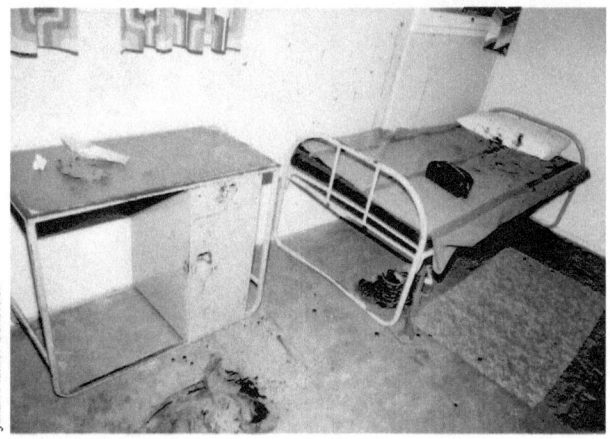

The blood-spattered room of Private Eggleton. This treatment was considered fair and reasonable by the people I was working alongside.

# The early years.

My ABC-trainee days. Lee Faulkner, Bruce Redman and me at the back. Three years of all care, NO responsibility.

Finally I was doing what I had long dreamed of: filming for the ABC. This is my first shooting assignment from a helicopter. Sucking lemons wouldn't have wiped that smile from my face.

## My first overseas assignment.

With a horseman in Xinjiang province of China, a cinematographer's paradise.

A falconer and a really big bird in Xinjiang province, northern China.

Mike Charman, Richard Corfield and me, just before I spotted the camel train in the distance.

## An ordinary boy; an extraordinary job.

Me standing outside TA55 in Los Alamos, New Mexico, a few minutes before the incident.

With Kosovo farm workers. The motorcycle battery is just visible strapped to my waist.

Setting up to film the remarkable Billy Wara. We are sitting below Uluru, which is just out of shot.

The Big Three — climbing, magic and photography — each shares equal billing on my list of passions.

One of the many climbing scenes I did with Glenn Singleman. His wife Heather is below. Little did I know the camera was about to die on me. We had to return a fortnight later and reshoot this entire scene.

My magic shows in Timor were from the back of UNICEF aid trucks. Look at the kids' faces.

'Quick, film the sunset!' How many times have cameramen around the world heard directors yell that? The only thing that gets a director's pulse going more is a soaring eagle. An eagle at sunset could easily reduce a director to a blithering mess.

## A bit of the old man in me.

The Bell 47 was my favourite chopper to shoot from because I could get outside and become a human camera mount. This is with Lord Robert Winston on a BBC co-production.

Lifting, always lifting. If it's not camera boxes, it's something else. This is at John Lever's croc farm near Yeppoon, Queensland.

Julian Shaun Fawcett Mather, my dad.

the Danube in northern Bavaria. Gunter hated every moment there; alone, eleven years old, singing Gregorian chants at five-thirty in a freezing cold cathedral for one hour every morning. His mother demanded nothing less. Worst of all, of the two hundred and seventy choirboys Gunter was the only Protestant; the rest were Catholic. Most if not all of his experiences in Regensburg will remain 'in the vault', as he put it. I was beginning to appreciate the complexities of my new friend.

The whole experience of black holes was ultimately positive. It won many international awards, including one for cinematography. I had formed a good relationship with Richard and Gunter and not long after arriving home a phone call came telling me I had been accredited by the Australian Cinematographers Society. I was now Julian Mather *ACS*. In the world of cinematography I had just received the highest stamp of approval from my peers. My head swam with the possibilities that might come my way. I was very excited but business is business as far as the ABC was concerned, and they rewarded my efforts by assigning me to a two-week tour around Queensland with the ABC promotional van. I was given the job of operating the junior newsreader camera. The big van would set up in a town and while Bananas in Pyjamas danced on stage I would sit kids down in a mock news set, give them a Miss Muffet news story to read, hit the record button then repeat it all again. There was no chance of my ego getting away on me. The ABC saw to that.

Working in the Brisbane branch of the ABC was different to the Sydney ABC. There, larger departments worked to larger budgets. Their cameramen had more comfortable schedules and the luxury of a personal-issue camera. Brisbane cameramen, along with most other capital branches, were the poor cousins to Sydney. Downtime didn't exist and we were always shooting something: news, current affairs, magazine shows. Almost every new day meant a different camera that felt and operated differently from the previous day. In the subtle art of cinematography small technical anomalies can magnify to substantial errors on the screen. Not having your own camera was less than ideal but it was all we knew. However, constantly shooting on a range of programs gave the Brisbane cameramen a distinct edge over their Sydney counterparts: speed.

Again, television and filmmaking are an expensive business. If you can save programs money, you become that little bit more attractive. If you step this argument up a notch to the international level, it explains why there are an inordinate number of Australians shooting feature movies in the very competitive Hollywood industry. Australians work fast. The system here was to watch the daily rushes exactly as they were shot; no corrections were made for it being a bit over- or underexposed, or the colours being a bit out. Consequently you learnt very quickly where you were making mistakes and where they could be corrected in post production if needed. The term for this is 'knowing where you are on the negative'. It's the confidence that comes from knowing just how much you can meddle, just how far you can push the boundaries and still have things look good.

The American system is different. It is based upon the people bankrolling a production wanting to be reassured that their money is well spent. The daily viewings there were corrected, or graded. Producers with big cigars *felt* better if the pictures they saw were glossy and beautiful. Consequently the director of photography rarely knew if he had made a mistake and was denied the knowledge that would come with it. Australian cinematographers are well respected. That said, it was back to the junior newsreader camera for me.

Most annoying about this particular promotional trip was the short hours. Downtime can be a dangerous thing if you work away a lot. You need a Plan B. I've always had a Plan B. To have no Plan B leaves you with two options: sit in the motel room and stare at the bricks in the wall or sit at the bar and watch your money disappear down the drain. Over the years my Plan B has changed. Once it was restoring furniture. We'd get plenty of strange looks when we'd turn up at a property for an interview and the owner wanted to know why we had a cedar chest of drawers tied to the roof. For years hotels across Australia must have wondered where the fine layer of red dust across the room came from; you can't sand and not have some dust. When my house renovations slowed I took to printing black and white photos. As motel bathrooms were usually designed like prison cells with little or no light entering, it occurred to me they would make perfect darkrooms. A couple of pillows stuffed in the window slot, a few camera boxes to make a bench, electricity and running water at hand. Once I'd located all the pieces of the enlarger scattered throughout my equipment cases, I was in business.

I'm not the only one who did this. Ex-ABC cameraman and Oscar winner John Seale, one of the world's top cinematographers, drove people in adjoining hotel rooms to distraction. The constant whistling of the kettle was a mystery until it was discovered that he was a mad keen sailor who was building his own wooden yacht. He was hand-bending strips of timber for the hull by softening the wood in the kettle's blast of steam.

This promotional trip around Queensland launched a new Plan B which, as it turned out, was quite a long-running one. Georgia and Sophie's birthdays were close together so Vicky had planned a combined second and fourth party. Preparations were quickly growing beyond our initial plans and we needed some entertainment. Vicky reminded me of a few years that I had spent following a childhood interest in magic. Yes I had, but that was a long time ago. My father was responsible for my early interest. He would frustrate my brother Shane and me, year after year, by making cigarettes vanish in his hand. When he felt we had paid our dues through years of begging, he finally showed us the secret. What struck me, even as a ten-year-old, was that although the mechanics of the trick were simple, the effect it had on people was powerful. As a kid I was way too shy ever to perform. Vicky suggested I revisit this interest and do a few tricks for the kids at the party. Reluctantly and nervously I agreed.

The local library had a few magic books in the kids' section that I checked out and packed in my suitcase for the trip. Since Dad was ultimately responsible for my predicament, I had him build me a few effects. As is my way, I rarely just dip my toes, and I threw myself whole-heartedly into the project. A few tricks blew out to a half-hour show with props and costume. I was well out of my comfort zone and trembled with nerves. I hated being the centre of attention and wondered why I was doing this.

The living room show was colourful but awful. To say I was wooden is an affront to puppets across the world, but my immediate retirement from showbiz was shortlived. My career revived a week later with a request from a mum to do her kid's birthday and so the trickle of requests started. To cater for this underwhelming but secretly exciting demand, I took more books away on trips. I would write new routines and practise them on the road. The word always got out that I did a few tricks and small performances followed. Plan B had a new incarnation.

The astronaut John Glenn, asked what he felt as he sat in the Apollo capsule awaiting launch of the first manned flight to the moon, is reported to have said:

'I felt exactly how you would feel if you were getting ready to launch and knew you were sitting on top of two million parts, all built by the lowest bidder on a government contract.'

Every now and then I have defining moments. This one occurred on a Saturday shift shooting local news. Phil Smith, the journalist I was working with, was keen for his nine-year-old daughter to see what Dad did at work, so she joined us for the day. In town for a visit was the replica *Endeavour*, an exact model of Captain Cook's ship. Weekends are when politicians give the cut under their nose a chance to heal and more time is allocated to what are termed 'colour stories'. Shooting these news stories is formulaic; we spoke to the captain, asked to speak to the newest or longest-serving crew member, asked a visitor for impressions of the ship and that's it.

On the dock Phil said to his daughter, 'So there you go, isn't it amazing to think that all those years ago people crowded onto small wooden boats and ventured off to places unknown? It's as amazing as man landing on the moon.'

'Don't be silly, Daddy; people haven't been to the moon.'

Phil and I looked at each other and the realisation that had just registered mirrored in our eyes: we were of a different generation.

A few months later I played on this new insight that common knowledge wasn't necessarily that common. Richard Corfield, Gunter and I were in Houston, Texas, shooting the oddly named documentary *In Space No One Can Hear You Pee*. It was another of Richard's human face of science shows that followed Dr Vaughan Clift, an Australian working on the NASA astronaut program. I relayed the *Endeavour* story to Gunter and Richard, and they thought I was overstating things, so we put it to the test. Checking into the nearby NASA Ramada Inn, we said to the young female receptionist, 'You should have our reservations for Armstrong, Aldrin and Collins.'

'No, sir, nothing here.'

'It could be under Apollo tours,' we offered.

'No, sir, nothing at all.'

That look, the one that betrays your hopes that you aren't really getting older, the same one I had seen in Phil Smith's eyes a month earlier, just flashed across Richard's and Gunter's.

Formerly a glamorous Sheraton Hotel from the Apollo days, this two-level lodging was now falling down around us. We were woken the first morning by an unusual alarm. The rooms immediately below had been converted into a meeting room booked by a Southern Baptist Revival Church. The electric organ, drums, tambourines, and singin' and a clappin' started at 7am. The infectious enthusiasm of the music set us in the right frame of mind to meet Vaughan Clift. You wouldn't have wanted to meet him before your first coffee of the day. Vaughan never stopped. He spoke constantly, at a million miles an hour, and loved his area of research: non-invasive ways of measuring and monitoring the health of astronauts in space. He was such strong talent on camera that the original script for the program was thrown out. This is one of the reasons I liked working with Richard Corfield: he was willing to take chances and take the consequences either way.

Like the church singers below our rooms, Vaughan had an infectious enthusiasm. Gunter put a hidden microphone on him, I made sure I had plenty of tapes and batteries and we just followed. For a week we had a personal guide around Johnson Space Center. This is the home of Mission Control. Remember those famous words, 'Houston we have a problem'? This is who they were talking to. The science took second billing to Vaughan's character. He told us the secret to being an astronaut was not being super fit, though it helps. It wasn't having a PhD. It was being prepared to live in Houston. He said, 'When we arrived it was week after week of 38 degrees and 95 percent humidity ... then summer came. It was like moving through a huge public shower with the hot taps on.' He was speaking the truth. The humidity played havoc with my camera. Before leaving the chilled air conditioning of the motel room each day, I had to bag the camera in a garbage bag and seal it. That way, as the camera warmed up over the next hour the condensation formed on the outside of the bag, not on the lens.

Gunter, Richard and I got a first-hand look at the astronaut training program. The highlight was going aboard a space shuttle. It was very small and cramped. The cockpit reminded me of a 1950s cargo plane. All the control panels had recessed switches and were designed to be stood on; in zero gravity all surfaces become the floor. Our one big regret was that we ran out of time to do the required training to take a flight on the infamous 'Vomit Comet'. This is the

Boeing 707 plane that simulates the weightless conditions of space. We gave our camera to a NASA cameraman to shoot for us. When I watched the footage later I was really glad I didn't go; half the people on board were lying in the fetal position dry-retching.

I had taken to travelling with a basic assortment of tricks from which I could build a small show. My interest in magic continued to grow and I was happy to perform my shaky and nervous shows whenever I could. Vaughan's eight-year-old daughter was having a party and I was asked to perform. All her friends were children of NASA scientists. It turned out I wasn't much of a match for these pint-size geniuses and they were close to chewing me up and spitting me out. I didn't like that experience so I vowed to prepare myself better.

Houston is one place to which I have no desire to return. The Texans themselves were, in general, lovely people, but as using the indicator in a car was seen as a sign of weakness and one in seven vehicles carried a gun in the glove box, it wasn't my sort of place. Besides, Texas is no place for a vegetarian. Head west, young man, and we did. The second part of our shoot was just next door in New Mexico, my favourite of all the states. It's a landscape of mesas, buttes, deserts and snow-capped mountains. We hit Albuquerque and headed north along the Rio Grande to Santa Fe – the US's oldest capital city, settled before the *Mayflower* landed – and on to Los Alamos National Laboratories, home of Little Boy and Fat Man, the nuclear bombs dropped on Japan. Its primary purpose today remains unchanged: this is where America makes its nuclear weapons, or what the PR spin refers to as 'the science that saves lives'. The US ceased all underground nuclear testing in 1992. Testing continues in earnest but at what they call subcritical level, meaning they don't get the atoms excited enough to run amok and start the chain reaction that causes the really big bangs.

Making an atomic bomb is straightforward: take a lump of plutonium and pack some high explosive around it and hit the trigger. The force of the explosion compresses the plutonium and causes the teeny tiny molecules to go crazy and kaboom! We were interested in the ka, not the boom. The ka bit produces a really high magnetic field which was the perfect place to test something Australian scientists were working on: nano wires. These were wires so small you couldn't see them, so small that only one electron at a time would be able to pass along them. So what? If only one electron at a time could pass, then you could conceivably count them as they went, which is essentially the function of a computer chip: it's a counting device. Then you could replace chips with these minute wires. For you and me that means things like thinner and thinner laptops.

Los Alamos is a laboratory that has grown into a town of twenty thousand people. It's high above the desert, higher than Australia's Mt Kosciuszko. It's surrounded by a backdrop of pines, with shops and playgrounds scattered among buildings important to US national security. It was really quite hard to define where the lab started and ended. By now I was realising that being an Australian in the US was easy and fun if you were there on holiday. All anyone ever wanted to know was if you knew the Crocodile Hunter, to which you always answered yes. Working in the US was another story. As far as anything to do with national security went, being an Australian meant, in their vernacular, 'zip'. At Los Alamos we were Uncleared Foreign Nationals and as such we were identified by green caps, to be worn everywhere we went. Our escorts wore blue caps. Their motto was: blue without green should never be seen. (I did mention their motto was arse-about but no one could come up with a suitable rhyme for blue.) We were not allowed anywhere without our escorts, even the toilet. I'm not joking. They told us not to complain; this was very relaxed compared to the tail end of the Cold War only a decade earlier. Implicit in our security induction was NO FILMING without an escort. This was cumbersome and seemed heavy-handed, but it was their place and their rules.

The bulk of our filming so far had centred on our scientists preparing for the 'shot'. This was jargon for the explosion which was happening at a test site named Ancho Canyon. A decade of work by a team of Australian, Japanese and US scientists culminated in this one shot that would give them a window of about one-millionth of a second to get the data they needed. That they wanted it all to go smoothly was a given.

A week after arriving everything was set for the shot the next day. At six in the evening all the scientists of Los Alamos returned to their families and we handed in our green caps, said goodnight to our escort and started the drive back down the mountain to catch a good night's sleep for the big day ahead. We had only rounded a few bends when I spotted a huge American flag that was wafting gently, backlit by a setting sun above the pine trees. I've got this thing for US flags; photographically I love the impact of the red, white and blue, especially if the sun is playing with it. My enthusiasm for this piece of cloth had already registered with Gunter, who pulled off to the side of the road. Do we or don't we? I knew the permit said NO FILMING without an escort but it was just a flag, for heaven's sake.

Between us and the flag was a mowed park with a children's playground. There was nothing of any security importance here. Collectively we agreed they were taking it all a bit too seriously. Besides, in Australia security meant making sure your mate's dog didn't steal the sausages off the barbecue. In Australia we could walk right up to the prime minister's car and stick the lens against the glass, so in full view of the passing cars we got out the camera and made the most of the setting sun.

Five minutes turned to ten and nobody had approached us. Directly behind me was a facility with razor wire fences and guard towers. Men in military uniforms looked down. I knew they could see me because I made eye contact. They didn't seem to mind so I rolled off a few shots of the yellow light glinting from the razor wire, a few more shots of the guard towers. Now we were certain this whole security thing was a big game that we had been suckered into.

While the light was still pretty we decided to get a few more much-needed general shots of Los Alamos. Gunter swung the car up a roadway that took us to the front entrance of this razor wire fortress. The sun slanted across a foreground sign that said 'Los Alamos National Laboratories TA-55'. This was the shot we needed: it would be a terrific opening shot. It spelt out where we were and the razor wire and towers said something important was going on in here. At the time, the significance of that last sentence didn't fully register in my mind. Smug in the knowledge that we'd tidied up a lot of loose filming ends in one short stop, we started for home.

Before our car had reached the end of the road we were forced to a halt by two black vans with darkened windows. One drove across our front at an angle and screeched to a stop, the one behind pulling up in a mirror position. Gunter said, 'This is not so good.' The side doors of the vans opened and half a dozen men in camouflage uniforms surrounded the car, each carrying M16 automatic weapons. I knew these guns quite intimately from my army days and I looked to see where the safety catches were set. They were still set to 'Safe', where I'd hoped they would be. This was just a low-level incident but having loaded weapons pointed at you when you're an Uncleared Foreign National in the land of Stars and Stripes and apple pie is unnerving. We sat there waiting for instructions. I whispered to Gunter, 'Don't say anything; they're still probably upset with Germany about the war.'

'Shut up, you idiot,' was his reasonable response.

Towards the car walked a man with a gun on his hip who motioned for us to roll down the windows. I managed a feeble 'Gidday' – that often worked to disarm Americans. Australians were still flavour of the month there, but not this time. Nope, not a bite.

His outstretched finger beckoned and he said, 'ID, sir.' We handed our passports over and Richard found our letter of invitation.

In one breath and with a southern twang our interrogator began, 'Says here, sir, NO FILMING without an escort. I don't see an escort in the car with you. Do you have an escort with you, sir?'

Richard has a lovely, gentle, clipped English accent that is quite whimsical. He started, 'Well, no actually, but —'

'Sir, Los Alamos National Laboratories is a secure facility. You have operated outside the terms of your agreement. Please wait in the car.'

Our main escort was summoned. We had a long wait as he lived an hour and a half away in Albuquerque. It was also Friday evening, so this was going to ruin his weekend. It was a given he wouldn't be happy. As we waited, our Aussie larrikin charm offensive was in overdrive. The security man's stern demeanour dissolved when he realised this carload of idiots was no threat. In his slow drawl he candidly spelt out the situation as he saw it: 'Seems to me you boys picked about the worst place in all of Los Alamos to set your camera up. You boys know what TA-55 is? TA-55 is the United States plutonium facility. We make all the plutonium that goes into our bombs here. Lots of bad people would like to get in here. We're pretty serious about keeping them out. Yes, sir, you sure did pick a bad place to put up your camera.'

Our escort eventually arrived and the formalities resumed. He was given a dressing down in earshot of us and told to be in ready phone contact to deal with the consequences that WOULD come from this incident. We were handed back into his care to be seen off the property. He kept saying, 'W-H-Y?' and pointed to the fact that there might not be an end to our program, as by the next day our permits might have been rescinded.

Saturday came and, being the weekend, we were hopeful that the previous night's indiscretion would wait until Monday to be addressed. Plenty of high-level Los Alamos scientists worked the phones on our behalf; they, of course, wanted our program to continue as it was very positive for them, though that didn't stop them from tsk-tsking us.

The canyon provided a natural place to conduct large aboveground explosions. A steel-framed rig about the size of an industrial dumpster bin supported a pack of high explosive the same shape and size as a car tyre. In the centre of this was our Australian scientist's tiny wire, invisible to the naked eye. In a matter of hours its destruction would answer many questions for them. Hundreds of intricate wires clustered into colourful snakes that disappeared down tubes leading to an underground command centre. Here large semi-trailers laden with electronics and computers were ready to collect and process the results.

Our situation had created an extra imperative to keep things moving but you don't rush things when you're working with large explosives. Running the canyon site and in charge of the explosives was big Jim. Jim was a tall and lanky man with a weatherbeaten face. He was part Navaho Indian, wore tight-fitting paisley body shirts and carried a thirty-centimetre Bowie knife strapped to his belt at all times. In his presence I felt I had walked onto the set of a Western. Jim ran a tight ship and you were never in any doubt that if you were in Jim's canyon, you did as Jim said. He told us two things: if I say run, RUN, and secondly, be aware that the canyons were home to fleas that were carrying the bubonic plague. Jim was a busy man but even he found a moment to tsk-tsk us.

It was past midday and everything was on track for a 3pm detonation. Nothing had happened in relation to our security breach the previous evening – no phone calls or nasty emails. The explosives were set and all the last-minute checks were happening underground. We took a few moments to relax for the first time since the day before. In the long shadows cast by the canyon walls we chatted next to the tunnel entrance. A car arrived and we watched as it stopped at the security gate. The security guard conversed with the driver and turned to point to where we were sitting. The green Ford Taurus with government number plates parked nearby. A man in a suit carrying three manila envelopes approached and asked, 'Messrs Corfield, Ericoli, Mather?'

We acknowledged our presence and he handed us each an envelope marked with our name. Inside was a single sheet of paper that read:

Dear Mr [INSERT NAME],

I was alerted this morning by a representative of Los Alamos National Laboratory's security force that you were at TA-55 without escort. Due to the egregious nature of this violation and your lack of compliance with protocols that had been previously explained to you, approval for your visit terminates today promptly at one pm. You are expected to vacate Laboratory property by that time, regardless of the status of your videotaping.

The suited man said he couldn't enter into any discussion; his job was to see us out the door. A cluster of concerned scientists formed and though assuring us they would try something at this last minute, their tone said they had conceded defeat. We gathered our gear and began packing the car and saying our goodbyes. Again we apologised for our mistake. Jim appeared from tidying up the explosives and asked what was happening. The situation and its impending resolution were quickly explained. The suited man checked his watch and pointed to the hour: 1pm. That was that. We began to move towards the car when Jim climbed up on some low steps and bellowed, 'Two hours to detonation. Canyon is in shutdown. No one is to enter or leave!' Yellow warning lights began to flash and the security guards closed the big steel gates. Jim flashed a quick smile and the suited man rolled his eyes.

Underground two hours later, with the explosion directly above, we witnessed the anticipation, tension and joyous relief as years of work culminated in one-millionth of a second. Two days later we were called to appear in person before the head of Los Alamos Communications. They couldn't see a funny side to any of it. So ended my first and only visit to Los Alamos.

I never found out if it was coincidence or if I was being punished in some way for the Los Alamos incident, but after six years of solid documentary work and the experiences I craved, it was like the tap had been turned off. Local news and current affairs were my lot for about a year. The Brisbane newsroom was a good place to work but as a cameraman I found no challenge in sitting outside courts all day or covering political press conferences. With tons of energy to spare, I found this very frustrating. It was not a complete waste of time, as there was always something I could learn, plus I never lost sight of the fact that the ABC was my employer and this was what they needed of me at that time. Still, it was not the direction in which I wanted to go.

I thought Vicky would have liked having me around a bit more. Up to a point she did, but living with me when I was grumpy wasn't fun. I was desperate for a challenge. My passion for magic was solid and I started to expand my interests. Circus sideshow acts caught my attention. The only circus skill I had was the simple juggling I had taught myself on my climbing trip to Yosemite years earlier, but it was a start. Juggling balls progressed to juggling clubs, which naturally led to juggling knives and fire. Often I'd spend time between jobs juggling in the ABC car park. Co-workers showed an interest and before I knew it, the ABC Juggling Club was born. At its height about fifteen people participated. As with everything I'd done before, I threw myself fully into it. Unicycling seemed the next step. Like juggling, I never had natural ability for it, just a determination to do it. I found it very hard to master but after months of effort I could finally ride from one side of the ABC car park to the other, a distance of twenty-five metres. Not much, I know. My ambition was to be able to unicycle in one spot so I could juggle at the same time; presently my audiences needed to run with me, which had its drawbacks.

I was extremely pleased with my efforts. I knew no other unicyclists and had no idea of how I was progressing. Maybe the internet could put me in touch with someone. I searched 'Queensland unicycle' and, bang, there on top of the search-results page was 'Qld Unicycle Club'. It had names and phone numbers, some even near me. I was surprised at how popular it was. There were equipment and clothing pages and, even better, weekly social rides with a coffee to finish. My elation quickly drained and I slumped in the chair when I discovered that these people were riding – I couldn't believe what I was reading – forty-five kilometres. All I could manage was twenty-five metres between cars. Why waste effort on something I had no aptitude for? I gave up on it. A few days later the penny dropped. You knucklehead, I thought, it was the University of Queensland Cycling Club, written as Qld Unicycle. My enthusiasm returned and I regularly took the disassembled one-wheeler away with me in my suitcase on trips around Queensland; another Plan B. I can't say for sure but I think I hold the title of Cloncurry's only known unicyclist.

After eighteen months the documentary drought broke and the phone started ringing again. Wendy Page was a producer on *Australian Story* and she was heading to the Kosovo–Macedonia border where an enormous refugee crisis was building during the Kosovo war. A week later, Wendy, I and a team of CARE aid workers from Australia were headed for Skopje on the Macedonian side of the border. The office was adamant that we take a satellite phone and I was adamant we didn't. I had a strong argument. Our reason for following CARE workers there in the first place came off the back of an incident earlier that year. An Australian CARE worker named Steve Pratt had been arrested by Yugoslav authorities and imprisoned as a NATO spy. He was a former Australian infantry officer and at the time of his arrest his satellite phone was used as evidence of his guilt. CARE ... previous army experience ... satellite phone ... do you see a pattern? We went without a phone.

It was a tough shoot made harder by Slovenian Airlines losing all of our bags. I had my camera, just. It's standard practice to carry your camera with you on board the plane. I had only one battery and one tape. Begging wasn't beneath me so I managed to cobble together enough gear from the other international crews there. I had the camera connected to a motorcycle battery around my waist. Two pieces of wire, sticky-tape and some paper clips worked as a temporary power lead.

Three days later some of the gear arrived but not our suitcases. We were in the same clothes we had worn leaving Australia and we stank, but this was not the sort of place to complain too loudly. Our young CARE workers impressed me, particularly Mark Brooking. Two weeks earlier he had volunteered for CARE Australia despite never having done this sort of work before. Six days ago he was watching television in Balmain with his mates. Now he was running a refugee camp intended for five thousand people and already up to fifteen thousand had arrived, and they kept on coming, bus load after crowded bus load. So many people were crammed on board that the humidity inside must have been horrible. Past the condensation running down the inside of the glass, people stared vacantly; children, women and the elderly but very few young men. This was the soft end of ethnic cleansing. A burst of escaping air heralded the opening of the pneumatic doors, then a wall of hot, stale, smelly air whooshed past us as the buses emptied. Moving was hard for many as they were ridiculously layered with extra clothing, as much as possible; they had only been allowed to bring what they could carry.

Wendy was finding the experience more difficult than me. I was able to balance my experiences by doing magic in the camps.

When necessary I found it easy to go into work mode and put my emotions in a box and lock that door. But refugee women saw Wendy as someone who might be able to help them. Old women who had been bashed with rifle butts sought medical aid from her, women who had lost their children pleaded with her for help. There was nothing she could do but squeeze their hands and walk away. Wendy tried not to but she cried a lot. I hadn't experienced a large-scale human drama before and I was struck by how 'normal' everything seemed. By that I mean world events seem to me to be filtered and processed by the media by the time the news reaches me in my living room. There seems to be urgent drama and intensity when I watch it on the screen. Here there was no soundtrack in the background, just taxi drivers laughing nearby. When people wailed to my face I couldn't help but inch back from the bad breath that accompanied their words. The breeze was cool on my face and the dew wet my shoes through and chilled my toes. The mundane detail didn't vanish in these circumstances.

Of all people I should have known the sanitising power the camera has on images, but I was quite struck by how utterly normal the component parts of this drama were. In a way to compensate for this, I began to shoot a lot of close-up details: a discarded lolly wrapper or a car radio punching out Kylie Minogue tunes. Most of these never made it in the final story. The battle for every second of TV screen time is hard-fought and anything that doesn't advance the narrative is cut. For my own purposes, though, I find these shots useful as mental joggers for my own thoughts when I view the rushes on our return.

Our clothes finally arrived and we made a last visit to the camps. An Irish CARE worker offered to drive us. Donkeys with carts, fallen rocks and broken-down cars ensured the drive was eventful. We were in the back seat and as the speed stayed between 140 and 160 kilometres an hour regardless of conditions, I was getting very uncomfortable. Wendy didn't seem perturbed at all. I urged the driver to slow down but he laughed me off. Again I told him to slow down, it was way too dangerous. Again he laughed me off. I screamed at the top of my lungs, 'STOP THE FUCKING CAR AND LET ME OUT. I AM NOT DYING IN A CAR CRASH!' Wendy looked shocked and the Irish driver went red and slowed. I meant it. I had not come this far in my life to die in a vehicle.

Trips like this are very exhausting and average ten to fourteen days away. Even though you end up sitting around and waiting a lot, there is little real downtime; you are forever discussing the story and its needs and there is always something to shoot: that one child's face might add a touch of poignancy to the story. Sleep is often hard to come by. Even if you manage a good eight hours, a lot of that is spent trying to slow your rushing mind. By the time you fly home you are well and truly over the person you have been working with constantly for the last few weeks. Still, you need to debrief and unload, and the plane flights home are the place to do it.

Sometimes my ability to detach myself emotionally worries me. I find it very hard not to stop and help a stranger push a broken-down car – injustice moves me to action, and I like supporting the underdog – but faced with someone's emotional distress I can easily flick a switch and distance myself. I often wondered if I had an empathy disorder. But I was a good foil for Wendy, who had impressed me with her strength and her ability to cry openly when faced with people's misfortune. She's sharp as a tack, always right on top of the story, and was very good at making the right decisions at crucial moments. I respected and liked her, which is so important. To work with somebody, living in each other's pockets day in and day out and not like them, was not for me.

Some cameramen think differently and enjoy the daily friction. Others have no choice: they are on an overseas posting to one of the ABC's many foreign bureaus and they get lumped with some very prickly journalists for up to three years at a time. It's one of the reasons I never applied for an overseas posting. Over the years I have turned down interesting jobs because of the people's names I saw on the call sheet next to mine. That may sound like a luxury and maybe it was, but I knew that friction on the road makes the story suffer, and in the end bad stories would reflect poorly on me. Professionally it makes a lot of sense to work with like-minded people.

Wendy and I compared notes on how far we had gone to get a good story. It seemed the perfect moment to tell her a story of my own, one I didn't have to travel far for, one I hadn't told before.

Long before we met, Vicky was a gregarious and intelligent teenager living in a conservative small New Zealand town with her large family. As the oldest of her brothers and sisters she found herself taking on more responsibilities as her parents' relationship headed off the rails. Her schooling suffered and she matured beyond her years, way too fast. She had a daughter. As was the protocol at that time, everything was brushed under the carpet and baby Helen was given up for adoption. Vicky was comfortable knowing her child had gone to a loving family and, though never forgetting and often wondering, she got on with her life. It was the birth of our children that made her thoughts restless and she was able to make contact with Helen, first by letter, then in person.

It went well, ridiculously well. From their first meeting at 2am in a deserted Wellington airport they were like long-lost sisters. There was no doubting they shared the same genes: similar looks, similar love of talking. I was nervous that it would be awkward and emotionally rocky, but I needn't have been. We fitted seamlessly into her family and they into ours. Helen was still to meet Vicky's family, a family so different to mine. My family members are like individual moons orbiting 'planet family'. All of us are held together by gravitational forces, we all know where the others are, and our paths regularly cross. Vicky's family is 'the planet'. It's one in, all in. Her family reunion to meet Helen was always going to be stellar.

There was Vicky, Georgia, Sophie and me. Vicky's dad was there, as was Vicky's mum and her partner. So was Vicky's biological father, a recent and unexpected addition to our family. He had skedaddled before Vicky was born and after forty years he decided to make contact. I thought it unusual to invite him but this is a family that likes to get things out in the open. Another unlikely guest was Helen's biological father and his family. And of course there was Helen, her children, and her adoptive parents, with Vicky's brothers and sisters and a few aunties and uncles thrown in. Both Vicky and Helen love a sense of family. Well, they got it. This is a family that can push differences aside and get on with life. It's a wonderful thing to be a part of. There was only one negative in all this: I was only in my late thirties but Helen's children took to calling me Grandpa. That was going to have to stop. Having new family in New Zealand was exciting and would eventually play a role in my work.

Back in Brisbane my first story after returning from Kosovo was at the Buranda Lawn Bowls Club. Times were changing and a quorum of younger women bowlers were bucking the rules set generations earlier that required women to have to ask permission before being allowed to start a game, and prohibited women from wearing their polishing cloths hanging from their pockets like the blokes. Opposition came not from the men but from the older generation of women bowlers who liked things just the way they were. I shot the story with the cooperation of the rebellious women and the male-dominated club leadership.

The older women refused to play ball with us. They had clustered in one corner of the club. As I left I approached them and explained my position: we were doing the story and they had every right not to cooperate with us. However, I did need shots of them playing so I was going out onto the footpath where I was legally entitled to shoot from. From a distance I would get enough shots then leave them be. It was not my choice, but it was the only option.

No one said a word. I made my exit and set up on the footpath. The older women's group emerged and I rolled the camera. Through the viewfinder I saw their leader storming towards me. Following her was a younger woman gesticulating wildly and saying, 'This is only going to make things worse.' The older woman came right up to me and started trying to pull the camera down by the lens, and she hit me and knocked my hat off. Of course I rolled over all of this and it opened the story as a descriptive example of how tensions were running high at the club. Only five days earlier I had been in a war zone where I felt quite safe and I'd come home to suburban Brisbane only to be set upon by an eighty-one-year-old woman.

The Kosovo story was a quick turnaround story by *Australian Story* standards; I watched it go to air a week and a half after returning. I was in yet another nameless motel room in the small country town of Murgon in southeast Queensland. My room adjoined the drive-through bottle shop of the motel. My whole evening passed to the endless background sound of vroom ... screech! ... clatter clink clatter ... laughter ... vroom vroom. From the end of my bed in this room smelling of stale cigarette smoke I watched the story on a small TV set with snowy reception. It was then I let out some of the uncried tears for the refugees whose problems had not been allowed to penetrate beyond my electronic and glass shield. It was an engaging half-hour and I felt proud to be doing this sort of work where maybe I was making a difference; people may have been moved to volunteer their time or money. Also, for the first time in my career I was happy with what I had shot.

I've always been my harshest critic. This wasn't the glossiest work I'd done, it wasn't the most gut-wrenching I'd done, it wasn't the most technically or physically difficult I'd done, but in my mind it was certainly the best I'd done. Why? Because I'd listened, really listened, to the story and what Wendy was trying to achieve. This marked a distinct turning point in my shooting style where I relaxed and stopped trying to make the situation fit the look I was after. It had taken me a while to come to this shift.

Oddly out of place in the cheap utility of this motel room was a dog-eared *Architecture* magazine. I chuckled to myself as I read of young architects winning awards. Architects and cinematographers, it seems, are very alike. Both are creative and technically based. Both rely on outside funding to realise their ideas. Movies are expensive to make, buildings are costly structures. Both are collaborative industries. You can't do it by yourself. And practitioners are both, early on in their careers, hell-bent on ignoring the client and creating monuments to their own egos at someone else's expense. I speak from experience.

Now I was confident enough in my work to shoot any style, off the cuff, as needed. Focusing on the technical leaves you no time to listen to the story and the clues people silently transmit about where to stand, what's happening next. Knowing the story well became my imperative. Mind you, it pays not to become too relaxed.

My next shoot required a lot of attention to detail, the same sort of attention I should have been giving my boots, at least according to the shoe-shine man in the men's room at Chicago's O'Hare Airport: 'Oh man, let me put some colour into your boots, look at them heels, you should be embarrassed.' He cajoled me into the high seat and put twenty minutes of sweat and effort into them as I told him how they had ended up as patches of grazed leather. That's what spinifex and boulders in Central Australia do. A few days earlier my toes were literally burning under the hot cowhide. It was thirty-eight degrees on a rocky outcrop north of Tennant Creek. Even the frequent gusts of wind were hot. The only relief they provided was to blow a few of the hundreds of flies onto the next person. I was there to film the last annular eclipse of the millennium as part of a documentary called *The Sun*. It was an international co-production that became the last program I was to shoot on film.

There still rages a debate as to whether film is superior to video. From an aesthetic standpoint film is divine; from an economic position alone this nineteenth-century technology is doomed. By the end of *The Sun* I was happy to see the last of it, only because the budget didn't allow for a camera assistant. Video cameras allow you to shoot around forty minutes before changing tape. Each film magazine lasts only ten minutes and you usually have just three of them. Sure, with discipline you can limit a location to thirty minutes of filming, but that wasn't the issue.

Schedules usually have multiple locations per day with inadequate travelling time between them, so normally you're running late to the next location. Then setting up for an interview takes twice as long as you expected. We were way behind before we even got to where we were going. The time I would normally have allocated to setting up lights and working out shots was spent with my hands in the black bag. This light-tight bag, used for changing film reels, has two elasticised armholes into which your hands go. By feel alone you remove the exposed film from the magazine and load on a new reel. Your hands sweat and it's easy to drop the centre of the spool. If you do, and I often did, one hundred and twenty metres of film starts to cascade off. It's an awful feeling that I got to know well. An experienced assistant can do it smoothly in a few minutes; out-of-practice dunderheads like me took ten minutes per magazine. By the time I had finally finished unloading and reloading, everyone else was set and ready to go and I hadn't even begun to think about the shot. With this added workload, long days and a full-on schedule, I was knackered after the first week.

Japan was the first stop on *The Sun* schedule, which would eventually culminate with the solar eclipse in Central Australia. We went one thousand metres under the earth to the world's oldest lead mine started fourteen hundred years earlier. It's now home to the aptly named Super-Kamiokande. This is an effective use of the prefix 'super'. Enormous underground caverns as broad as a football field and about as deep house equally enormous tanks of ultra pure water, so pure if you were to drop a spanner in, it would strangely enough dissolve. These mind-boggling tanks are there to catch teeny tiny things called neutrinos. They come from our sun and exploding stars and are so unbelievably small and benign that they pass through the earth without stopping. You have thousands passing through you at this moment. Don't ask me how but over a year scientists are able to capture a few thousand and somehow contain and study them.

More amazing than this ready-made James Bond film set was that we travelled around Japan, with our twenty cases of gear, by train. It was a nightmare. Turnstiles weren't wide enough, elevators were the size of broom closets and escalators were unavoidable. To move fifty metres sometimes required us to unload and load our trolleys three or four times. We resorted to hijacking escalators and shooting the cases down like balls in a bowling alley, scattering the commuters below. The super-efficient bullet trains would stop for twenty seconds to allow passengers on and off. The four of us – Richard Campbell, Geoff Burchfield, Gunter and I – took five cases each and would literally throw them through the door as shocked Japanese commuters dodged the missiles. On board the train is when things got interesting. Some trains were purely commuter services and had no storage space at all, and generally they were packed to the rafters. The only place to put the bags was in the narrow aisle. The Japanese were so polite. Without a word they climbed over boxes, not fazed at all by the undulating staircase.

The compact efficiency of Japan was traded for the volumetric excess of the United States. We crisscrossed the country guzzling up gallons of fuel on wide freeways and busy flight paths. Sixteen months of my life have been spent shooting in the US and a fair whack of that time has been spent sitting on a plane. Most plane trips are uncomfortable and uneventful, sometimes not. When a pilot with a sense of humour makes an announcement I gratefully listen. Coming in to land at Washington DC, one advised passengers, 'The houses are starting to look really big now so that's my cue to ask you to put your seat belts on nice and tight. With the exception of small children, everything you brought onto the plane must be stowed in the overhead bins or under the seat in front of you. Do not stick your arms or head outside the window at any time.'

On a Chicago to Los Angeles flight a thin, distorted voice came over the intercom: 'It's the captain speaking. In nineteen years of flying I've never had to make this announcement. Would you keep your eyes open for a black cat.' A family had brought their pet on board secreted in their hand luggage. One of the kids slid the zip a few centimetres to sneak a peek and the cat made his escape. From my seat at the back of the plane I looked over the headrest in front. The length of the cabin was alive. Everyone was wriggling and bobbing and searching; it looked like popcorn popping in the pan. By the time the cat had been found, escaped, found, escaped again and found it was a frightened, hissing, spitting, clawing demon.

The announcement that affected me most happened en route to Washington DC. We had been shooting the US component of *The Sun* doco. The following day would be our first day off in two weeks. We were at the very front of the economy cabin and in a relaxed mood, especially Gunter, who had tucked away a few beers. On the other side of the fabric curtains that separated us from the first-class cabin an obnoxious blonde woman, partnered by her equally obnoxious husband, had turned that part of the aircraft into their own party. It had become rowdy to the point that other first-class passengers were escaping to the empty seats in economy for some respite.

Gunter and I were quietly reading when the obnoxious blonde appeared from between the curtains and announced to the entire plane, 'We've got a request from *first class*. It's someone's birthday and I want the whole plane to sing "Happy Birthday".' She was met with dead silence broken only by Gunter saying, 'My friend here, Julian, he's a magician. He'll come and do a show for you.' I stared daggers at Gunter and he shot me back a smile that said too late for that now. Before I could protest she was gone. A minute on the curtains parted again and in her best ringmaster's voice she announced, 'For the pleasure of *first-class* passengers only, Julian from … ah … ah … England!' Gee, thanks Gunter. He had a grin from ear to ear that sucking lemons wouldn't have removed.

When I moved forward it was obvious that not all the first-class passengers were party to the party, so to speak. I was just another unwelcome intrusion into their peace and quiet that had been hijacked by this boorish woman. I did a few tricks with dollar bills and coins and was about to wrap it up when I felt a poking in my lower back. I turned to see the boorish blonde's husband, a buffoonish man with red cheeks and a glass of wine, who said, 'Have you *ever* done magic in *first class* before?' Ignoring him, I tried to get through the remaining thirty seconds when I felt a finger jabbing at my lower back again. That's it. I don't have to take this anymore. With 'Piss off, you wanker' perched on the tip of my tongue I turned. What? In a slightly surreal moment, a very, very short, old and grumpy nun in a black and white habit snapped at me, 'Get out of the aisle, you're blocking my way.' With that I said goodbye and returned to a chortling Gunter.

Before I could get a word in, the curtains parted and Mrs Loudmouth butted in: 'If you boys are lucky I might be able to get you some FIRST-CLASS champagne.' 'Piss off, you wanker' readied itself for launch again but take-off was aborted by a courteous acceptance from Gunter. We sipped our bubbly from plastic cups and didn't hear boo after that. A few days later we celebrated my thirty-seventh birthday back in Albuquerque at a favourite Mexican restaurant. That I had a favourite restaurant there and not in Brisbane registered. I was away a lot.

Before heading back to Australia for our date with the solar eclipse, we needed to do a quick shoot in New York. Walking the streets there is always eventful. This day I saw something that left me in awe. I ran block after block trying to keep this guy in sight as he ducked and dived through traffic, between trucks and past roadworks. He was a bicycle courier with one leg. His remaining foot was strapped to the pedal. Along the length of the bike frame hung a crutch. At his destination he sprang with ease from his bike and chained it to a truck. Using his crutch he hopped giant strides and slipped out of sight into a doorway. Whoever he was, he made an enormous impression on me. I almost felt as though I had been slapped in the face. This person did not view life through their own perceived limitations. I still did. This stranger became a point of reference for me in many future decisions.

Back in outback Australia, on the hot hilltop waiting for the eclipse, my decisions about correct exposures had been made. Simple maths that I had gone over and over and over in my head, checked and double-checked, gave me an 'f stop' number to set my lens to. An 'f stop' is one of those curiously named things that frightens off a lot of people from really understanding photography. It's just a measurement of the amount of light you let into the camera but it has been poorly named. The entire eclipse would take a little over two hours and, using a technique called time lapse, it would run at just eight seconds of screen time.

Slowly the light dimmed but the sky and clouds remained bright. Everything descended into a surreal twilight zone although the shadows were still quite sharp. It was very eerie. All the crickets started chirping and mercifully all the flies disappeared. The annularity, where the moon is directly in front of the sun, lasted for just one minute. I got goose bumps. There was nothing to tell me the camera was doing its job apart from a small green light that flashed every twenty or so seconds. I'd covered all my bases and was confident the shot was going to be stunning. Then the crickets quietened, the flies returned and I headed home.

The commercial flight taking me back to Brisbane departed from Alice Springs. I was feeling chuffed with myself and how well everything had gone over the past month in Japan and the US. This was the cherry on top of the cake. The whole shoot, particularly the time-lapse angle, would make an interesting article for the ACS magazine. On the back of a napkin I started jotting down the formula I had used to arrive at my exposure. Oh no. My stomach sank and I reeled forward and groaned. The person next to me asked if I was alright. In my calculations I had made a simple mistake but despite all the checking and double-checking, I had become oblivious to it. My exposure was six stops overexposed. Believe me, this wasn't good. Two, three, maybe four is fixable, but six!

The wait for the inevitable phone call was excruciating. The executive producer said just three words: 'It looks beautiful.' Huh? I'd timed my stuff-up brilliantly. If there was ever a time to be six stops overexposed, that was it. What I'd failed to take into account was the eclipse from its lightest to darkest moment was a brightness range of six stops. My wrong exposure became a correct one, only in a different part of the shot. That was uncomfortably close to being a rooster one day, feather duster the next.

Making television is akin to building a finely balanced house of cards. The smallest indiscretion can cause it to collapse. Having your name on the offending card is not good because this is an industry that looks for scapegoats. Making a mistake and learning from it is experience, making the same mistake twice is your fault. Once, running down a city street, I was in a pack of cameramen chasing someone leaving a courthouse. The Channel Nine cameraman's shoelace came loose and he tripped, smashing his camera on the bitumen. From that day on I have always tied double knots. It may seem silly but it's always the silly little things that get you.

In early 2000, months had passed since I'd worked with one of the Richards. It was Richard Smith's turn this time and we headed back to Central Australia to shoot another international co-production called *Extreme Australia*. Leigh Wayper was our soundo and, like Mike Charman, whom I had worked with in China, he had had an interesting career start with the BBC in Britain. A huge circus spectacular was broadcast live to air and the opening was an ambitious shot that wandered with the crowd as they queued for tickets and entered the tent. Little vignettes of conversation were crucial to its success so the young Leigh was fitted up with a hidden microphone and he mingled to capture the intimate sound effects. Rehearsal was called and Leigh took up his position. Ten minutes turned to twenty, twenty into forty. It was bitterly cold and Leigh was frozen. He returned to the van to find everyone enjoying warm drinks. Rehearsal had been done and dusted in five minutes and no one had thought to tell Leigh. Miffed, he made the blanket statement to his bosses, 'I *never* want to work on *any* circus production ever again!' Another circus production did follow soon after and, as was Leigh's wish, his name was left off the list. 'Bad move,' said Leigh. It was the iconic comedy series *Monty Python's Flying Circus*.

Richard had lined up a potentially good interview with a man named Billy. Billy amazed me with the way he could walk barefoot over the red hot sand, deftly dodging the spinifex spines, his speed never fluctuating, his direction never straying. This was nothing new for Billy Wara, an elder of the Arrernte people of Uluru. *Wara* means 'tall' in Arrernte, and Billy was tall and spindly like the desert oaks nearby. His dark skin looked darker, if that was possible, against the white stubble of his beard and the shock of white matted hair that extended back from his traditionally half-shaven crown. Billy was old. How old was a bit of a mystery, but his lined face and the way he seemed such a natural part of the timeless landscape suggested ninety wouldn't be far off the mark.

We set up for an interview with Billy on the sand dunes in front of the iconic Uluru. What interested us for the story were the traditional ways of living off the land and the sense of change he had known. He told of hunting kangaroo, mala and bilby, none of which are seen around the Rock anymore. Letting handfuls of red sand run through his fingers he illustrated the Dreamtime story of how Uluru was formed. Then he told us an amazing story that I felt privileged to hear, about his first meeting with a white man. He was about ten years old and a man arrived with three camels in tow. Billy was shy so he hid behind some grass and just stared at this strange vision. Greetings with other family members over, the man went to secure the camels for the night. In relieving the camels of their loads, the heavy saddle bags slipped and went crashing onto the man, momentarily pinning him to the ground. In the confusion the tether rope slipped from the man's grasp and entangled the camels' feet. As he went one way to untie the knot, the camels went the other. Billy cackled with delight as he recounted three camels bound together at the hoof toppling like a large tree being felled. This white man had a name. It was Harold Lasseter, who perished trying to find his legendary lost reef of gold.

Billy also told of other people from his area who had never seen a car before, coming upon their first tyre tracks. Not knowing what to make of the two endless lines they convinced themselves it must be some serpent spirit. Too afraid to cross this serpent for fear of being devoured, they turned one way and walked and walked and walked. Still the serpent blocked their path. They turned and walked the other way for days. Still the serpent stopped them. Eventually they returned to their original point of contact, gave up and went home.

Listening to these stories it struck me that six months earlier I had been sitting in a space shuttle and now I was talking to a man who had had no concept of modern technology for a large part of his life. In the same year I had felt safe in a war zone yet been assaulted at a benign lawn bowls club; that mine was an unusual job was not lost on me. I termed these realisations MOCs or moments of contrast. There were to be many more.

Billy's interview was television gold. Richard was on the phone to keep the executive producers happy that their money was being well spent. The humidity became debilitating as we headed north and a few days later we were recuperating on a welcome day off. We were in Kakadu National Park. On a nature trail close to the motel I came upon a huge flying fox colony and for the small amount of effort required, I went back for the camera. Leigh was using it to check back over the week's worth of tapes, logging each tape for the editor's convenience. I grabbed the camera and a tape and hotfooted it to the bats, shot what was useful, then returned the camera to Leigh.

Back in my air-conditioned room the phone rang. It was Leigh with sickening news: I had taped over the Billy Wara interview. Despite all the protocols and safety checks we had in place, it had happened; a series of assumptions had created this catastrophe. Ultimately I was responsible but it was Richard who was answerable to higher up. Each tape has a little red safety tab that when pushed in stops the tape from being recorded on again. Wrong. A pushed-in red tab can also be pulled out again. Whether that's intentional or accidental is irrelevant. It signals that the tape is able to be recorded on. That is confusion and from confusion will eventually come tears. From that moment on I have ripped the red tab out of every tape that I have shot. That way there is no confusion. This frustrates editors and administrative staff. Each tape costs about forty dollars and ripping out the tab precludes it from being recycled. I'm willing to cop the flak over this because I don't want another Billy episode. About six minutes of Billy's interview remained but many of his great stories were lost forever.

# 10

## Although the photographer and the art thief were close friends, neither had ever taken the other's picture.

I love New Zealand. There's so much to love about it. The people for starters; Vicky is a Kiwi. On top its highest mountain, Mt Cook, I once witnessed a bumble bee as he laboured up the eastern flank, past my shins, then zoomed down the west side. Was he aware he had taken the hardest possible route to cross New Zealand? Just another example, I thought, of New Zealanders' strength of character. Then there's all that glorious scenery. Anytime I get the chance I return.

Glenn Singleman had another BASE-jumping film on the boil. His previous documentary, *BASEClimb*, had been very successful and launched his corporate speaking career. 'If you can jump off a chair and at the same time pull a handkerchief from your pocket, you have the physical wherewithal to BASE jump from the highest cliff in the world,' he would challenge his audience. 'You just need to manage your fear and that can be learnt.' Glenn's new wife, Heather Swan, had heard Glenn deliver this message hundreds of times and issued her own challenge to a slightly shocked Glenn: 'Then teach me.' So was born *BASEClimb 2*, and I was on board.

Returning to the Mt Cook region to climb was part of the schedule and I was keen to get back onto the snow and ice. First up was a trip through the spectacular Starlight Cave system at the top of New Zealand's South Island. The entry to the cave took our breath away. Harwood's Hole is a two-hundred-metre-deep vertical drop straight towards the centre of the earth. The shearers' quarters at the nearby sheep station of Canaan Downs served as our base. I've never been so keen to make the daily commute to work.

Each morning we divided up the camera and caving gear into large backpacks. There was to be no walking for us; we had mountain bikes. Hundreds of freshly shorn sheep sprang and bounced as we pedalled through the paddock that led to the flat trail. With its soft carpet of leaves, the track weaved through towering silver birch and past glassy mountain lakes; a most peaceful start to the day. Harwood's Hole has an external opening the size of an Olympic swimming pool and widens as you descend. After the first forty metres of the abseil, the twist in the rope slowly spun us around in free space. Deeper and deeper, round and round, we descended until an angled slope of loose stone chips signalled the journey's end. Nearby, a wooden cross supporting a punctured caving helmet commemorated an unlucky caver and showed the power of a small stone at terminal speed; this was no place to linger.

We followed room-size caverns that narrowed and narrowed before opening again, always a stream of water underfoot. Watertight Pelican cases protected the cameras and lights, for which I'd packed enough battery power to do four five-minute scenes. It was a wonderland. Huge stalactites formed mysterious curtains to navigate. Pools of bottomless crystal-clear water glowed emerald green under the power of my lights. The intensity of the colour fixated me. I didn't want to fall in but I was fascinated where it might lead. We filmed going through a 'squeeze', a constriction in the cave large enough to allow only an adult wriggling on their stomach. I'm not prone to panic but came close to it this time. Through the three-metre-long rock tunnel flowed the ever-present ankle-deep stream.

The narrowing in the cave system's airflow meant a stiff breeze existed in, through, and out of the rock aperture. Lying on my stomach I could see faces past the squeeze peering back. Unlike the feeling of freedom I experience living life in the vertical while climbing, here I felt trapped. (I had ventured into a squeeze in a simple cave system in north Queensland once. I was by myself and I panicked. My history wasn't encouraging.) The roughness of the limestone on my clothing slowed me down. I heard Glenn's voice ahead: 'This next bit's interesting. You've got to put your face in the water to be able to move forward. Don't stop once you've started.' He was right. The rock angled unusually and the only way forward was as he said. My helmet scraped the rock overhead as I tried to lift my face out of the few inches of water. I wasn't enjoying this.

Cavers prefer to use a small flame burning on their helmet rather than torches as the flame provides a gentle, even illumination preferable to a harsh narrow torch beam. As the bulk of my body had reduced the air gap further, the air rushed noisily over me and snuffed out my flame. In darkness with my nose and mouth under water I felt a rising panic, but panic gets you nowhere. Using that realisation I refocused and inched my way forward and out. Before this moment I had quietly questioned Glenn's reasoning for including caving in his film, apart from its inherent picture value. As it was I had just experienced the central theme first-hand: if you can manage fear by breaking it down into component parts, you can rise above your perceived limitations.

My respect for Glenn's wife Heather was strong. She'd attained a law degree through the police force and walked the beat in the bad parts of Sydney. She'd also toughed it out in the argy-bargy of a corporate job. She was no softie. With no climbing or parachuting experience she had invested huge trust in Glenn to join him on his quest to climb and then jump off the highest cliffs in the world. I was right behind them except for one thing: my children. They asked me to share their commitment to the project but I couldn't. Even though I was travelling and taking risks, my priority was now my family and I needed to manage my desire for personal achievement within these boundaries.

Glenn and Heather had five children between them. I was fascinated by how they reconciled any conflict they might have felt between their ambitions and their responsibilities as parents. There was a very real possibility of death on this venture. Addressing this issue in detail would make a strong thread to their film but they disagreed and treated it as a bit of a no-go zone. It wasn't as though they had dreamed this adventure up overnight. It had a very real genesis in their unique personal story and their arguments were strong and well thought out on an emotional and intellectual level. A missed opportunity, I thought. However, this was Glenn's film and the role of a cameraman is to cinematically realise the director's ideas and pack their own ego away during the shoot. Neither was Glenn a filmmaking novice. He had well and truly paid his dues. I was very supportive of Glenn's decisions but made it clear that when it came to personal safety my family was utmost in my mind.

The most important part of a BASE jump is the launch. Something as minor as having one shoulder a bit low, which would barely provoke a 'don't slouch' in daily life, can have dire consequences when you are hurtling only metres out from the rock. This small error magnifies into opening the chute, turning it back into the wall prematurely. Heather needed to practise the technique of launching herself from a cliff. The safest, fastest and easiest way to get her 'exits' correct was bungy jumping. We booked a commercial bungy operator outside their normal operating times. Two sides of a spectacular gorge were connected by tensioned wire cable. A gondola suspended under the cable served as the launch platform for the 130-metre drop. Full of trepidation Heather began a series of jumps. She showed promise and quickly graduated to a specially made, never-before-tried parachute harness that would allow the elastic bungy rope to be attached to a point in the middle of her back. The standard bungy attachment is around the ankles, which prevented Heather from feeling realistic BASE-jumping exits. With the extra freedom of the new harness, Heather did a textbook launch.

A winch was alongside to bring the jumpers back up after their jump. As Heather was clipping in for the ninety-second ride on the airy elevator, we laughed and congratulated ourselves on the successful harness design and filming so far. Heather quickly arrived level with us, suspended stomach-down in the harness, feet towards us, head away. Glenn was beaming with pride and playfully grabbed her foot and swung her to face us. The mood went cold. Her face was contorted in pain and she began to scream. Glenn was an emergency room doctor and the seriousness of the situation was written across his face. He examined her and at the same time tried to provide comfort as her husband.

There was no point in calling for an ambulance; it happened to be the ambulance driver's house we were staying in and he was away on a distant job. We found an old mattress to make our van into an impromptu ambulance. Heather's moaning and screaming continued, made worse by thirty minutes of rugged 4WD track before hitting the bitumen. Invercargill Hospital was closest but still hours away. Once there, tests revealed a one-and-a-half-centimetre tear in Heather's duodenum which required emergency surgery. We waited. The hospital generously accommodated us in a comfort house that was unusually located between the morgue and the STD clinic. Heather came through with flying colours but was badly shaken by how easily things could go pear-shaped, even under relatively safe conditions.

A period of soul searching followed for the adventurous couple. Heather's inner strength triumphed and they continued, eventually setting a new world record for the highest BASE jump. Opinions were polarised over their adventures – they were irresponsible foolhardiness to some, an inspiration for most. Over many years I've seen the tenacity, commitment and personal sacrifice they have made. To be given the opportunity to work alongside people of this calibre is part of the attraction of being a cameraman and also part of the problem. While they and all the others are 'doing', I'm witnessing from the sidelines. I would often lie awake tussling with this thought. In the light of day the reality that I had one of the best jobs going couldn't be ignored and I went on doing what I did best, being a cameraman.

Within a fortnight I was in Dili shooting a documentary on the plight of East Timorese schoolchildren trying to get an education without books, pens, chairs, teachers or schools. The Indonesian military had done a thorough job of torching the place during its recent fight for independence. In stark contrast to Glenn and Heather's impressive yet hedonistic pursuit of danger, the blackened walls of East Timor's burnt-out towns were reminders that many more people don't need to seek danger; they have it thrust upon them.

One of the terrific things about the ABC in Brisbane is the people who work there. It's a pity I got to see so little of them. Ours is a transient job; when I was back in they were often out. That's why I was so happy to be in Timor with a wonderful ABC producer named Gary Johnson. What Gary lacked in hair – everything – he made up for in talent and compassion. If sincerity were measured in ounces, he'd have tons. Within days of us arriving, the Timorese children had taken to calling him Meester Baldy.

Also on the shoot was Phil Smith, the journalist whose daughter's belief that man hadn't landed on the moon was so insightful for me.

Phil was a lover of all things military and he had spent time as an officer in the army reserve, where he contracted that most unfortunate of military afflictions: OROA, otherwise known as overreliance on acronyms. With army to our left and army to our right, he was often AWOL in a world of LocStats and LZs.

Operating in and around Dili was relatively safe since the TNI, Indonesia's military, had moved on. The only real act of aggression we encountered was a stone-throwing monkey who made it very clear he wanted to be left in peace. I was happy this was no longer a war zone. It has never been my ambition to be in one. I'd had my fill of army life. Besides, we had two immediate and formidable problems to overcome: the United Nations and Timor Lodge Hotel.

The United Nations is essentially a portable government. My opinion of them from what I saw in Timor wasn't good. I thought they were excessive in self-spending, expert in bureaucracy, arrogant by nature and rude in delivery. They made our job of filming difficult. That I could accept, as we were not a high priority. It was the lectures we received from them about the forty-kilometre-an-hour speed limit that angered us. As we putted around taking hours to get anywhere, time after time we saw shiny new UN Range Rovers doing 100 kilometres an hour past small children walking on the road. We took to waving them down and Phil would unleash a torrent of acronyms letting them know we were going to lodge complaints. With whom we weren't sure.

Timor Lodge Hotel was a collection of ex-mining-camp prefabs shipped in from the Northern Territory. The show was run by a couple of dubious-looking Australians supported by an army of local Timorese collectively labelled 'security'. But where was security when you really needed them? Packs of aggressive dogs roamed the compound and terrorised us if we dared walk outside. I took to carrying a wet towel rolled into a kangaroo's tail – a skill I had learnt at primary school – to defend myself on the way to breakfast for our daily audience with Stefan, the Turkish cook, and his specialty dish, barked bin (baked beans). Our rooms were tiny. For small rooms they sure did have a lot of rules pinned to the inside of the door. Rule No 2 was an eye-catcher: NO PROSTITUTES OR TRANSVESTITES ALLOWED IN ROOMS. During the daily tropical deluges water filled the rooms. I'm guessing reception had given up on dealing with this complaint as their responses were always accompanied by a chuckle: 'Not all rooms have showers, you know,' and 'Life jackets are located under the beds.'

School upon school we visited was a burnt-out shell. Education was valued here, so classes continued. Open-air classes were held under the deep shade of mango trees with rudimentary blackboards nailed to the trunks. Every village school we went to welcomed us with toothy smiles, except one. A class of four-year-olds burst into tears at the sight of my big camera. The teachers apologised and asked us to leave the camera outside; it reminded the children of the men who had come with guns. That was the cue I was waiting for to pull out a few magic tricks. Within minutes I had thirty little kids giggling, their tears forgotten. The effect that a few simple tricks and a willingness to communicate a smile had on these kids was intoxicating. I wanted to do it again. With Gary's goodwill we made time in our schedule for half a dozen small shows. We invited entire villages. It was a double act they came to see: the intriguing smooth head of Meester Baldy and the ball-tossing antics of Meester Meestree (their name not mine).

The back of an aid truck worked as a stage from where I could perform a twenty-minute show. No one spoke English but no one minded. Once the laughter started it was infectious. Even then, mid-juggle on the back of the truck, the potential for my new-found skills began to fill my head. That night my mind wouldn't relax. I mused on the Kosovo story and how I thought maybe someone watching it would be moved into action. But that was indirect and still a 'maybe'. Today I was smitten with the power of direct action. All I did was make some people laugh; I didn't improve their water supply or put a roof over their heads but I had found a tool that suited my personality and could be used to make a difference. Something in me started to stir.

Pondering my new-found insight would have to wait. Wendy Page called asking me to accompany her on a shoot in England. We had worked well together in Kosovo and I trusted her judgement so I accepted knowing little about the story. The turnaround between the Timor shoot and this one was tight, just two days. Wendy was to go a few days earlier, set some things in place then I would meet her there. I said a brief hello to my family then, in a bit of a travelling daze, headed back to Brisbane's international airport.

Checking in for flights with a small mountain of equipment cases rarely goes smoothly. The rules change airline by airline, person by person, day by day. Pre 9/11 it used to be a lot easier, particularly in the US. There they have airport staff called Skycaps who can check you in kerbside. Our excess baggage bill was always one hundred dollars; that's the amount of cash you included in the folds of your ticket before handing it over. Without a moment's hesitation or a set of scales in sight, all the cases were tagged and taken away. Post 9/11 that all changed big time; all the 'giddays' and 'maaates' in the world didn't help. Not only did they extract top dollar for every extra kilogram, as an Australian they saw me as a 'foreign national' in possession of cases full of electronics and wires. I thought John Howard holidaying with George Bush at the ranch meant we were all friends. It didn't. I was accorded membership of the SSSS club. Those four letters on the bottom of a boarding pass highlight you as a security risk so you receive all the extra attention of bag checks, bomb residue checks, and Q&A sessions. I've often wondered if my indiscretion at Los Alamos had me on some database of undesirables.

Standing at the British Airways counter in Brisbane, my check-in was taking an unusually long time. A growing number of staff were attending to my booking. 'It's just a glitch with the system, Mr Mather,' they reassured me. It didn't worry me. I had developed a very relaxed attitude to travelling over the years. I'd do everything possible to try and get on a flight but if it went without me, it went without me. I knew the producers and office staff would be doing all the stressing and any on my part was excess to requirements and therefore, I reasoned, wasted energy. One of the simplest ways to make almost every flight is to get to the airport early. Most problems can be sorted if you give the airline staff time to fix them. Some camera crews see it as a badge of honour to arrive with only minutes to spare, the later the better. This is somehow viewed as a mark of professionalism. That's not me. I had plenty of time and wasn't feeling stressed in the least.

The duty manager was summoned; more discussion, more pointing, more hammering away at the keyboard. A young girl who looked like the work-experience person peered over their shoulders and said, 'That's tomorrow.' She was right. I had arrived a day early for my flight, which even for me and my desire to arrive early was taking things a bit too far. I collected my gear and headed for the taxis and home. 'You look exhausted, mate. Where have you just come in from?' the taxi driver quizzed. There goes my chance for a quiet ride home, I thought to myself.

I met up with Wendy at Heathrow and she filled me in. She was doing an *Australian Story* about a man who'd helped to revolutionise police practices around the world. He'd been praised for his pioneering work in restorative justice, a process whereby offenders are brought face to face with their victims. The extraordinary thing was that while he was in demand to train police officers overseas, in Australia his work had been obstructed at every turn. He was a former police sergeant from New South Wales by the name of Terry O'Connell.

We headed up the M40 to Oxfordshire, the heart of the Thames Valley police district, the largest in England. Here Terry O'Connell and his ideas had been welcomed with open arms. Our first job was to get some rest. Wendy had found a four-hundred-year-old bed-and-breakfast on a working farm. We knocked on the solid timber door and readied our best smiles. A woman named Miriam opened the door. She was a wiry, early-to-bed, early-to-rise sort of person. Wendy chirped up, 'Hi, I'm Wendy and this is Julian.'

Miriam put her hands to her thin face like she'd seen a ghost. Her mouth dropped down at the same time that her eyebrows went up. 'You're not two women, oh my God, one's a man.' She then raised her hands above her head and starting shaking them. In small yelps she said, 'I'm flipping out, I'm flipping out,' then turned and left us. A gently spoken, greying man in a padded hunting vest and wellington boots appeared and offered an apology. 'If you'll excuse me for a moment, my wife's flipping out.' A typo had me on the booking sheet as Julia, not Julian. The inn was full and she had arranged a share room for our first night. So began an entertaining few days with Miriam and Mike, our eccentric English hosts.

There was nothing eccentric or quaint about our work there. In the morning we traded the verdant lawns and quacking ducks of the farm for the gritty, dirty side of English urban living. The housing commission estates were high-crime areas so seeing them first-hand in the company of police was reassuring. It was like being in an episode of *The Bill*. Our days were spent riding around in the back of police cars, Pandas as they call them. We attended a fracas in the High Street where drunken yobs were slugging it out. There was the comical situation in which a car thief, fresh out of prison, had his car stolen. Without seeing the irony, he demanded the police do their job better.

One of the side effects of looking through a viewfinder while in a moving vehicle is motion sickness. I was particularly susceptible to it. Outside it was cold and raining, inside the police car it was hot and claustrophobic. Keith and Pete, our police crew, loved turning the heater dial until it would turn no more. I subscribe to Spike Milligan's theory that the best cure for seasickness is to sit under a tree, which is what I did. Pete, Keith and Wendy would go off for half an hour then return to pick me up from my bench, until the winding estate streets got me again.

The lights were still on when we arrived back late at Miriam and Mike's. Our day's work naturally steered the conversation towards law and order. Miriam's eyes lit up. 'My cousin was a headmaster and he resigned when the cane was abolished ... nothing wrong with a bit of hitting.' Her pitch increased and she stood for effect. 'Besides, it's not the hitting itself, it's the ... the ... the ... *anticipation* of the whack, that's what's effective.' Wendy and I snuck a glance at each other. Miriam had agitated herself into one of her moments again. 'And what's more,' she added, 'they should bring back the stocks for teenagers.'

Next day we had plenty of opportunity to consider this remark. Hundreds of eleven- to seventeen-year-olds at Drayton Comprehensive School were not going to miss an opportunity to have their face on Australian television. This school just outside of Banbury had problems: fifty percent of the kids came from single-parent families, locals said it was a breeding ground for a new generation of artful dodgers, and the kids were streetwise and lippy. Celebrity chef Gordon Ramsay went to school here in the eighties. The school was also trialling restorative justice. Expulsions and suspensions by the school had dropped sixty percent since its introduction.

Responsible for overseeing this program was Police Constable Graham Waddington. He was the school's own policeman. This was his place of work. We first met him in a staff meeting that was interrupted by a subject master who slid in like Kramer in a *Seinfeld* episode and announced, 'He's struck again.' The staff let out a collective extended sigh. The phantom defecator was back. In an unspoken drill the teachers went off left, right and centre to deal with it. Faeces-smearing and arson were signs of sexual abuse. PC Waddington told us they thought they knew who it was, a boy whose council flat was visited by police on a weekly basis for drug offences. On the last visit police found home-made porn videos of the father and his girlfriend. They were scattered among all the kids' videos and toys.

That diversion sorted, we filmed PC Waddington in action. A class of motley fifteen-year-olds with little respect for authority had the sting taken out of their collective tails as PC Waddington did what he does best: relate to kids. His message of the moment was to stop sniffing aerosols. This was a major problem at the school. He didn't talk at the kids, above them, or beneath them; just to them. He didn't pull his punches, the law was the law. It was a lively forty minutes and they gave plenty of lip. Everyone, including me, was hanging on his every word. I felt cheated when the bell rang; I wanted to keep listening to him.

Among the screeching and clatter and chaos of fifteen-year-olds exiting a classroom it happened. Unannounced, without breaking stride or making eye contact, three students with the light touch of drug dealers left aerosols on the teacher's desk. I thought, wow, one bloke, forty minutes, three young lives affected for the better. It is probably the one single moment in everything I've seen and done that has profoundly changed my thinking. What I saw was the power of direct action and it resonated with me. I'd already started thinking about this in Timor. I recognised in myself a desire to make a difference in people's lives. Today was the first time it occurred to me that the camera might be holding me back.

We left Drayton School and PC Waddington. It was our last night with Miriam and Mike. I was keen to tell of this amazing copper I had met but Miriam was keener to take up where she had left off the night before. She assumed she had found sympathetic ears and unloaded herself onto us. 'Gypsies are vermin and anyone caught stealing should have their fingers cut off, like in Arabia.' Wendy and I exchanged glances again. 'Goodnight, Miriam.'

Next day I said goodbye to Wendy. There was still work to be done but budgets at the ABC were starting to tighten and there was no money left for me to stay on. With a small camera and a big commitment to seeing the story through, Wendy stayed while I flew home.

My enthusiasm for the insight I had gleaned from PC Waddington remained. I didn't really know what to do with all this energy so I just thought about it a lot and, where I could, passionately recounted my Timor experience. For me this was unusual as I'm not a big talker. My story caught the ear of the executive producer of the current-affairs program *Stateline*. What really attracted Kirsten McGregor's attention was that I had some video footage of me doing shows on the back of the aid trucks in Timorese villages. In the cash-strapped world of ABC local current affairs that titbit elevated a passing conversation into a potential TV story that would fill a few minutes of airtime. Kirsten suggested that while my enthusiasm levels were high, we should do a quick interview. I knew exactly where they were coming from. Nine out of ten people will passionately recount things off camera but as soon as the camera rolls they replace that passion with caution and measure. The result is a wooden performance.

With thousands of interviews under my belt as a cameraman, I knew the drill, so we set to doing it straightaway. The cameraman and journalist opposite me were colleagues. I put on an air of nonchalance. After all, this is what we did every day. Really, I was terrified. It reminded me so much of climbing and how it strips you bare of any pretence. While climbing you're at the pointy end of things and you can either do it or you fall. There are no excuses, no elaborate ruses. Your climbing partner sees you for who you really are. Succeed or fail, climbing is very cathartic and liberating.

I didn't feel liberated in this situation. I felt bare in front of my work colleagues, my armour of glass and electronics gone. I felt they had high expectations for me to breeze through this. Why, I'm not sure. Maybe I was used to being seen to be in control, a by-product of knowledge and confidence in any given field. I was anything but confident in front of the camera. I felt like a fish out of water, just like the hundreds of politicians, captains of industry and senior bureaucrats I have watched perspire and go dry-mouthed.

I saw the red light on the camera glow and I was on. I opened my mouth and disconnected words came out, words that weren't mine. That's not what I meant to say. I found myself listening to the sound of my own voice, not thinking about what I was saying. I became self-conscious about my posture, how I was holding myself during the pauses. I qualified every statement where a short sharp answer would have done. The passion had evaporated and I said stupid things I thought people would want me to say. I had just been introduced to the terror of being interviewed on television. How many thousands of people had I glibly told, 'Don't worry, mate, it's a piece of cake.' It wasn't.

The power of any possible message I might have conveyed was diluted by my nerve-racked performance. How many of the people I had filmed in interviews had gone home and winced at seeing their sub-standard performance on the screen, just as I did? Fragile ego aside, I realised that as a result the production suffered as well. Lively interviews are inspiring; pedestrian interviews waste screen time. I had to ask myself whether the way I conducted myself as a cameraman was part of the problem and could I come up with any solution. I put my thinking cap on.

While I thought, lots of Australia passed by my window. I moved on to shooting *Outstanding Australia*, a picture-driven series on Australia's national parks. I love national parks and I love pictures so, as far as I was concerned, I was the right man for the job. My friend and Timor colleague Gary Johnson was producing, my conspirator on the Billy Wara tape erasure, Leigh Wayper, was doing sound and the presenter was Ranger Tim, a well-known kids' show personality from Channel Ten. The locations were, well, outstanding and so was I, particularly on this day. I was standing on the skids of a helicopter, flying metres above the glassy water with red canyon walls flashing by on each side. We had come to Nitmiluk National Park a few hundred kilometres south of Darwin. Many would know it by its former name, Katherine Gorge.

Some places scream out for aerial shots, it's a no-brainer, but things hadn't changed since the Mt Mulligan days. Gyroscopic mounts and the powerful helicopters that carry them still consumed huge chunks of the budget and were always passed over in favour of cheaper options. Bumpy-looking aerials still frustrated me. The mount I had constructed for the Mt Mulligan shoot was not worth pursuing so I applied myself to finding another economical solution. The answer was right under my nose, literally. Me. If the camera was strapped to my body and I tensioned myself on a supporting line to hang out and forward, my body could become the mount. As long as the airspeed was kept down to about sixty knots and the pilot called the turns to me over the intercom, the shots were gloriously smooth. It looked just like flying.

I adopted this same principle to overcome the problems of shooting inside cars. Big cameras and small cars don't mix. External car rigs are available but are cumbersome and time-consuming. Using my knowledge of climbing knots I could tie myself to the outside of a car in a few minutes. With instructions to the driver to drive wide of signposts and trees, great shots could be had for a fraction of the cost and time. Even though I had factored safety into my designs with simplicity, triple backup and quick release in case of emergency, what I did broke every occupational health and safety rule in the book. Common sense, experience and intuition were my guide, always whispering in my ear: 'Is the shot worth it?'

Better than all the wonderful places we were visiting was the relationship I was building with Tim. He's a naturally funny person, the type that just by his presence won't allow a mood to stay flat. He also had something I wanted: experience in inspiring children. Along with his TV commitments he went to schools promoting an environmental awareness message. I couldn't believe my luck. In my spare time I had started approaching Brisbane schools and performing my 'Use Your Noggin' show. Using magic and juggling as a vehicle, I told kids that there was a difference between magic and tricks. Beware of people saying they can use magic to make you better if you're sick, or that they could really talk to ghosts. I never told them what to think, just to apply some critical thinking. The message was simple: think it over, look it up, ask questions. I had a few dozen shows under my belt but I was very much the novice. Tim, on the other hand, had hundreds of shows notched up. Not only did I have someone to milk for ideas, but for the first time I had someone to talk to about my own ideas.

We connected instantly and easily and quickly found another common trait: an ability to dream up an idea and worry about the details later. Poor Gary just rolled his eyes and said, 'I can tell you two are up to something.' A quick call was made to the Katherine South Primary School saying the ABC would come and do a show. Their response was enthusiastic but we would have to be there before parade ended in fifteen minutes. Tim and I raced to the school. As we parked the car we could hear the announcement on the PA system that the ABC was coming to do a show. Without breaking stride, Tim took over the microphone and ad-libbed. We hadn't really planned anything but I took his lead and the one hundred and eighty kids and staff lapped it up. Tim and I repeated this at schools in Victoria, New South Wales and Western

Australia. I could see I was on a journey somewhere. I didn't know the destination, but I was enjoying the ride.

Photographically my career was still on the ascent. One of the things that bugs most cameramen is a lack of consistency in a program's visual style. Simply, budgets run out and rather than using the cameraman who started the shoot, the program picks up someone local to shoot this bit and that. The result is a mishmash of shooting styles. To be honest, does the viewer at home notice? Probably not, but as a cameraman, it makes you want to cry. To be offered an entire series to shoot, in the ABC at least, was a luxury. The first seven episodes of a new series named *Dynasties* were mine if I wanted them. That this was a Sydney-based production that should rightly have gone to a Sydney crew made it that much more attractive. Of course, I jumped at it.

The series looked at some of Australia's most remarkable and influential families: the Macarthurs, Myers, DeBortolis, Wrights, Duracks, Downers and Murdochs. The opportunity to spend a day with the tough-as-nails Dame Elisabeth Murdoch was one of the highlights. On a freezing cold day at her family home, Cruden Farm on the Frankston Peninsula in Victoria, I asked the slight but sturdy woman if we could put the heating on. Essentially I was told to toughen up. Heating, she explained, was often frivolously wasted. That was all well and good but I was a Queenslander and I was freezing. If Rupert plays hard ball I can see where he gets it from. When she left I set up every light from my lighting kit and let the thousands of watts of energy bring the temperature in the room to above single figures.

We had a few frosty receptions on the shoot, especially from the Macarthurs, as there were was some friction within their family and it was central to their story. Why they agreed to have us there is beyond me, but they did. Behind their smiles we could tell we were about as welcome as a fart in a space suit. Over the years I had toughened up considerably so that being around personal friction like this, although I still wouldn't actively have chosen to be there, no longer cost me any lost sleep.

Where I did lose a bit of sleep, to my surprise, was with the Downer family. I found the matriarch of the family, Lady Mary Downer, to be a woman of substance and very likeable. Her son, Australia's former Foreign Minister Alexander Downer, had a strange effect on me. We spent time with him at his home in the hills of Adelaide, in his electorate, in his Parliament House offices, in his car. By the end of a few days he still didn't even know my name. It was like I was invisible and I didn't like that. I understand that the day-to-day hurly-burly of politics renders the cameraman faceless; we are hidden behind a lump of glass and the glare of bright lights, and the interviews are usually short and on the run, what we call door stops. We often use this to our advantage as we can leave the humdrum of small talk to the journalists. But this was different. Rather than the hit-and-run type meetings with most politicians, we were spending longer periods of time with Downer and I began to like him. I didn't think I would. I never cared much for his views or politics, or his pompous private schoolboy image that comes across in the media. There's some truth there but he's much more than that. He's very intelligent, funny, profane and likeable. That he couldn't muster the effort to remember my name did throw me a bit but I got over it. Like kryptonite to Superman, Downer's unconscious dismissal of me had robbed me of some of my inner strength and my self-esteem wobbled a bit on that shoot. But I had plenty of energy for some things, one of those being the ABC's integrity.

I've made my fair share of mistakes and the ABC doesn't get it right all the time, but overall the ABC promotes a culture of accuracy, honesty and fairness. As a front-line representative of the ABC, I dealt daily with the job of repairing the damage done to the general public's view of the media. The 'get a story at any cost' mentality of large sections of the industry incrementally raises the level of distrust towards us. I acknowledge that ABC staffers don't have an economic imperative looming over the security of their jobs, and that is a luxury that affords us a little more idealism. Still, much of what we do and the way we do it goes a long way towards rebuilding the tattered bridge of trust between the general public and the media. I find myself constantly relying on the goodwill of the public just to do my job because we certainly can't lure them with money. So when I see someone destroying that goodwill, especially for short-term gain, I get annoyed.

Lady Mary Downer is a tough woman. She lives by herself in a beautiful family home high in the Adelaide Hills. She gave us complete access to her house and family history. Her one request was that we didn't show the exterior of her house. She was elderly and scared this program might encourage burglars to do the place over. It was an utterly fair and understandable request, especially considering what she was graciously providing us in return. We gave our word. During the day the freelance producer requested that I get an exterior shot of the house. I reminded him of our agreement with Lady Downer. 'Oh, I'm not going to use it,' he insisted, 'it's just good to have in the edit suite in case I need it.' I refused and got on with the job at hand.

The day was stinking hot and Lady Downer had found towels and bathers for everyone to cool off in her pool. I still had to finish off shots of the many family photos and portraits lining the walls. From an upstairs window I saw the producer hiding in the bushes. With a small handycam he was sneaking shots of the house. I stormed down and fair near knocked his block off. He looked at me like I was some puritanical nutter. I'd given my word, that was important to me, and I was stuffed if I was going to let him add to the mess that I have to deal with daily. It's not surprising that we never worked together again.

# 11

# What do you call a Frenchman wearing thongs?

PHILIPPE FILL-LOP.

Or Mathieu Ricard, as it happened in the US university town of Madison, Wisconsin. Mathieu had been a doctor of molecular genetics before making the unlikely career change to thong-wearing, robe-clad Tibetan Buddhist monk. For a decade he was the Dalai Lama's French translator. His small roll-on cabin bag made me envious. (I dream of one day being able to leave behind the mountain of gear, and travel with nothing more than a book, a ticket and passport.) The small case held his few worldly possessions. In this materialistic world was he really happy? He was. I could be accused of making patronising generalisations but I knew he was. Science had proved it. He was officially the world's happiest man. What a chance combination. In one person was respect for scientific research and a measurable capacity to be compassionate towards all humankind.

Wearing a wig of painstakingly placed electrodes that would monitor his brain activity Mathieu, a master meditator, would go into a meditative state within seconds and the screen would literally light up. By concentrating on thinking only good thoughts, Mathieu, in essence, was overdosing on happiness. Sophisticated brain scans highlighted the exact bits of his brain responsible for his blithe state. It was now possible to map happiness in a person. This research already has many applications. Imagine you've just paid millions to an advertising company to promote your new car and they assure you their subliminal messages will put people in a happy buying mood. The same ads are shown to people while undergoing the brain scans and it shows otherwise. You're going to want a refund on your million dollars. Human emotions and the science underlying them were the central thread to a series called *Primal Instincts*.

This was a long shoot, eight weeks back and forth across the US. My travelling partner's passport identified him as Warwick Finlay but the world knows him as Wok. He's a sound recordist with a zillion years' experience and cunning to match. If you've met Wok and have at least one working ear and a heartbeat you will have heard his proclamation: 'Being part of a documentary film crew is the second-best job in the world.' What a conversation starter. Even the most socially inept can hit that one back over the net. Who's got the best then? According to Wok, it's Sir David Attenborough. To his way of thinking both of them do the same thing – travel the world to unlikely places and meet unlikely people – only David Attenborough doesn't have to carry the twenty cases of gear. Even if I didn't agree with Wok, it might go unnoticed as cameramen and soundos go under the collective moniker of 'the crew'. Often there is the presumption that what one says goes for both. In this case it did. If you thrive on experiences, don't so much care for great personal wealth, want to travel, meet everyone from prince to pauper, get access to inaccessible places, have someone organise it all for you and you don't mind carrying a box or two, then shooting documentaries is the job for you.

Early in the trip we had a day off in San Francisco. I went for a run with a few friends: sixty thousand of them. The twelve-kilometre-long colourful and eccentric Bay to Breakers run is the biggest foot race in the world. Running while away on shoots helps clear my mind and counters the sedentary nature of plane travel. My body didn't agree. Next morning I woke sick, really sick, and it continued for three days. Shooting schedules take a massive amount of work to coordinate and rain, hail, shine or sickness they go on. The only way I could cope was to light an interview, frame the person in a wide shot, lock it all off and for the next forty minutes until the tape needed changing, I would leave the room, find some grass and shade, and rest. (I was to find out later that the ABC had a replacement cameraman ready to fly in. It was thought I had contracted the SARS virus during an outbreak in San Francisco at the time.)

A few days later I came good but it did highlight a problem of these trips: fatigue. At best it's six days on, one off. There are many times you miss a day off and it's nearly two weeks of twelve- to sixteen-hour days before a rest. Those days are mentally exhausting. Just getting from A to B is taxing, which is why on this long and well-funded shoot, we had producer Paul Faint and associate producer Anna Cater making up our team of four. There were seventeen flights and as many locations. Later I found a note in my diary: 'I'm tired. I have averaged three hours a night for the past five nights.' Sleep, when you get it, better be good.

Rested and enthused, we made for Chicago and the notorious slum area Cabrini Green. In the 1960s, large public housing tenements were built there but it was to be a social experiment gone wrong. At the height of its lawlessness Chicago police refused to enter for fear of their lives. Things had quietened for our arrival but the apartments were still unpleasant, rundown and scary. Seven people had been murdered there in the last two weeks. There were more real gunshots outside the residents' doors than there were on the nightly TV police dramas. The families there were trapped by their socioeconomic situation and lived in an environment fuelled by anger, another of the emotions investigated in our series.

The local kids participated in anger awareness programs at the local Byrd Community School. They looked and acted like normal kids but the metal detectors and physical bag searches mandatory before gaining entry to the school suggested these five- to nine-year-olds had seen a lot more than my daughters Georgia and Sophie had. Their early exposure to drugs, guns and violence didn't stop them liking magic tricks. I launched into a quick show but had my rapt attention stolen by the PA speaker that crackled into life: 'Students, stand and face the flag.' 'The Star-Spangled Banner' struck up and with hand on heart everyone proudly sang along. My moment was gone and we got back to filming, which is apparently why we were there.

Any chance we could we opted to drive rather than fly. Flying, with all the checkouts, hire-car drop-offs, check-ins and flight delays can end up taking longer for shorter trips. We followed the Ohio Turnpike across three states. We were in my favourite of all cars, the hire car. I don't care what model, I never feel as relaxed driving as I do in a hire car: a full tank of fuel, if it breaks down someone drives a replacement to you, and a little bag to put your rubbish in. I've thought of having one on permanent hire at home. Every Sunday night while I was sleeping the hire-car firm would back the old one out and slip a new one into its place. That, to me, is driving bliss.

Lorain County on the shores of Lake Erie was the home of James and Mary Filliagi, a down-to-earth couple living in a small tidy house only fifteen metres from a railway line. He had spent thirty-five years in car assembly plants and she dished out meals at a local school. They were working-class people living in an unappealing landscape of broken-down storefronts, out-of-plumb power poles with their cables strangling the view and factories spewing out steam. They also had a son on death row. Jimmy 'the Fuse' Filliagi had murdered his ex-wife Lisa in a fit of rage. In a landmark legal case he claimed a controversial biological defence: Jimmy claimed he was 'born bad' and was 'genetically predetermined' to bouts of anger. The courts didn't agree.

Jimmy's parents enjoyed having fresh ears to tell their story to. The best part of a day and night passed, much of it on their couch, surrounded by childhood photos of a murderer-to-be. There was much more to tell and they insisted we stay for dinner. Turned out vegetarianism wasn't big in this part of the country either. Around midnight we went to leave. Mary knew we were to visit Jimmy in jail a few days on. She was envious. Her visits were rare and allowed no physical contact. She hadn't touched her son for seven years. Opening her arms to Paul she gave him a big hug and said, 'Give this hug to my boy Jimmy and tell him I love him.'

While 'media friendly' and 'Australian court system' aren't often found in the same sentence – I've spent hundreds of hours on footpaths outside courts because cameras aren't allowed in – the American system is far more accommodating. We needed to get shots of Jimmy's attorney in court. The cigar-chewing James Burge was sixty, fit, immaculately dressed in fine Italian suits and, as he confessed to us, an obsessive compulsive on medication.

At the Lorain Courthouse the judge's assistant invited us into an office and immediately directed me to another door. 'Just go through,' she said. Laughing about something insignificant, I left the others and walked on through. I almost died. The door separated the judge's chamber from the courtroom. In mid-chuckle I had burst into an active courtroom, just a pace to the side of the judge's right shoulder. Everyone went silent and looked at me. Bug-eyed and my ears burning I went straight into reverse without turning and gently pulled the door closed. I said to the judge's assistant, 'Why did you do that?'

'You wanted pictures in the courtroom, didn't you?'

A brief discourse followed in which I explained the sanctimony of courts in Australia. She told me I had total access, anywhere – just don't make too much noise.

I inched my way back into the courtroom, off to one side, to wait for Jim Burge's case. Currently in session was an extradition hearing in which an African American prisoner was defending himself. Dressed in grey and white striped prison clothes and manacled from wrist to ankle, he bumbled through his argument to be extradited to South Carolina where the death penalty didn't exist. The judge dismissed his claim and as the prisoner was being led from the court he said loud enough that I could hear, 'Go kiss your white ass.' The judge responded by adding to his sentence another thirty days, but as he was in for life this was a bit of a technicality. I had been in many courtrooms before but never seen it from this view, the judge's.

Another judge, Edward M. Zaleski, had sentenced Jimmy Filliagi to death. Again, it would probably not have happened in Australia, but he agreed to re-enact the sentencing for us. It was quite sobering to hear. 'Would you like it again?' he suggested. Well, yes. He read it four times so we could shoot from different angles. I was stunned by his cooperation. As he left the empty court the judge thought to offer, 'We have the evidence box. Would that be useful?' What that entailed none of us knew but we'd all been around long enough to know that you say yes and sorted it out later. Five minutes passed and a young woman entered with a cardboard box. 'Just make sure it all goes back in when you're finished,' were the only restrictions. Evidence bags containing the bloodstained clothes, the flattened lead slug removed from Lisa's head, chilling photos in which her open-eyed body stared directly at camera and macabre shots of every stage of her autopsy were left in our care. This openness and access didn't stop at the courthouse, it extended to the crime scene as well.

It was after five and people were driving home from work. The street we were parked in could have been the setting for any number of middle-class family sitcom shows. There were two houses involved in Lisa's murder, one where it started and one where it ended. We waited outside the latter. Into the drive pulled a car and out hopped a man in his forties. Anna and Paul walked over and introduced themselves. Within five minutes they were back saying that this man, named Brian, had agreed to have a foreign film crew take over his house, completely unannounced, and film a murder re-creation. All credit to Anna and Paul. Little had changed in the house except for interior decoration, so we were able to authentically retrace every movement, which we knew so well from our morning with the evidence box. When Brian found out that his towel cupboard was where Jimmy had put the gun to the cowering Lisa's head and pulled the trigger, he started to wish he hadn't agreed.

Brian's house was the easy one. Two doors up was where Lisa called 911 pleading for her life. At the time it belonged to Lisa's partner Eric, and it still did. Eric had refused to speak to any media since the trial seven years earlier, but that wasn't going to stop Anna and Paul. I don't know how they did it but half an hour later we were at Eric's house. Caution turned to friendly assistance when he realised we were not there to sensationalise his misfortune. Another late finish and another missed dinner. Eric insisted we stay and he called out for pizza. At eleven-thirty that night, I sat on yet another couch, chomping pizza and washing it down with beer, as photos of a murdered woman watched over these strange proceedings. The couch phenomenon never ceases to amaze me.

May 29, 2003 was fifty years to the day since Sir Edmund Hillary climbed Mt Everest – yet another reminder of my regretful meeting. It was also the day I visited Jimmy 'the Fuse' Filliagi on death row, a prison within a prison within a prison at Mansfield Correctional Facility in rural northern Ohio. Concrete block walls, light blue in colour, with vertical strips of heavy security glass, flanked us on the long corridor leading in. Everything was smooth and featureless. In sound recordists' parlance the room was 'live'.

To you and me that meant it sounded hollow and echoed. Wok wasn't a happy chappie on the walk in. The sounds of clunking magnetic latches echoing throughout signalled his job would be that much harder. Big letters on the door read DEATH ROW. We were there. The warden met us and outlined the terms of our meeting. We had one hour exactly from the moment he passed the threshold of the door. Our room had a choice of powder blue or powder blue walls. It wasn't my idea of a background for an interview with a murderer, but I could make it work. Everything was set and we waited.

Jimmy was escorted in. He was much heavier and jowlier than in the news footage we had seen of him as a handsome younger man. His hand extended out to us but was cut short in its trajectory by the prison manacles that made his movements short and sharp. What struck me immediately was how much he looked like my brother Shane who, like Jimmy, had had wild and troubled teenage years. My brother, whom I'm so proud of, turned out great and Jimmy was here. Time was pressing so we started rolling and asking questions. At Jimmy's insistence, nothing was off limits. 'What have I got to lose?' was his reasoning.

'Hands up I did it,' he started, 'and I gotta pay.' His name 'the Fuse' came from the troublesome switch that was in his chest. You could hit him, spit on him and he'd stay cool, but poke him in the chest as you made your point, that was anyone's worst mistake. He had been in hundreds of dust-ups from an early age and wondered how he had managed not to kill anyone sooner. We'd almost begin to like the guy and he'd lose us just as quickly. He hadn't loved Lisa for six months before he killed her. At the time, 'She was just a piece of pussy and I could get plenty more of that.' He told us the morbid realities of his short future that included twenty-two hours a day in isolated lockdown. Ohio State offered prisoners the choice of lethal injection or the electric chair. 'Real men take the chair,' he said. 'They take the chair to win the respect of fellas who won't be around to tell the story. How's that for a fucked-up reality?' Jimmy had made his peace and looked forward to the day his suffering would end, so much so that he had become 'a volunteer', an inmate who had waived all appeals and in effect 'queue jumped' to the Death House, as it was called.

Our hour was quickly up and the warden made true his promise. Jimmy shuffled towards the door and Paul stepped in his path. 'Your mum asked me to give you this.' Paul leaned in and passed on the big hug to the tough but powerless man. Jimmy smiled and that was that.

Paul pondered on the slightly surreal moment he'd just had and I couldn't help but compare my life with Jimmy's. My twenty-year milestone with the ABC had recently passed and I felt I had another twenty exciting years ahead. My future was full of opportunity and hope. All Jimmy could look forward to was being let out of his cell for two hours a day until he was executed.

Where anger had secured Jimmy his one-way ticket to jail, happiness had created a different sort of prison for New York man George Holden. George was morbidly obese. The pleasure receptors in his brain went into overdrive at the sight, smell and even the mention of food. He'd eaten all the pies and licked the plate clean along the way to happily eating himself to death.

Our first meeting with George wasn't the best. The noisy doorbell at the small weatherboard house woke the entire house: grandpa, uncle, nephew, sister-in-law and George. I'm guessing a 'get up and get going' attitude wasn't a big part of George's childhood. It was 11am. A crusty-eyed George opened the door to find us standing there with a small mountain of equipment. With nonstop apologies he gestured us in. Creaky internal stairs led up. They had threadbare covering and a halfway landing where the steps turned at right angles. 'Don't step on the landing, take a big step over it,' George cautioned. A thin sheet of warped plywood had settled over time to show the telltale outline of an irregular one-metre-diameter hole. George confided later that the old boards had given way under his weight, his massive body plunging to his thighs, stopped only by the circumference of his girth being way larger than the structural beams he came to rest against.

George was a big African American man. Because he was a big man he had a big car: a big black Cadillac that was left-hand drive, which excited me. To an Australian cameraman a left-hand drive car is bliss. The viewfinders on the type of cameras used for TV are on the wrong side, the left side. Take my word, the difference is enormous. Without resorting to time-consuming expensive alternatives, shooting in Australian cars limits you to unflattering profile shots of the driver. A general rule of thumb for framing up a shot is to be able to see both eyes when a person is talking, and that's what I could easily do with George in this spacious, swaying, gas-guzzling late eighties Cadillac. We were headed to a smorgasbord restaurant to film his eating habits. En route we collected George's gay partner, David, a waif-thin effeminate man sporting a green safari suit, wide-brimmed hat and patent leather shoulder bag. They were quite the couple.

No pain, none of the unusual body contortions, no twelve kilograms of camera pummelling my shoulder as the car took the bumps, I was comfortable and enjoying the ride down the Brooklyn Expressway in the rain, though not as much as George. He had just lit up a marijuana joint the size of a cigar. Plumes of smoke curled and quickly filled the car interior. At that moment I was struck by another MOC (a moment of contrast) in my job. Ten years earlier I had been sitting in the same relative position beside Sister Anne Maree as she readied for take-off on the Longreach airstrip. Then it had been a small white woman, now it was a big black man. She was a selfless person on a mission to give of herself, he on a hedonistic pursuit of self-gratification. Sister Anne Maree had crossed herself and exclaimed, 'Lord bless us safely and get us all to Sunnyside.' George sucked in a lungful and as he handed the joint back to an eager David he said, 'Sweet Jesus, taste the nectar.'

The longer I worked the more 'sinner and the saint' type moments I had. This continually drove home to me how unusual my job was in its breadth, but not depth. Many people have commented that I must have acquired a large depth of knowledge over the years; quite the opposite. The way cameramen flit from one job to the next, not really involved in the research or planning stages of the story, means we have a shallow floodplain of facts and figures to draw on. Only I can't get to them in time. I am forever clicking my fingers saying, 'Oh, I know about that ... I worked with that person, what was it they said?' By the time I remember, the conversation has long moved on. This contributes to my being a poor conversationalist, something Vicky knows only too well. I drift off topic very easily as I start trawling for a thought, then someone will say a trigger word and my brain spins off on that tangent imagining possibilities. Some take my silence as rudeness or lack of interest. I like to say it's the curse of a creative mind but really there are no excuses. I just don't think I have a zippy enough brain. Mine is more like George's Cadillac: overloaded and lumbering.

The moments of contrast continued. One month I was in the middle of the Indian Ocean on the tiny Cocos Keeling Islands, the next I was in the middle of the Pacific Ocean on the Hawaiian islands. Meeting me there was one of the Richards again, Dr Richard Smith. It was unavoidable but we had to spend one night in Waikiki, the showcase of the Ugly American Tourist. I've stayed in the cheapest hotels in the outback right through to the cheapest hotels in big cities, I've had cockroaches in the kettle and pubic hairs in the bed sheets, but this hotel was the filthiest I'd ever seen. It was the sort of place where you wipe your feet on the way out.

We quickly escaped this waffle-devouring, loudmouthed slice of humanity to the cobalt-blue depths of the ocean. Surrounding us were million-dollar game-fishing boats in the Kona Classic, one of the world's premier game-fishing events. They were hunting the magnificent blue marlin. We, however, were on a seven-metre research boat hunting larval marlin. Dr Andrew West was a world authority on these juvenile fish and it was his boat, or at least that's what he told us at the start. Turns out it wasn't his boat. He was typical of many researchers I have met over the years; he was severely underfunded and it was his passion for his work that kept him going. This always struck a chord with me. Embarrassed by the idea of his regular boat being seen on television, he begged a friend for the use of this one on the condition that he get the motor serviced; it wouldn't idle and was hard to start. Time got away on Andrew and he neglected the service.

Andrew was the one person in the world able to hand-catch larval marlin. His tools were a hand-held net and a pair of polarising sunglasses. With the engine just a notch above idle he would stand on the bow of the slow-moving boat and scour the waters ahead. It seemed impossible. Larval marlin are the size of an underperforming guppy – about the size of a cigarette butt – and the ocean is considerably larger. Hours passed and the novelty had worn off this trying to find a needle in a haystack game. Sound recordist Anthony Frisina was burning nicely under the clear skies, Richard was worrying about the time and I was concerned about my dwindling camera battery supply.

Andrew gently lowered the net once more then yelled, 'Let's go.' In that benign, casual movement he had just done what few in the world have: caught a newborn marlin. And I had done what no one ever had – filmed a baby blue marlin for television. We had to move quickly as the little fish would last no more than twenty minutes out of the ocean. Richard and Andrew suited up for getting underwater footage while Anthony and I set about filming close-ups of this tiny animal. Through the camera it looked like a Disney animation of a baby fish. Its eyes were disproportionately large in its little body. Already it had an unmistakeable dorsal fin.

Richard was an experienced underwater cinematographer and Andrew's specialised knowledge of fish behaviour augured well for them to get some rare footage. Within minutes, Richard, Andrew and the little marlin were snorkelling away in the clear water.

Anthony and I busied ourselves getting out of the sun and finding a cold drink. Happy that we could switch off for a bit while our two underwater experts took over, we started chatting. Twenty minutes later we checked on their progress. In the distance were two small dots waving to us. What looked like glassy still water was hiding a strong current and it was taking them away. Anthony and I looked at one another as if to say, well, you better start the boat and go get them. It was then we discovered our combined lack of seamanship. Somehow, somewhere, an assumption was made that Anthony and I knew something about boats. What I knew about boats you could stick in a matchbox and still have room for the matches. Anthony didn't rate much better. Camera crews do share a common trait of being fairly practical and able to work out things in a nuts-and-bolts fashion, though. We'd seen boats started before so that didn't seem too difficult: prime the fuel line, find neutral, press the start button and full steam ahead. But this boat had missed its service. It was not going to start, at least not for us.

There was an auxiliary nine-horsepower outboard motor alongside the main motor. Unlike the shiny new boat it was attached to, it looked decades old. It was. The rubber throttle on the steering arm had turned to tar which stuck to our hands like black grease. We took it in turn to pull on the start cord but couldn't get it to kick over. Finally it screamed into life emitting a cloud of blue smoke larger than the one from George Holden's marijuana joint. We set a course for our receding black dots and the boat laboured towards them, the undersize emergency engine coughing and spluttering.

As things settled I noticed the black tar had found its way onto the seats, onto the gleaming white walls of the console, onto the shiny control panel. Every time we moved we spread more of the cancerous goop. It was impossible not to. We seemed to be gaining little ground when 'snap', the steering arm of the outboard motor broke off in Anthony's hand. Decades of neglect were starting to show. The throttle, now welded to Anthony's hand with black goop, was attached by a few cables to the engine, which I now steered by physically holding the engine's cowling and turning as needed. By the time we reached the waterlogged pair they were physically spent from swimming against the current trying to reach what they thought to be a couple of idiots in the boat. Andrew wasn't happy as he climbed in, and was less so when he found his boat covered in black tar.

Richard is an amazing man. He's intelligent, talented and, like Glenn Singleman, has an amazing tenacity, an ability to keep going in the face of all logistical odds. When all else around them says turn back, these guys keep going. Had we been born a century or two earlier these guys would have been the Captain Cooks or the Scotts of Antarctica. They reason using sound logic and are not enslaved by convention. They both live by the rule you've got to get out of your comfort zone if you're ever going to move forward. The downside is the attendant stress that accompanies it. Richard's took the form of a loss of appetite and slowly rubbing his forehead. By shoot's end he was noticeably thinner and slightly balder.

Richard easily does the work of a handful of people, drawing his energy from his passion and vision, but no matter how diligently he applies himself to crossing the t's and dotting the i's, he's no match for the permit system that awaits any filmmaker. Permits and the requirement to have them are slowly strangling the ability to make factual television. It's not just the number of permits needed, or their dollar cost, or the administrative time involved, it's that once you have a permit, there is no guarantee you'll be able to film when you get there. Often ignoring the correct procedures and just taking your chances on the day produces better results.

We headed to Mexico to shoot a story on Mayan culture that took us into rarely visited ancient tunnels running under the Pyramids of the Sun and Moon at Teotihuacan. These tunnels were visited by few and getting there was a coup. Richard had also acquired the necessary permits for the Mexico City Museum of Anthropology. We were accompanied around by two museum representatives and an armed guard. Unlike most museums and art galleries worldwide, here there were no restrictions on the amount of light I could shine on the artefacts. I had lights and cables going everywhere and the most reaction I got from any staff was a yawning nod.

Later in the day I plugged a battery charger into a wall socket to replenish my dwindling power supply. The security guard rushed over and unplugged the charger, at the same time indicating that I should stop filming. Garbled words on the walkie-talkies filled the cavernous hall and more museum staff showed up. I was at a loss as to what I had done. We were directed to our copies of our expensive and comprehensive permit, one that permitted us to film the museum's entire Mayan exhibition. Our oversight? We had not specified 'charging of batteries' on the permit and therefore it would not be allowed. Eventually it was sorted at the cost of a few lost hours of valuable filming time. Richard rubbed his forehead in disbelief and wondered what troubles lay ahead for us in New York, a city in love with permits.

Before New York, though, we headed to Mexico's Yucatan Peninsula, to the site of the meteor impact that was said to have caused the extinction of the dinosaurs. Our work there took a few days and, as was often the case, only the aerials were holding us up. Richard had hired the best charter firm in the city of Merida. As it was situated at the main airport, we could do the hour-long flight then easily catch our commercial flight back to Mexico City.

The general aviation hangars looked like they did at any other airport so the charter company's office came as a surprise. A nondescript door led into a split-level space with Doric columns, polished marble floors and trompe l'oeil walls. I'd been in many charter companies and none had looked like this. I began to quietly wonder what cargo they might transport that paid so well.

In a manner reminiscent of a 1930s musical, our pilot made his entrance down the small but grand staircase. He looked like a Mexican pilot should, with a black moustache and gold jewellery. His limited English was double our ability with Spanish. We made it clear that we needed to catch a flight to Mexico City later so if we could, we'd look at the maps, make a flight plan and get going. He said he had no maps. Obviously our Australian accents made our spoken English a little difficult for him. Slowly and clearly we repeated ourselves, to which he replied with a big smile, 'I understood you. I have no maps.'

It seemed unlikely but we had managed to book possibly the only air charter company in the world that operated without maps. Richard began rubbing his forehead in disbelief. On a nearby coffee table I found a local tourist magazine and flicked through to the map section. The best map available to us was a half-page one that showed the local tourist spots. It sported little icons of palm trees, flamingos, Aztec temples and frolicking beach-goers. With a pen we drew a route and emphasised the main destination was the town of Yaxcopoil, where the researchers had drilled a one-kilometre shaft down into the centre of the meteor crater.

At the plane our pilot proudly displayed the specially designed window that hinged upwards to allow clear shots. We were paying extra for this privilege. While strapping myself in, I caught the eye of a twenty-something-year-old local man standing next to my open door. I smiled and nodded that I was fine and didn't need his assistance. The pilot said in his heavy Mexican accent, 'Is Ronnie. Please, you must get out. Ronnie must get in.' I was apologetic as I felt I had embarrassed him. I got out and helped him into the small back seat alongside Richard. Who's Ronnie? I thought to myself. Often I miss out on key bits of information as there's always something that needs filming. He must have been another of the scientists I hadn't met. The plane took to the heavens on a very potholed runway. The early afternoon heat and humidity made the flying very bumpy and I knew immediately it would be almost useless for shooting aerials. I was still wondering who Ronnie was.

I opened the special filming window and quickly saw the locking stay had lost its mounting screws. The plane was bouncing along at two hundred kilometres an hour and the window flapped violently and noisily. I looked to the pilot for assistance and he just smiled a big cheesy grin which did nothing to help. Maybe Richard could help but he was bent over rubbing his forehead. I gestured to Ronnie to help. He was able to hold the flap steady. The bumps were getting worse and we were getting tossed around by the thermals.

Starting an orbit around a township, the pilot fingered the map on the word Yaxcopoil. We had just spent two days in the small village of Yaxcopoil; below us was a town of several thousand.

'No, no, not Yaxcopoil, not Yaxcopoil,' Richard said.

'Sí, sí, is Yaxcopoil,' countered the pilot, still fingering the map.

'No, no,' returned Richard.

'Sí, señor, is Yaxcopoil.'

As we flew continuous bumpy orbits around the township Richard and the pilot discussed the merits of map reading. Richard was sure we had taken a wrong turn at the flamingo icon and we were currently over the icon of a petrol pump.

Time was getting away as we hopelessly circled the same wrong town with yet no useful footage in the bumpy conditions. Clearly the pilot had no idea and Richard returned to rubbing his forehead. A decision had to be made which way to go and Ronnie made it for us. The first I knew of it was the smell, next the surging and retreating wave of thick yellow green liquid coming from under my seat. Ronnie had projectile-vomited in the back seat of the small plane. It was like someone had stuck a stick of dynamite in a can of pineapple pieces. Richard had taken some direct hits and all credit to him for trying to rescue my camera bag from the rising tide of Ronnie's lunch. Richard resumed rubbing his forehead in disbelief and I think I heard him moan. There was no option but to head back empty-handed.

As we washed ourselves at an outside tap on the ground, I quizzed Richard about Ronnie. Who was he? Richard had no idea – he thought I knew. It turned out Ronnie was the nephew of the receptionist. He was bored, so came for the ride. As our Mexicana Airlines took off with us on board, through the window we saw our small plane sitting with its doors open, airing out. Surely our filming in New York would go much better.

Steam was coming from Richard's ears when we walked from the New York mayor's office where our filming permit was waiting. To get to this stage had taken months of original documents being security-posted between the US and Australia. ABC lawyers had been dragged in, the head of television needed to sign off, all of this just to get a few shots of what is essentially a busy city street. The issue was the tripod. Many places, central London included, ban tripods because the streets are simply too busy. Thinking ahead, Richard had about a dozen locations added to the list, just in case, but Times Square was the goal, as was the New York Stock Exchange. At the mayor's office there was no permit waiting for Richard Smith from the ABC, Australia. Richard explained every step of the long and costly process he had followed to the letter. Still no permit. Just as he was about to rub his forehead and let go an involuntary moan he spied a corner of a form jutting from a pending tray. 'That's it, that's it,' he said to the uninterested woman.

'Oh, yes ... Richard Smith from NBC in ... say where? ... Autalia?'

She read it exactly as it was typed on the form. Close enough thought Richard and as he clutched it dearly I could see his blood pressure lower. In the next breath the woman motioned for its return. With a red marker she drew a thick line through one of the locations and handed it back. Times Square had been ruled out.

'What does that mean?' asked Richard.

'You can't film there. Not today, not tomorrow. They're filming *Spiderman* all over the city. They've got streets blocked off everywhere. They've got set-ups all over Times Square. Sorry, honey.'

Schedules are schedules. Ours said Times Square that night so we went ahead, dodging the police and using the tripod as little as possible. It reached the point where the good-natured cops couldn't see the funny side any longer and we headed off. The shots weren't what we wanted but we needed to get some sleep before the Stock Exchange the following morning. It was about 10.30pm when Richard's phone rang. It was the person organising our Stock Exchange visit: 'Hi, I forgot to mention, your cameraman has to wear a suit. Have a nice night.'

They say New York never sleeps, but the people who sell suits do. Our only chance was early next morning on the way to the Stock Exchange. I knew New York quite well and found a place that opened early, but every suit had unhemmed sleeves and cuffs. There's nothing that gaffer tape can't fix. Our window of opportunity closed in on us. There wasn't enough time to select, purchase and gaffer tape up the legs and sleeves of the suit. Richard groaned and rubbed his forehead. No doubt about it, with an increasing number of obstacles and shrinking budgets, making factual TV was getting harder. Watching Richard doing battle on a daily basis confirmed what I already knew: I was never cut out to be a producer. I've tried it a few times and it left me cold. One shoot in New Zealand indicates why.

I was always happy to be in New Zealand's capital city, Wellington, especially now I had Vicky's daughter Helen and her family to visit. The ABC crew met them, as that afternoon they became our rent-a-family for some scenes we needed. Everything went well apart from the younger kids calling me Grandpa again.

The next few days were a whirlwind and typical of many New Zealand shoots we were doing then. A waiting helicopter took us and all our gear across the stunning Marlborough Sound on the north end of New Zealand's South Island. The chopper headed to the remote fishing village of French's Pass where we put down in someone's yard next to their pig pen. The pigs looked up in disbelief at the big red thing coming from the sky but they were the only ones. No one from the ten or so houses came out. I would never have thought you could land a helicopter in a domestic yard unnoticed. There we met local Maoris and traded our chopper for their car keys. They went ahead to the remote and stunningly beautiful Stephen's Island while we drove their car and picked up some local shots. The chopper returned for us and took us to Stephen's Island for a traditional Maori welcome. A feast followed. For the rest of the day and night until 3am we filmed a prehistoric lizard called the tuatara.

A short sleep, quad bikes, helicopter again, commercial flight to Auckland, hire car, and onto a boat that took us to Kawau Island where more quad bikes waited. A quick meeting with new researchers and we quad-biked our way over mountainous terrain to film the trapping of rare brushtailed rock wallabies. Laid-on adventure, laid-on transport, laid-on access to places and animals few get to see – this is why I loved working with the science unit. I would never give this up. The only regret I had over these New Zealand trips was failing miserably, time after time, in the small part we had to play at traditional Maori welcomes. We could stand proud until we were required to sing a song that held some meaning for us. Invariably it was a flat, out of tune, half-hearted rendition of 'Advance Australia Fair'. It was embarrassingly bad, especially as it always followed a beautiful, traditional Maori song delivered by a sweet voice. That always caused me to choke up. Enough was enough; I wasn't going to let this happen again.

On a subsequent New Zealand trip our focus was on an animal central to Maori culture, the pacific rat or kiore. The original Maori forefathers brought with them two animals, the dog and the rat. If they could find out where the rat came from, it would provide a clue as to the origins of the Maori. Auckland-based anthropologist Dr Lisa Matisoo-Smith was the central character in our story. Her knowledge of Maori culture was welcome, as there were some culturally sensitive areas to be negotiated in this story.

We had ten days before our traditional welcome by the Maoris of Whangarei, ten days to finally get this right. With me were producer Louise Heywood and reporter Jonica Newby. Both were smart, talented women and both, it turned out, could hold a tune. It was to be their responsibility to represent the ABC while I would provide motivation and support from the ranks. Something about the power of the haka and the gentleness of the Maoris' singing stirred a lot of emotion in me during these ceremonies and I'd convinced myself that it wasn't what you sang that mattered, as long as you sang with sincerity. Somehow, maybe in a moment of combined weakness, Louise and Jonica bought into my untested theory. Long drives between locations were the perfect opportunity for them to polish their act. When the day arrived they were well rehearsed, though a little nervous.

As we approached the cultural centre of the Ngatiwai people, warriors approached us waving clubs and spears. The haka was performed at full tilt. (I don't think it is ever done any other way.) They laid down challenge tokens that we were to pick up to show we came in peace. The Maori women began the welcoming call and the warriors backed off as we slowly advanced. Inside we were motioned to stand opposite rows of Maori elders. Prayers and speeches were offered to us in Maori and beautiful, beautiful singing followed. My eyes welled involuntarily. Louise and I gave a brief speech and about thirty pairs of expectant eyes waited for our song. Five times before I had seen that same expression turn to one of shock and bemusement as the Aussie monotone took to the stage. Not this time, no more turgid anthems, we were just about to knock their socks off. As Jonica and Louise made moves to start, anthropologist Lisa leaned and whispered to me, 'What are they going to sing?'

I proudly returned the whisper: 'Bonnie Tyler's "Total Eclipse of the Heart".'

Lisa's eyes widened and she lurched forward and politely elbowed her way through Jonica and Louise. She spoke a few Maori words and began a gentle traditional Maori song. I've since realised that's what traditional cultural meetings require: traditional songs. Apparently, lyrics full of sexual tension, where someone is a powder keg and their lover is giving off sparks, where it all ends in one big bang, aren't a big step forward in trans-Tasman relations. Maybe my belief that sincerity would conquer all would never have survived that 1980s pop song. Just like the PR man back in Los Alamos, Lisa asked, 'W-h-y?' This is exactly why I'm a cameraman and not a producer. Not only don't I like the endless organisation and administration that befalls producers, I'm often too quick to say what's really on my mind. 'Diplomatically retarded' is a term I've heard used.

# 12

# Death is caused by swallowing small amounts of saliva over a long period of time.

It's simple maths really. Twenty years at, let's say, three hundred days a year shooting, each of those days shooting a minimum of five scenes. Conservatively I've shot at least thirty thousand set-ups. After a while you get the hang of things. My professional confidence was at an all-time high. I felt as though I could walk into any situation and photographically I could handle it. And that was a good position to be in. One of the stresses of this job is that there is rarely a second bite of the cherry. I know history repeats itself but when it's unfolding in front of you and there is a nightly bulletin to be fed, you'd better get it right. First time. Even during preplanned shoots like interviews, often those people are available one time only. You need to get it right first time. The cameraman's world is not one of first and second drafts, rewrites and input from others. It all happens quickly and you've got no one to turn to for advice.

When we arrive on location, say someone's office, I make my introduction brief then set to work. Great sound recordists like Gunter and Wok are like gold here; they 'work' the talent, relaxing them and providing a buffer for me to quickly assess a raft of things. What natural light is there? Where are the power points? Are there noisy air conditioning ducts? Do I have to match this to a previous interview? Their eyes – are they deep-set, bulging? Any unflattering acne scars? What are they wearing? Dozens of considerations tumble around in my head and like an account balance printing out at an ATM, the answer emerges. Rarely does this take me longer than ten seconds. The physical setting of lights and blacking out of windows takes longer, though, much longer. And this is time people aren't willing to give in today's time-poor societies. Interviewees take this as an opportunity to deal with their backlog of emails, hence I am not an expert at lighting people; I'm an expert at lighting empty chairs. Experience has taught me how to overcome these artistic and creative hurdles and to do it fast, the number-one quality of the modern cameraman.

Early on in my career I wanted as much prior knowledge about a location as possible so I could previsualise scenes. Not now. I love going in blind and seeing how I can overcome the problems. Often I will take no lights at all to force myself to think outside the square, always testing myself, always looking for a challenge. I got what I was after in spades at the world's longest-running sleep experiment that happened deep inside a Philadelphia hospital. There people voluntarily tortured themselves, existing in an artificial environment where they never knew if it was day or night. This helped scientists find an answer to the question 'how little sleep can we get by on?'

The high-security sleep research unit is situated in the central part of the building where there is no chance of anyone accidentally opening a window to daylight. Surrounding it is the psychiatric ward through which we had to pass. Under no circumstances, we were instructed, should we talk to any person in the psych unit, even if they appeared sane and dressed like a doctor. The sleep unit was darker than I imagined. The only lighting came from a few laptop computer screens. There's nothing like meeting somebody for the first time when you wake them from their sleep, especially if they have been in a strange world existing on four hours' rest a day for the past month.

'Wake up, Jenny,' the researcher gently said to the lump under the bedcovers. Jenny was shocked to see a camera pointed in her face but I was even more shocked. Jenny was African American, as were all the other subjects of the study. Dark room, grumpy dark-skinned people, no lights; I had wanted a challenge and I had it. Using some computer screens, the glow from a mobile phone and a few tricks of the trade as light sources, I made it work. Often producers commented that the way I did things was different and new to them. I have always subscribed to what legendary photographer Ansel Adams said: 'There are no rules for good photographs, only good photographs.' Being my own authority was satisfying.

But challenge to me is like a drug and I found myself needing larger hits to stay on top and that wasn't happening. The reality was that things had creatively plateaued. I was on the treadmill. Mind you, if I had to be on one, this was the one. I had, as did Wok, the second-best job in the world and I never underestimated the value of that. But for me, if I am not creating in some form or another, I am a miserable sod to be around – just ask Vicky. I'm not suggesting I knew it all, it's just it was becoming more of a battle to land a gig on the programs I found stimulating. It was easier to coast along, so I did, and as soon as I did, the mistakes started. I knew this would happen, as I'd seen it happen before in climbing. Most accidents in climbing happen on the descent, once you've reached the top. After you enjoy the view from the top for a while and you feel satisfied you've reached your goal, you feel the hard work is over and switch off a bit. That is often a fatal mistake. Without full concentration and attention to detail, the easiest of moves can cause you the greatest grief.

So it was another day, another story, another check of my battery and tape supply as we headed out, this time to Amberley air force base near Brisbane. The F111 squadron were preparing for the Singapore Air Show and practising their 'dump and burns' at low level. These are where they ignite dumped fuel in a blazing twenty-metre flame trailing the aircraft. It was also the last flight for an American exchange pilot after a year in Australia. You're right, where's the story? It was of borderline value but the program I was shooting for was the chronically underfunded Queensland current-affairs program, *Stateline*. Their ridiculously small budget dictated that a cheap story was a good story.

Waiting for us at the air base were pilots, commanders, wing commanders and the base commander. This very commanding group formed a half-circle around the back of our car as the journalist and I made our introductions. The journo continued the chitchat as I gathered the gear. I opened the camera box and quickly shut it again. I felt the urge to dry-retch. I'd left the camera back at the ABC. Over my shoulder a dozen highly trained, disciplined ultra professionals waited on me. Bad, bad timing – why today? Why couldn't it have been a dozen chronic dole bludgers? They at least would have given a rousing cheer. I confessed my sins in a way my friend Jack King had shown me through example: directly, honestly and with a view to offering a solution. Luck was on my side. The afternoon's story could be brought forward and there was to be a second flight rehearsal in the afternoon.

We put our skates on, collected the camera from the ABC studios and made it to our rescheduled story on Huntington's disease. Not only did this require an approach opposite to the one needed for cocky fighter pilots, technically it was a tricky interior shoot. Gone were the days of having the luxury of a sound recordist when shooting local news and current affairs. Tightening budgets meant I handled quite tricky sound jobs as well as filming. There are lots of switches and lots of chances for things to go wrong.

Everything went as well as we had hoped and we high-tailed it back to the air force base with ten minutes to spare. The thundering roar of jet engines worried me. I was right to be concerned. A pilot named Curly ran over to us and said, 'Quick, they've gone up early, you'll just catch the dump and burn if you run.' Faster than a speeding bullet I was over there, then Curly called me back. 'You've got to get hearing protection, it's an OHS requirement.' We ran into an open doorway and scribbled above a dotted line to get a set of ear muffs. Everything I had learnt came into play and the camera was up and running none too soon. To my right was the impressive sight of an F111 barrel-rolling only fifty metres from the ground. It righted itself then lit the afterburner right in front of me.

All of this thundering, impressive, boy's own adventure action was recorded but … it was the size of a match head on the screen. In the rush I had forgotten to switch over from the wide-angle lens I'd used on the interior locations of the Huntington's disease story. Not to worry, my other lens was in my backpack and I could change a lens lightning fast, except the pilot was faster. He hooked the plane into a tight turn and dropped the landing gear for an impending touchdown. At least I'd get that. I lined up a beautiful touchdown shot. The editors would thank me for that. At the moment the puff of white smoke would have indicated touchdown, my camera jerked violently and I heard, 'Gotta remember the OHS rules.' The ear muffs had fallen from my head and Curly the pilot decided to push them back on at that very moment. There were file shots of F111s landing, no big deal. We'd get the interview and fashion a story around that.

With the young American pilot in a rush to get somewhere and as the OHS ear muffs had precluded me from wearing my headphones to check sound, I hadn't realised the microphone batteries had died. There was no sound on the interview. There was only one thing to do. I immediately rang the program's executive producer, downplayed the value of the story and encouraged her to drop it from the weekly rundown, which she did.

Tens of thousands of unpredictable filming jobs for the ABC and my mistakes could be counted on one hand. I was happy with that. That another should happen so soon shook me a bit. *Talking Heads* was a weekly program that looked into the lives of some of Australia's prominent personalities. With ABC budget cuts it went from being a studio-based program with a large crew and a multimillion dollar van to a small set-up filmed by a pair of field cameramen, like me, with tired and ill-suited equipment. But as was always the case, they wanted it to look just as good, if not better. I was asked to help create a visual style for the program and using ingenuity to overcome a lack of resources we came up with a rich and appealing product.

Occasionally I filmed for the program, one of those episodes being the celebrity chef Ian Hewitson. To make life easier for the producer, good ol' Jack King, I went all out and set up the cameras in a configuration that gave Jack a little more control, like he'd had with the original large van. To do this the cameras were operating at their full capacity or, as it turned out, a little over. Nobody got a hint that anything was wrong, not me, not Jack, not the senior technical person there and certainly not Ian Hewitson. Everything, outwardly at least, looked terrific, so much so that I was continually complimented on a fine job.

Ian Hewitson gave a very personal interview in which he broke down talking about the death of his first wife. The interview had to be halted to allow him time to recover. Treated respectfully his emotion would make powerful viewing. At the end of the interview it was back-patting all around until the tapes were checked. To everyone's surprise there was nothing on them except fuzz and squiggly lines. It's always the small things that get you. One cable, one I'd put there to make Jack's life easier, was plugged into the wrong hole and it brought the whole show down. I assumed total responsibility and still needed to break the bad news to Jack. I decided to use Jack's own approach of honesty, directness and offering a solution. That didn't seem to strike a chord at all. It wasn't a high point in our relationship and Jack had yet to tell Ian Hewitson, which wasn't going to be pretty. Ian had just made the point that the last time he had worked with the ABC was fourteen years earlier and the experience had been a bad one. They call learning from your mistakes experience, and that's what I've conveniently put this down to.

My photographic plateau continued with peaks here and there. I wasn't about to complain. In my spare time I made up for this lack of challenge by creating my own. My motivational magic shows for primary schools were chugging along. These shows were always free, as I have had a long-held view that education is a community responsibility. I could do my bit and have a lot of fun at the same time. It was 2005. By this time had done the show in over two hundred schools across the country. Dear old Dad was full steam ahead making magical props for me. Using his artistic eye he provided me with a growing range of weird, wonderful and unique magical apparatus that helped me entertain and motivate the kids. Dad was still the only person I knew who shared my two passions: photography and magic. I was very protective of my time with him.

People would often ask me how I managed to fit so much into a week; just don't sleep. This started me thinking and evolved into a talk I began giving to high-school students called 'Five Things I Wish They Had Taught Me at School'. I simply related the approaches I used to turn an idea into a reality. Both my primary and secondary shows were a hard sell at times. Ironically, people put the shutters up when they heard the word 'free'. I had to draw on a lot of inner strength to see these ideas through. Being rejected still didn't sit well with me.

The phones kept ringing and the work kept coming. *Australian Story* producer Ben Cheshire called asking if I knew anything about a couple named Glenn Singleman and Heather Swan. I sure did and was happy to work with them again on this *Australian Story* episode. Some shoots are beset by problems from the outset and this was a doozy: sound recordists having heart scares, cameras having major meltdowns, lost sound on interviews (see, it's not just me), national parks refusing filming permits, helicopters being fogged in. There was one setback in all of this that I'd never experienced and will never experience again.

BASE jumping is illegal in New South Wales national parks. Overcoming this restriction is not that hard; jumpers make illegal jumps in the still of first light. Small cameras, a light climbing rig to secure myself near the valley's edge, mountain bikes to get us there and a bit of sleep beforehand were all that were necessary. It was 5pm on the day before the jumps. An early dinner was planned so I could spend the evening preparing the gear. I had always been a stickler for top-notch preparation.

Nearing the town of Blackheath my phone rang. It was Vicky, crying. Through sobs she told me Dad had died. I went very quiet. I was shocked by what I felt: nothing. Well, not nothing, more a numbness, but there was no wave of grief, no welling of the eyes, not a snuffle. What sort of a callous bastard was I? I've questioned my lack of feelings before and here it confronted me head on.

The others in the car asked what had happened. Their immediate response was 'We've got to get you to the airport and straight home.' My response was no, which I could see shocked them a bit. But I knew my family. We're not the type to sit around the table holding hands and wondering why. We would deal with it privately. That is the Mather way. Even Vicky agreed. Besides, Ben had suffered so many setbacks on this shoot to date, I felt I should stay one more day to see it through.

Everyone's show of support was terrific but I still needed to prepare the gear. This took hours and gave me ample time to reflect on the sort of person I was. I'd never lost anyone really close before. This wasn't like my dog dying. You only get one father. This wasn't a dress rehearsal for the real thing. My head was filled with thoughts of Dad but my heart was numb. It neared 11pm and I was all set for the morning. There was one last thing to do: flick the light switch and catch some sleep. The lights went out and the emotion was turned on. A torrent of grief escaped my body. I literally roared with pain, like a handful of my guts had been grabbed and slowly twisted and twisted upon itself. I just started talking, apologising to Dad for all the things I had done wrong by him but were left unspoken. It really hurt. My photographic mentor and my magic confidant were gone as well as someone who was always unconditionally proud of me. So this was grief.

I learnt something about myself that night, something I already knew but never fully appreciated: my intensity and my project-driven nature. If I start something I never leave it unfinished. I couldn't even grieve for my father until I'd tidied up every loose end. It's both a blessing and a curse.

I'd lost someone with finality and in a natural order. That was a lot easier to accept compared with a parent faced with the loss of their child. This was the situation of Lee and Christine Rush, the parents of Scott Rush, one of the Bali Nine, convicted of heroin smuggling and now facing execution by the Indonesian government. They didn't trust me, I was absolutely sure of that. We'd just met in the foyer of a Bali hotel, exchanged handshakes, moved to a bar, ordered some Bintang beers and the whole while they didn't say a word. Lee was wound up tight as a steel cable and his first words were, 'I don't trust you,' followed by 'at all.' Seemed pretty clear to me. That I was there with *Australian Story*, a program with a pretty clean journalistic record, meant nothing. Producer Helen Grasswill had skilfully nurtured and secured the story with the Rushes. It was a journalistic coup. Sitting next to me now she was working hard to allay their concerns.

Christine was convinced but Lee was having none of it. He was only there because his legal team thought it a good idea. The family had been naive to the ways of the sensationalist pack-hunting media and had been bitten. The situation was very tense; you could hear his teeth grinding. Helen's words were washing over him and we were losing him before we'd had a chance to begin. Here we go again, I thought, I have to battle to do my job simply because a growing part of the media thinks the ends justifies the means. That I had to have my integrity questioned before I could open my mouth pissed me off. Lee was entitled to his own opinions but not his own facts. Helen and I were not journalistically bankrupt.

Lee remained steely faced. Helen's words didn't fit with Lee's language, through no fault of her own; he was a bloke's bloke. It was time to play my last card. I said to him, 'Shake my hand.'

'What?'

'Shake my hand,' I said, extending mine towards his.

His strong, rough grip was what I expected. Looking straight down the barrel at him, I said, 'You're only going to make me say this once. You have my word we did not come here to do you over.' It seemed to do the trick. It took another two hours and one or two more Bintangs but slowly, eventually, we gained their trust. Now I had to live up to it.

The story here was not Scott; it was his parents and the nightmare they were living. *Australian Story* interviews put people through the wringer. They are long: long for me sitting hunched over a camera, longer for the person who eventually transcribes the tapes to paper, longest of all for the person being interviewed. It has always been an intention of mine to have a plastic medal made up inscribed with 'I survived an *Australian Story* interview'. Recipients would be entitled to take part in the Anzac Day march, as they had served above and beyond the call of duty. There are two places you get to talk about yourself, incessantly, hour upon hour: in the psychologist's office and during an *Australian Story* interview. Both allow a person to fit together the pieces of their own personal puzzle and, more often than not, both end in tears.

Lee Rush was one tough nut to crack. He was so aware that anything he said might have a possible negative impact on his son Scott that he vetted almost each and every word, slowly and painfully. He came across as emotionless. How would anyone relate to him? Then he said something that sent shivers up my spine. He'd had a dream in which Scott was taken into a jungle clearing to face the firing squad. He ran forward and grabbed one of the soldier's guns and pointed it at Scott. 'I brought you into this world, son, and it's going to be me who takes you out of it.'

I felt the tears roll down my cheeks. This poor tormented man. I had already met Scott and again it struck me, like it had when I met Jimmy Filliagi, how he could easily have been my brother in his wilder youth. For what was a stupid mistake by a naive boy, a huge price was being exacted. Scott would pay at worst with his life, at best with twenty years of it, and his parents were being torn apart, something I could visibly see happening. Lee and Christine could have been any of the parents doing the weekly sausage sizzle at my kids' sporting club. It struck me that I was not immune to any of this, which is quite scary. Scott was a gullible boy in a reckless time of his life – just how gullible I was about to find out.

Over the course of the week my obsession with magic came up. Lee and Christine were excited. Scott had always been fascinated by magic tricks as a kid. Would I perform some for him? Maybe they thought this would give him a point of focus to help him through.

Kerobokan Prison itself was oppressive. Money needed to change hands to get in, another exchange of money so Scott could be 'found', another exchange of money to rent woven mats to sit on. The last one was a fair call. Around us wasn't a pretty picture: ponds of fetid black water, crumbling murals, cockroaches and the stench of garbage in the stifling, breezeless humidity.

Scott wasn't interested in hellos, just food. Internal prisoner politics meant he hadn't eaten yet and it was already 3pm. Down went the muesli bars, down went the pastries and lollies. Visits were around thirty minutes so Lee quickly introduced the idea that I would perform some magic. Scott was dead keen. Kneeling on the mat surrounded by Scott, Lee, Christine, Helen, Scott's Uncle Glen, a growing number of prisoners, some prison guards and a few appreciative cockroaches, I put a bit of joy into Scott's day. Scott's laughter was cut short by the clanging of a tinny-sounding bell. I left him with an unopened pack of cards and a promise that I'd send him some magic books. (I did. Whether or not they made it to him I don't know.)

Much of what I say while performing my tricks is said unmistakeably tongue-in-cheek. Scott took it all very literally. He believed everything I said. Later that night he'd managed to get a phone and called me. 'How'd you get those words to write themselves on those cards?' I tipped him the secret – who was he going to tell? – but he still didn't believe me. He was sticking to the ridiculous explanation I had given at the time. That was all part of the fun, I explained, but he wasn't having it. Aha. I began to see how Scott might have got himself into this great big mess in the first place.

# 13

## Give me the folly of enthusiasm over the indifference of wisdom any day.

Professionally these were sad times for me. I was losing my enthusiasm for the job. I didn't want to. Being a cameraman, in particular an ABC one, had shaped who I was. I loved the creativity, the travel, the people I worked with. I wanted challenge but I craved one thing more: enthusiasm; I was addicted to it.

To have a dream and see the potential laid out before you is exciting. I saw that back when I was seventeen; the land of photojournalism where stories were told with pictures was across the water somewhere. Getting there was straightforward enough. In front of me was a bridge heading that way but it wasn't yet finished, just the pillars were in place. All I needed to do was work out how to join the pillars, which of course would take hard work followed by more hard work. Enthusiasm made the task a whole lot easier. Enthusiasm is an anaesthetic for hard work. Where do you get enthusiasm? Mine comes from looking ahead; it's the excitement of always learning something new, of finding a new book that could hold secrets within its pages, of visualising where

I saw myself in a few years' time. It's a mix of hope and potential, and I love that feeling more than the activity itself. So, like an addict faced with losing a supplier, I started looking for new ways to get another hit of enthusiasm. Strangely, that came from being able to make people laugh.

I say strangely because I am not a naturally funny person. My default position in life is a notch above miserable. People have often told me I come across as surly and unapproachable when I am actually feeling quite good. The room doesn't light up when I walk in nor do I have a quick wit. However, I do have a good sense of humour and I found performing magic was a way to liberate it, especially with children. Being able to take to the stage and keep four hundred children, their teachers and their parents laughing, solidly, for forty minutes was a good feeling and a nice thing to be able to do, but it's not what I was after. My ambition was not to be an entertainer – nor do I think I had any particular aptitude for it – but that I would use entertainment as a bridge to something more personally satisfying was becoming clear. What that 'something' was started revealing itself here and there.

My school shows were steadily growing. One was at Greenslopes Primary, Brisbane, where about twenty percent of the students came from refugee backgrounds. One of these, a little boy of five from the former Yugoslav Republic, was having a tough time adjusting to life in Australia. He didn't speak a word of English, was very withdrawn and in the four months he'd been at school he hadn't smiled. The teachers were seriously concerned for him. Midway through my show two teachers pushed through the sitting children to attend to him. He was having some sort of fit. As it turned out it was a laughing fit. An infectious wave of smiles washed over the room, all delighting at this little fellow's coming out. I was unaware of this until it was explained to me later. Driving home I felt that rush of enthusiasm again, an enthusiasm for the potential that my magic could be used for something more than entertainment, an enthusiasm that maybe I could achieve what PC Graham Waddington had achieved, directly affecting the lives of kids. Meanwhile the ABC had not lost its enthusiasm for sending me away.

Trepidation is part of the package that comes with every new travelling partner, particularly nowadays as we mainly work in two-person teams: cameraman and journalist. It's refreshing to have new stories to listen to and new ideas to glean something from but it can also quickly turn sour. When hostilities arise on the first phone call, it doesn't augur well. That's what happened here. Counter to all the rules I'd set myself about choosing travelling partners carefully, I went ahead and I'm glad I did. The Princess is an affectionately derisive name for *Australian Story* producer/reporter Belinda Hawkins. Don't extend her any sympathy, for she refers to me as the 'sweaty technician'. She started it.

Childish name-calling like this is a way of coping with the stresses of intense shoots in foreign countries. Relationships between camera crews and producers had generally started to fray because of a growing lack of money to make ABC programs. There was less of it going around and there was a lot of cutting corners. People like Belinda and me found ourselves at odds with each other, forced into defending our own corners by a system that no longer had the money to properly fund programs. Though we were both committed to making the best stories possible, at times we were at each other over how our limited money should be spent. A long flight to Cape Town gave us time to iron out our differences and we realised we could work well together as a team.

Teamwork was central to the story we were doing. Each year a different country hosts the World Homeless Soccer Cup. This is street soccer with only four a side. Forty-eight nations send their socially marginalised to compete for gold in a sort of outcast Olympics. In 2006 it was held in South Africa. Australia sent a team and *Australian Story* sent us. Wherever they went, we went,

Australia's finest homeless with the Princess and the 'sweaty technician' in tow, camera and microphone at the ready.

We followed the ever-optimistic coach George Halkias as he negotiated airports and their requisite unhelpful staff. With him was the team he was unquestioningly devoted to, eight young men with various grasps on reality. Brian was a gangly likeable goth who battled anger outbursts and had separation anxiety from his pet rat and cape – yes, cape. The team elder, 'Bushy', could have had an academic career but his train got derailed. The youngest was sixteen-year-old Manny, a Sierra Leone refugee who had seen his father executed.

It was a rollercoaster ride of emotions and confrontations. We were joined for a few days by a freelance South African sound recordist, Tony Wende, who happened to be an erudite and eloquent author of three novels. In a former life Princess was an English teacher with a hankering for Latin. They were old friends, having worked together in wartorn African countries previously, so for a few days I happily took on the role of outsider to this mini literary cartel. They enjoyed cutting me down with their rapier-like wit and playfulness with language, something I was no match at. It was all in good humour and something positive came from it: the idea for writing this book was seeded. Any complaints should therefore be directed to Belinda Hawkins.

Sometimes as a cameraman you have to wear a few hats. Coach George was seeing young Manny plunge into a crisis over his identity. There he was, an African refugee playing for Australia but feeling more akin to his black African competitors. He was struggling with this so George asked for help. I stepped out of my shoes as cameraman and into my magician shoes and entertained Manny. My little yellow lens cloth has a habit of vanishing from my closed hand and reappearing in the oddest of places. When it emerged from my mouth Manny screamed and ran back twenty paces, refusing to come any closer. For all the world he thought he had come face to face with the devil. That was the pinnacle of my magic career; I'm never going to get that reaction again. Manny, though, was back on board, and a wink from George was satisfying thanks enough.

Archbishop Desmond Tutu was visiting the games and I conspired to meet the great man. I broke away from the large media pack that followed him and attached myself to a group of dignitaries. For the moment I had slung my camera over my shoulder and behind me. As he came close I strode forward with my hand outstretched to shake his. He didn't meet my advance, rather choosing to look me in the eye and say, 'Please move, you're in my way.' I seemed to have this effect on members of the church – that is just what the small nun on the flight across the US said to me when I was doing magic for the boorish blonde in *First Class*. It wasn't quite the response I had hoped for from the archbishop. The result of the soccer competition wasn't what the Australian team had hoped for either. They finished well down the ladder.

Despite our rocky start and her insistence that the collective noun for cameramen is 'a whinge', Princess and I went on to do a number of stories together. We parachuted into the lives of MIA Vietnam soldiers, their families and that handful of veterans who can't live with the thought of having left their mates behind in the jungles and battlefields. True to *Australian Story* form there were tears, lots of them, some belonging to me.

Nguyen Van Bao was once the enemy. The Viet Cong. The VC. Charlie. The black-pyjama-clad communist who was on one side of the Vietnam War: the wrong side. Says who? The Australian soldiers who fought the good fight for US foreign policy thirty-five years ago. Politics change, young soldiers grey and youthful zealousness fades. Mr Bao was no longer the enemy. He was the ally of three Australian Vietnam vets trying to tidy up one of war's loose ends – the search for MIAs, those missing in action. Mr and Mrs Bao graciously welcomed us and my camera into their house knowing full well old wounds would open again.

Mr Bao relived his battlefield memories slowly and emotively for the camera. As he spoke I realised I was sitting on his couch so I had to do what I always did in this situation, look around at the family photos that would stare back as if saying, 'Who said you could come in here, stranger?' Low down on a post was a faded old photo of a beautiful young Vietnamese woman wearing an expression of obedience. I glanced across to the elderly Mrs Bao, who had taken up a seat next to Mr Bao, just out of camera frame. It was her in the picture. Belinda hadn't expected she would talk on camera and seized the opportunity by gently including her in the conversation. Even though the microphone was not in position for her (I was about to create another handful of technical problems for myself and the editor), I could see the tears welling in her eyes so I just tightened right in on her beautifully lined face. With her words came a river of sadness. Many of her family were killed. The pain she bore was deep and it was impossible not to be affected by it. I was trying to see through a veil of sweat and tears.

In March 2007, not too long after this, Princess and I found ourselves back in Asia on another *Australian Story*. We were in Indonesia following Australia's foreign minister, Alexander Downer, the subject of an upcoming episode and the man who'd given my self-confidence a slight knock years earlier. Most ministerial trips provide for Australian journalists to tag along if logistics permit. The initial plan was that the larger of the government jets be allocated for the four-day trip. Due to prior requirements a smaller jet was provided. Big or small, the air force plane was known as a 'VIP'. The smaller plane allowed only three spare seats for media. Belinda snagged one, I got the second and the last went to Cynthia Banham from the *Sydney Morning Herald*.

Travelling on the government's private jet is acronymic; you 'VIP' everywhere. 'VIP' will take us from here to there. 'VIP' is scheduled to leave at 5am. No doubt about it, 'vipping' was a nice way to travel. It's very fast, very plush, and much, much better than the discount economy I knew so well. Mind you, any sudden onsets of pomposity are quickly deflated. If your ego is fragile then pack it well because like excess baggage, journalists are on- and offloaded as ministerial needs dictate. Belinda and I learnt this shortly after arriving at our first destination, Semarang, where the Indonesian and Australian foreign ministers met to open a counter-terrorism training facility. Mr Downer's Indonesian counterpart expressed a desire to travel the next leg on to Jakarta with him. Dr Hassan Wirajuda was accorded VIP status and Belinda, Cynthia and I were 'de-vipped' and put on a commercial Garuda flight.

'I don't know what people have against Garuda. Seems alright to me,' Princess and I chortled in our business-class seats. From the capacious luxury of the front of the plane, the white linen tablecloths and the clink of metal cutlery dull out the pervasive scariness of flying that seems to come with the plastic cutlery, engine noise and overcrowding in economy. But for those who would travel in the same seats only days later, the executive class sticker on their boarding pass would be a stamp of death.

The next few days in Jakarta and surrounds were a blur of police motorcades (the only way to travel in Jakarta's traffic), press conferences and photo opportunities. Things hadn't changed since Downer last rattled my cage. I was still a nameless cameraman and my cloak of invisibility hadn't slipped. I was a bit miffed and now felt no connection with him whatsoever. You need to have some point of empathy with a person to have a desire to want to tell their story. I mentally switched off and prematurely set my sights on home. And it reflected in my work. I wasn't engaged in finding and following the story. My shooting was adequate at best.

During this time we had many snatched moments to get to know Morgan Mellish from the *Financial Review* and Liz O'Neill from the Australian embassy, both of whom would die a few days later in the same seats we had frivolously flown in. Morgan was the centre of a conversation Belinda and I had. It's one I argue endlessly with Vicky. Simply, I can't tell if a bloke is good looking or not. Morgan became a temporary test case.

'What do you mean you can't tell?' Belinda came at me with incredulous overtones. 'Look at Morgan – *you can't see* those beautiful eyes, that boyish smile, the close-cropped hair, the tall frame, the strong chest and no doubt the six-pack that lurks under his shirt?'

I took it as read that he was good looking. I remember thinking of him, you really are in a good phase of your professional life, a phase I could see slipping away from me. He was an interesting person working in an interesting place and he was immensely likeable. In an open and honest way he confided how he felt inadequate at giving on-the-spot public comment when we tried to interview him. He felt he couldn't articulate his thinking well (I knew where he was coming from) and rolled off a list of names of people whose capability he aspired to, among them Liz O'Neill.

Liz's was the first voice I heard when we arrived in Indonesia. The VIP jet had taxied to a stop, the doors had opened and the official guard of honour had assembled on the tarmac. Their faces all registered momentary confusion as a bloke in jeans disembarked first. I needed to get in front of Alexander Downer to film his exit. As I battled with a fogged-up lens in the overwhelming humidity, I tuned to the repetitious calling of my name. Duh, what, who? I looked over to see a smartly dressed woman who exuded control and charm. 'I'm Liz … you know, Liz from the embassy!' The penny finally dropped. I smiled and we both got back to the business at hand.

You felt you were in such good hands with Liz. She was very professional at her job, so much so that I was compelled to tell her, which I did. It was the last thing I said to her the night before she died. Even as I told her she was rocking from foot to foot, busting for a wee, the professional putting my needs ahead of her discomfort.

The unfortunate thing about all this is that no one from our group was meant to be on that plane. Everyone was scheduled to go the evening before the crash but heavy traffic and a presidential side trip to the palace extended that day's ministerial duties. Everyone missed the booked flights. Quick rescheduling was made for the next morning. All groaned at the prospect of a very early start. In a cruel twist of fate, Morgan Mellish was offered and accepted a last-minute Garuda ticket. It was a logical choice, a much safer bet than the cut-price carrier he was booked on. Belinda and I had our fingers crossed that we weren't going to be offloaded from the VIP flight.

The morning of March 2007 we sped towards the military airport, whizzing through traffic under a wail of police sirens. Belinda and I were in high spirits. We had been 'vipped' and were on the plane with Downer. Within the hour any jubilant feelings had gone, to be replaced by a large pit in our stomachs. The crash of the Garuda flight was on everybody's lips. We were sickened further upon hearing that business class had taken the brunt, including the *Sydney Morning Herald*'s Cynthia Banham, who suffered burns to seventy percent of her body and subsequently had to have both legs amputated. Cynthia is our reminder of just how fickle life can be.

I thought often of Cynthia, as I did Jimmy 'the Fuse' Filliagi and Scott Rush, all reminders that I should grab opportunities that came my way. If there weren't any, I made them. My constant quest for challenge wouldn't sleep. Being idle stresses me, I know that. I was also very keen to put my magic and juggling to better use. I'd put a lot of time and effort in and I was beginning to wonder what it might lead to, if anything. Erratic hours and extended trips away made it difficult. The answer, I found, was to start busking. My skills were good enough and I was comfortable in front of an audience but I was naive about what it took to be a street performer: total confidence and a rhino hide, neither of which had ever been my strong points.

To stand in a busy thoroughfare and start yelling for people to stop, that you are in fact worthy of their time, that your claims for your abilities will not disappoint them, and then ask them to pay for the inconvenience was the hardest and scariest thing I have ever done. I drew on some of the things I had learnt from Glenn and Heather, breaking fear down into component parts, but I felt very lonely out there. The only thing between myself and the busking experience was an imaginary line, just one step, but once you take that step the bridge is pulled back and you are committed to success or public humiliation. If you hesitate, even for a moment, you are dead. Audiences smell fear and desert you in droves. Whenever I could I went busking, always feeling sick to the stomach with fear. Why? I think for the feeling of achievement, of beating what might keep me down; that is what I liked. I had mixed success. Overall the crowd's response said it was worth pursuing. I was back on the Brisbane streets where I had shot my first protest rally in 1977, though this time I wasn't part of the crowd looking on.

Work as always was ready to whisk me away. Not long after this I was back in a room at the funky Standard Hotel on Sunset Boulevard in Los Angeles. Through my open balcony doors on the first floor I looked straight onto the action. Stretch limo upon stretch limo, the sound of a saxophone and the smell of dope wafting by, the panic of car alarms and sirens, impossibly beautiful people strutting their stuff as bikers paraded their gleaming Harleys ... and there's me tucked up in my room learning to twist balloon animals. There was confusion in my mind about what I wanted to be doing.

Later in the year I was in Rome, shooting a story about the impending Mt Vesuvius eruption. It's going to blow, soon. Geologically speaking, that's sometime in the next few thousand years, so said Professor Roberto Scandione, a theoretical vulcanologist. He also said, as we were walking back to our car after interviewing him, 'Do you know someone is taking bags from your car?' He was right. One hundred metres away in broad daylight our car was being broken into. I could see one man passing my light kit to another who put it in the boot of their nearby car. Soundo Rodney Larsen and I dropped our gear and ran, yelling. The heavy traffic and gentle wind swallowed our voices and the thieves kept on thieving, unaware we were closing in. This wasn't part of the plan, they should have run off by now. When we reached them the two stocky men were nearly as surprised as Rodney and I were. Everyone was now too close for comfort. They dropped the cases and locked themselves in their car. I pounded on the bonnet and Rodney looked for a rock to smash the windscreen. Their engine revved wildly and as they screamed off into the traffic, my consolation prize being that I managed to snap off their side mirror. Granted this was not how the safety manual would have said to behave when being robbed by 'Gypsies' – that's the police description, not mine – but they stole my photographic lights, anything but my lights. Twenty years it had taken me to get my light kit 'just so'. Without my lights I felt like Samson without his hair. I didn't know how prophetic this allusion would be. I seemed to have been robbed of something more.

# 14

## Life shrinks or expands in direct proportion to one's courage.

ANAIS NIN

My life was shrinking; my ABC life, that is. Two and a half decades of opportunity, fascinating stories and travel ended. It was as though the tap had been turned off when, in 2008, the ABC moved to outsourcing much of its programming to the independent sector. It was cheaper to buy it than make it. Wordy spin documents would have you believe otherwise but that's the way it is. The luxury that had been extended to me of working on programs usually crewed by cameramen from other states was withdrawn. I was grounded. A staple of local news and current affairs was my lot.

Mustering whatever positive outlook I could, shooting the Broncos Rugby League team at training sessions and the launch of the annual Fire Safety Week were not challenging me. As long as I smiled and everything was in focus, that seemed all that was required of me. Focus was easy, smiling wasn't. What I had always vowed would never happen to me did: the professional grump started to rear its ugly head. Not often, but enough to sound alarm bells. There was a quick fix for this, something I had done for a decade and a half. In our crew room we had an eclectic photo board of past adventures. There is one photo that would make me laugh, really laugh out loud. It was taken by fellow cameraman Brett Ramsay.

Brett had established himself as the master of revenge with this photo. He was on a New Zealand shoot with a sound recordist who was so tight with money that you could have turned him upside down and shaken the guy and you wouldn't have got ten cents out of him. Brett had forgotten to pack a happy snap camera for the trip and asked the soundo if he would use his camera to take a photo of Brett in front of a beautiful vista. The soundo explained he'd rather not as he had brought only one roll of film and had planned the spots where he was going to take each photo. Brett was gobsmacked but kept his cool demeanour as his deliciously wicked mind went to work. 'Sure, not a problem, let me take a photo of you anyway.' The soundo was pleasantly surprised that Brett had taken his act of frugality so well.

The trip went without a hitch and Brett continued to take happy snaps of the soundo in front of New Zealand's finest views. When the eager soundo picked up his processed photos, they were not what he had hoped for. Brett had framed all of the twenty-four photos to start at the shoulders: each one was missing the soundo's head. One of the photos had been pinned to the board, and the sight of it would always send me into fits of belly laughter and set me back on track, ready to return to doing what was still a really good job. Soon enough, I'd be off the rails again, battling between my ambitions and the cooling reality that opportunities for me within the ABC were disappearing.

Early 2008 was marred by the death of a great man. Sir Edmund Hillary died. A giant of a man was gone and for me a small weight of guilt lifted. I'd never been proud of my poor showing in front of him two decades earlier. I also felt guilty that I couldn't be satisfied with the work that was being offered to me.

Most of the time I felt under-utilised, as did many of my peers. Good stories came up, just not that often. *Australian Story* was doing a profile on Steve Irwin's father, Bob Irwin, and his decision to leave the Australia Zoo fold and start up his own wildlife rescue property. To my surprise he lived a few kilometres outside the small town of Blackbutt, two hours northwest of Brisbane. I was really keen to do the shoot to meet this thoroughly decent man and to partake in a small and relatively recent ritual I undertook each time I passed through the town of Blackbutt.

As we neared the town outskirts I would ask those in the car if they wanted to say hello to my dad. That was quick and easy; we only needed to wave as we passed the Blackbutt cemetery. This was Dad's town and I was proud to show off the newest attraction. A right turn at the Cenotaph and a hundred metres on was the Shaun Mather Memorial Park. My father, who had spent a lifetime avoiding any public recognition, had been honoured with a park. That this had happened made me immensely proud, and shocked. Obviously I had never known him as well as I thought I had. It was the same at his funeral; where had all those people come from? My dad had made a bigger impression than I had ever realised. Maybe if I'd stopped and asked, I'd have found out. I had never been the perfect son and he hadn't been the perfect dad, but our time together had been good. Later that day that's just what Bob Irwin said about Steve. We did have a good laugh when we compared the size of our parks. His son was remembered with a huge park, my dad with a small one. A bit more chatting made one thing clear: we had both decided to move on to new phases of our lives.

Looking back there seems an obvious path this was all following. I never really thought it would amount to anything. I am ABC through and through, I'm a firm believer in the value of public broadcasting – that idea of treating people as thinking citizens in a democracy rather than simply consumers in a marketplace (maybe overstated a little but the sentiment is there) –

and I loved my career. Most ABC people feel that way. There runs a deep culture of belief throughout the ABC that by being there you are contributing to something worthwhile. Presently that culture is being dismantled in a cold and faceless way, some say in the name of progress, others cry political will. Whatever the reasons, Australians will be poorer for it.

I also have an internal switch that has only two positions: on and off. I was caught by surprise when it flicked off for the ABC, something I never thought possible. It happened as I was sitting on my kitchen bench listening to a local ABC Radio station's special on creating a better public understanding of the courts and the judiciary. It was exceptionally well done and of great benefit to the community. It was everything the ABC was about, but it was radio and relative to making television, making radio is affordable. ABC Television, particularly on a local state basis, wasn't thinking like this anymore. It no longer wanted to make programs. Many of the producers I had worked with, people with mountains of knowledge and active minds, were suffocating a slow professional death – Jack King, Gary Johnson, Richard Smith ... Some jumped, others were pushed; all went with a sadness that it had ended this way. The truth for me was that the ABC could no longer offer me a career, only a job. I actually cried when the realisation hit: the ABC simply didn't need me anymore. I settled on leaving.

Once I'd made that decision I guess it was natural that I started looking for things to back it up. I didn't have to look far. I was rejected for a shoot in Bulgaria on the grounds that I hadn't undertaken a 'Hostile Environment' course. This course is mandatory for all staff before heading into a war zone, but a program has to pay for it. Bulgaria was not at war, there weren't even travel warnings about it on the Foreign Affairs website. I'm guessing insurance worries had a lot to do with it. There was also no money to send me on the course. It certainly didn't make me happy that as a former army sniper, climber and with two decades of foreign travel behind me I was now deemed unqualified for this type of work.

I started to think of the thousands of things that thousands of people in thousands of interviews had said. A few of those had stuck. Normie Rowe said he heard advice given to Shania Twain by her father – never sing a song you don't think you'll be able to sing when you're sixty. Would I be lugging the gear around at that age? I'd always hoped to but I'd discovered a new law of physics. A camera is featherweight when you're motivated and leaden when you're not. Some of the things came from the many clever people I'd been lucky enough to work alongside. Documentary producer Tim Clarke quoted a philosopher whose name escapes me: 'There are three things required for happiness: the ability to lead a considered life, friends and self-determination.' The first two were within acceptable limits but I craved the third. Three years in the army followed by twenty-six at the ABC qualifies as institutionalisation. For nearly thirty years I'd been told where to be and when to be there. As great as some of those locations were, I'd had enough. I wanted to know: could I make it on my own? It took nearly a year for the ABC lifeblood to finally drain out of me as I used up a stack of long-service leave I'd never accessed. It was December 2009 when my blip finally disappeared off the ABC radar.

Leaving the security of the ABC was a scary thought. Weekly there were freelancers knocking on the ABC's doors looking for stable work. The global financial crisis of 2009 had hit hard. It might seem foolhardy and even ungrateful to give up a plum job but you've gotta do what you've gotta do. I thought that maybe I could stay and do something else on the side but another realisation snuffed out that idea. It was that I had become part of the culture of spectating; I had a ringside view of life, that's true, but still always from the sidelines. I was at the back of the room being inspired by the people up the front whom I was filming. My new ideas required me to move to the metaphorical front of the room where things were achieved. It was clear I couldn't be in two places at once.

I had an idea and it came from another thing that had struck me time and time again, ever since working with the Myer family on one of the episodes of *Dynasties*. The Myer Foundation exists to give away part of the family wealth, primarily through a grants scheme to support philanthropic endeavours. I saw how you could take limited amounts of money and then value-add to them by applying some clever thinking. The money could then be used to promote good and improve human quality of life. I became intrigued by the notion of philanthropy. It took me a while to understand the difference between charity and philanthropy. There are people infinitely more qualified than me to argue the definitions but I'll give you my take on them.

One view says philanthropy is necessarily associated with the wealthy. Their donations are targeted to specific causes to bring about recognisable change in social conditions. Many rich philanthropists support the arts, religious, humanitarian and educational causes. These often require large donations over a period of time. The organisations that are subsequently created out of philanthropic giving then allow for charitable giving of smaller amounts by the individual.

I subscribe to another line of thought. I don't think wealth creates the distinction between philanthropy and charity, I think it is intent. Charity generally doesn't require foresight. We all drop a few coins in a tin because we want to contribute and Australians by and large are generous givers. As long as someone else identifies an area of need and sets up the infrastructure to address it, we are happy to support it; can't complain about that. Philanthropy, I think, takes that next step where you find a problem of interest to yourself, and looking ahead you identify social issues then use money to try to head off perceived problems. It is this foresight that I think is the hallmark of philanthropy. Collective pooling of funds by like-minded individuals can create volumes of money that can make a difference; therefore you needn't be wealthy to be a philanthropist. To my way of thinking it's wanting to make a difference and finding a way to do it that identifies a philanthropist. A line I like to use is: philanthropy is charity on steroids. Semantics aside, I needed to find a definition I was comfortable with to be able to discuss it.

Over the years, I spoke to hundreds of people in positions of influence and if there was a spare moment I liked to see what they thought about the idea of philanthropy. What surprised me was the majority had never really given it any thought. It would be one of those things they could attend to in retirement. This struck me as reverse thinking. They are well placed now, when they are in positions of influence and control, when they have their hands on the levers, so to speak, and access to resources. Now is the time to do it.

So I thought, how do you turn that around? How do you move the clock forward on people giving something back to society? I don't know why but I couldn't let go of this. First of all I knew there needed to be more talk about it. It's a discussion I rarely hear. I've never been much of a talker, though. Wherever this nagging idea took me I didn't want to head down the road of idealism. If I could come up with an idea it had to be very nuts and bolts and suit my pragmatic outlook. Another thing I knew was that it would be very hard to teach an old dog new tricks, so children would play a major role. How on earth was I going to take the very adult concept of philanthropy and package it in a way that could be understood and of some use to children? More than that, did anyone really care or was I simply having my mid-life crisis and heading off on an inconsequential tangent?

No matter where I looked I came back to the model of PC Graham Waddington and his work of going into schools and using direct action. I could see myself doing that, as my strength was effectively delivering messages to children. I wanted to let kids know that they can make a difference and they can start doing it now. The simplest explanation I could come up with was: if you give a man a fish you feed him for a day, teach a man to fish you feed him for a lifetime. But it wasn't original and, as it came with religious overtones, it wasn't for me. My message also needed to be memorable, so much so that if I was able to provide them with some sort of a mental trigger, they would maybe remember it as a working adult.

It was all heading for the too-hard basket when I realised I'd seen this sort of trigger in action before. Almost every few months over the past twenty years someone would walk up to my camera and flash five outstretched fingers to the camera lens, followed by a peace sign. It was the Channel Seven promotional campaign from the 1980s. This nonverbal gesture had been drilled into their psyche and the sight of a TV camera could still trigger a response nearly two decades later. I know the camera was the trigger in this instance but it made me realise the power of a gesture like this. Once I started thinking along those lines, the pieces of the jigsaw all came together. The THUMB program was born in about an hour. THUMB is an acronym for:

Think of others

Help when you can

Use your noggin to

Make the world a

Better place

It's a child-friendly version of thinking charitably then taking the extra step. Imagine the classic thumbs-up gesture of four fingers curled into a fist and the thumb pointing skywards. Starting with the thumb as number one, you then extend each finger in turn as you read each of the lines from the THUMB acronym. If I can use this visual imagery to reinforce the THUMB message in the minds of children throughout their primary schooling then I'm in with a chance that the thumbs-up gesture will remain for them an ongoing reminder that now is the right time to try and make a difference. My vision is this: in about forty years' time if you eavesdropped on a group of business leaders from around the world and heard them comparing what they made, you'd hear a hundred and fifty thousand, two hundred thousand, half a million and then it'd be the Australian's turn. What do you make, they'd ask, and she'd answer: What do I make? I make a difference.

A nice sentiment but how could I get it into schools? I'd have to disguise this character-building dose of brussels sprouts as ice cream. The showpiece of the program is the THUMB show, a magic and juggling laugh fest that promotes building strength of character through resilience, responsibility and respect. Then it encourages kids to try and make a difference. So far so what? Nothing particularly new, but what makes this unique is the way it gets the idea off the whiteboard, out of the classroom and turns it into a living, breathing, learning and teaching experience. This is where it gets good. I've come up with a way to give schools modest funding to help them realise an idea that a student or teacher may suggest after the THUMB show visits their school. It's what I call project ignition money. Every school will vary in how they run with this opportunity. Their project may be driven by a handful of eager students, maybe one driven by a teacher; indeed, they may just enjoy the show and its positive character-building messages and leave it at that. That is still a good outcome. However, to encourage schools to embrace this and to include the THUMB message as part of their school's ethos, there is the THUMB Award. Each year participating schools will be able to enter their project and maybe win the $5000 prize. The criterion is that they attempt to value-add to the benefits that money can generate by applying some clever thinking to their project ignition money.

What sort of projects? There is unlimited potential as it's anything that promotes good or improves the quality of life. It could be an energy-saving initiative for their school or something to benefit the local community. It could be a sporting program or tuckshop initiative to improve students' health. This is how I explain it to the kids. If you had $20 to help fix a problem in your school, how could you use the money? Imagine there's a path at your school that's got a crack in it and one bit sits a bit higher than the other. Every day someone trips over the crack and skins their knee. What could you do? You could buy lots of Band-Aids; plenty for everyone. What about spending that $20 another way? What if you held a competition and made the $20 a prize? You could win it by bringing in toys and books at home you don't want anymore; the person who brings in the most toys wins the $20. All the toys and books would be sold at the next school fete at the *Nothing over a Dollar* stall. If you made $300 at the stall you could use that money to buy sand and cement, rent a cement mixer, and get dads to come in on a school working bee. That way you could repair the broken path and there would be no more skinned knees.

From little things big things can grow. It's all about preparing today's students to be tomorrow's architects of social change. Along the way it will give us adults the chance to give back to our kids the one thing we seem hell-bent on keeping at arm's length from them – that deliriously life-enriching drug called responsibility. Am I crazy and naive? Time will tell. I told my idea to Frank Manthey, one of the colourful Bilby Brothers. People had said he was mad when he embarked upon his ambitious plans to help save the bilby from extinction. Frank said to me, 'The man who never failed never did anything.'

What I do know is that I have seen enough good ideas labour under the burden of over-administration. Underpinning all this will always be my memory of PC Waddington, his direct action stopping three aerosol sprays disappearing up the noses of kids full of potential. I've tried to track him down but so far have failed. He would have no idea that a chance meeting nine years earlier, a meeting that he has most likely forgotten, has spawned an unusual venture on the other side of the globe. I'd love to see his face.

Even though I've pushed the levers full forward, set the rev counter to high and let go of the brake, this project is going to take some time to get up and running and I've found you can't live on air. I've started doing family magic shows and kids' parties, which brought me to another realisation: being an ABC cameraman had a moderate amount of status attached to it. That I was no longer entitled to the hint of social privilege that came with flying the ABC colours was driven home when I performed a Christmas Family Magic Show at a very exclusive Brisbane club patronised by people with a lot of diamonds on display. I finished a successful show and one little seven-year-old girl, very well dressed, who had been having a good time in the front row, said to me, 'Do the trick with the yellow balls again,' to which I said no because that's what I always say; you never perform the same trick twice. Her response floored me. 'If you don't do it again we won't pay you.' It felt like something out of a Dickensian novel; a wealthy seven-year-old aristocrat threatening to withhold a few pieces of silver from the Gypsies unless they danced another jig. The truth was she was paying me, at least her parents were. I was working in the real world now, far removed from the security of taxpayer-funded pay cheques. It's amazing how quickly the thought of having no money can cause you to re-evaluate your ideals. I stared her down and hoped that I'd made the right decision about leaving the ABC.

So that is where I am at. Still a vegetarian, still committed to not dying in a car crash, and presently oozing enthusiasm and passion, which is great for me but poor Vicky still carries the burden of living with an obsessional person. She's still with me, which proves she is both delusional and loving. Our oldest, Georgia, is showing an interest in photography but she has to open that door herself if she is to go through it. If she did take it up we would qualify as a dynasty – three generations is all it takes. Our youngest, Sophie, is a fantastic writer, which fills me with hope.

Gunter Ericoli still records sound at the ABC. I forgot to mention that he is the undisputed world champion at fitting a mountain of gear into undersize cars. Gunter will remain a friend forever.

Richard Corfield no longer has woolly hair and has become one of the new breed of one-man producer/cameraman/soundo outfits. He's still enchanting people as he goes.

Richard Smith was deemed excess to ABC requirements and let go, much to the delight of *National Geographic*, who have their hooks into him.

The ABC couldn't find anything for Jack King and Gary Johnson's talents either. Jack's at university and Gary has gone into theatre.

Belinda Hawkins is still mired in others' misfortune, as that is and always will be the *Australian Story* way. As a former English teacher she has generously been on my case, correcting my grammar and bemoaning me as an uncouth Queenslander with a glorious absence of sophistication and a predilection towards scatological humour. This sort of writing, she tells me, will scare off the refined intelligentsia of Melbourne.

Scott Rush remains banged up in an Indonesian prison while his family continue their own sentence back here in Australia.

Jimmy 'the Fuse' Filliagi got the needle on 24 April 2007. Every few months I would check the Ohio Death Row website to see that he was OK and then one time he wasn't on the list. Sad is not the word, just disappointed. I always hoped that in some sort of fairytale ending he'd manage to beat the system.

In Italy somewhere my lights and stands probably have beans growing on them as they are otherwise useless in day-to-day Gypsy life.

And remember Wok, the soundo who always said we, 'the crew', had the second-best job in the world? Well, he recently got to work with the man we deemed to have the best job. I want Wok to have the last word.

> I found myself driving the great man around out the back of the Mary River in the Northern Territory. The BBC had engaged me to record the sound for the final episode of Attenborough's *Life* series. David was a lifelong non-driver so I took the opportunity to be his guide. On the first day of the shoot as we hurtled along a 'beef' road, David turned to me and said, 'Old boy, you have a great job.'
>
> I replied, 'Thanks, mate, I've got the second-best job in the world.'
>
> His interest was piqued:
>
> 'Who has the best?'
>
> 'You, and after fifty years I've finally been able to tell you.'

# Postscript

After an almost endless twilight of untaken leave, in February 2010 my ABC career turned off the lights and tucked itself in for a long sleep.

I looked forward to my farewell dinner with the trepidation I feel for funerals; part of me was to be buried. In between the endless plates of samosas and naan, the smiles, handshakes and yawns – it was a Friday night – I said my farewells and touched people, really touched people: hugs, holds, boyish mock wrestles and tousling greying hair. No one offered resistance. It was the ABC spirit manifesting itself as almost brotherly and sisterly love. It's very real and drives much of the ABC. I just hope in the race for efficiency by the national broadcaster this wonderful resource isn't overlooked.

# Acknowledgements

Thank you:
To my sister Vanessa, my brother Shane and dear old Mum,
I'm very proud of you all.

It's an odd thing, the cameramen I've worked alongside for a quarter of a century are the people I know least of all. Everyone is always off shooting. Regardless, you're friends first and foremost:

John Bean
Mick Fanning
Colin Hertzog
Julie Hornsey
Peter Moor
Ian Mosey
Liz Pickering
Brett Ramsay
Anthony Sines
Mark Slade
Marc Smith

www.ingramcontent.com/pod-product-compliance
Lightning Source LLC
Chambersburg PA
CBHW022047290426
44109CB00014B/1014